Introduction
to
Christian
Education

by
Eleanor Daniel
John W. Wade
Charles Gresham

STANDARD PUBLISHING
Cincinnati, Ohio   88581

Textbooks by Standard Publishing:

The Christian Minister
  Sam E. Stone
Introduction to Christian Education
  Eleanor Daniel, John W. Wade, Charles Gresham
Ministering to Youth
  David Roadcup, editor

Commentary on Acts
  J. W. McGarvey
The Equipping Ministry
  Paul Benjamin
Essays on New Testament Christianity
  C. Robert Wetzel, editor
The Fourfold Gospel
  J. W. McGarvey and P. Y. Pendleton
The Jesus Years
  Thomas D. Thurman
How to Understand the Bible
  Knofel Staton
Teach With Success
  Guy P. Leavitt, revised by Eleanor Daniel

Library of Congress Cataloging in Publication Data

Daniel, Eleanor Ann.
    Introduction to Christian education.

    Includes index.
    1. Christian education. I. Wade, John William, 1924-
joint author. II. Gresham, Charles, joint author. III. Title.
VB1471.2.D35   207   79-92587
ISBN 0-87239-394-1

Except where otherwise specified, Scripture quotations are from the New International Version of the Bible, © 1978, New York Bible Society International.

Scripture verses designated NEB are from The New English Bible, ©The Delegates of the Oxford University Press and The Syndics of the Cambridge University Press 1961, 1970. Reprinted by permission.

Foreword

An "Introduction" is probably the most difficult of books to write, in any field. We can't presuppose that the reader or student will know anything at all about the subject. And yet we dare not be superficial in our treatment, and leave the learner with only a host of vague impressions. To add to the normal difficulties, it's hard to take the work of a number of individuals and integrate that work into a whole that reflects a common philosophy and excellence.

Because I know how hard it is to do these things well, I have appreciated the opportunity to read this volume in manuscript. I've had the enriching pleasure of knowing several of the authors personally, and now the added pleasure of hearing their voices, speaking from the solid Biblical perspective of restorationism.

A number of things about this *Introduction to Christian Education* invite approval. The authors have rightly seen that we must begin thinking about Christian education by exploring the nature of the church. Understanding the church—our relationship with Christ as Living Head and with one another as members of God's family—is basic to effective educational ministry. Often in the body of the book beyond these initial chapters the authors return to related issues, and in these sections the work is uniformly excellent.

The authors have also shown consistent scholarship that is fully aware of both historic and contemporary contributions to our understanding of educational ministry. Historical background is invariably provided where it is important to gain perspective, and each section shows a good choice of bibliographical material. Focusing on readings in these suggested resources, as the author suggests, is a good approach for conducting a course. The guidance the references provide will also be valuable to the local church practitioner.

One of the great tensions felt in the church today is never quite resolved, and probably cannot be: This is the tension between what is ... and what might be. Some will find the detailed examination of contemporary educational programs in the church troublesome; they will doubt that we can squeeze the wine of the theology the book espouses into the older wineskins of the contemporary institution. At the same time, revolutionary kinds of changes are seldom helpful and often harmful. It seems to me that the authors have wisely chosen to explore the potential for good of what is, and not to describe for this kind of work the "might be" we all dream of. Still, the tension does exist. And because many of us may have to continue to live with that tension, it is helpful to explore how to make the best of what is possible for us now.

Personally, I believe that in the 80's we can expect—largely due to energy shortages and similar societal pressures—much more educational ministry taking place in neighborhood settings. These non-formal settings and their potential will require exploration ... perhaps as another study by these same authors based on the same solid theological assumptions.

All in all, I am pleased to express my appreciation to Standard and to each of the authors for what is certainly one of the very best introductions to Christian education available.

—*Lawrence O. Richards*

Contents

For the Teacher

Introduction to Christian Education is an overview of the educational task of the church. But it is more than an academic exercise—it is meant to be a practical primer in Christian education.

This book is the result of the efforts of seven writers who reflect their particular academic interests and practical experiences in their respective chapters. Despite their differences, these authors are consistent in demonstrating a strong Biblical basis for the practices of Christian education.

An introductory course in Christian education could utilize this text to accomplish three objectives.

1. To provide an overview to beginning students of what Christian education is and how it is accomplished.

2. To lay foundations for further study in Christian education.

3. To encourage students to understand how Christian education relates to their vocational choices.

The course could be divided into four sections corresponding to the parts of this book: foundations, materials and methods, administration, and beyond the local church.

The first part, Foundations of Christian Education, should emphasize precise definitions and identification of genuinely Biblical education. Five or six weeks may be devoted to this section. This section will best be accomplished with readings and by having each student write a short paper examining the nature of teaching in the church.

Part Two, Materials and Methods for Christian Education, will require at least six weeks to develop. Projects coupled with readings will contribute to adequate expansion of this section. The projects suggested at the end of each chapter provide practice of concepts discussed in the chapter.

Audiovisual materials should be selected carefully to develop the chapters on materials and methods. Early childhood, children, youth, and adult training filmstrips from International Center for Learning are helpful resources for this section. The International Center for Learning also produces 16mm training films for each age level. The "Teaching God's Word To . . ." filmstrips from Scripture Press give an effective overview for nursery through junior age levels. Involve the students in examining curriculum materials and preparing Bible lessons for each age level. Demonstrate the wide variety of visuals available. A field trip to observe adequate buildings and facilities would add interest.

The third section, Administration of Christian Education, will require four or five weeks to develop. Practical projects, suggested at the end of each chapter, should be coupled with the readings. Assign interviews with educational leaders, or invite a minister and a minister of education to share in a question-and-answer period in class.

The final part deals with extra-church organizations. Although the section is brief (a week or two will suffice), the reading is important. Another short paper on a topic of interest would be appropriate if time permits.

Building a Christian education file is a worthwhile term project. This author requires the student to set up his filing system and add at least a hundred items to it. A well-established file will prove to be a valuable tool for the future.

Above all else, work at modeling effective teaching—the kind of teaching outlined in Chapter Seven. Balance the course with reading, films, projects, discussion, outside resource people, and lecture. Help the student to experience effective teaching. In turn, he will teach in much the same way as he has been taught.

Contributors

Eleanor Daniel is professor of Christian education at Midwest Christian College in Oklahoma City. Her academic credits include an A.B. and M.A. in Christian education from Lincoln Christian College and an Ed.M. and Ph.D. in educational psychology from the University of Illinois. She has served as a minister of education in Illinois, Michigan, and Oklahoma, and has taught at Midwest Christian College, Lincoln Christian College, and the University of Illinois.

Gerald Denny is minister of education at Mount Carmel Christian Church, Decatur, Georgia. He holds the A.B. and M.A. degrees from Lincoln Christian College and an Ed.M. in educational psychology from the University of Illinois. He has served in educational ministries in Illinois and Georgia, and has taught for one year at Lincoln Christian College.

W. Edward Fine is minister of education at Central Christian Church, St. Petersburg, Florida. He holds an A.B. from Milligan College. He has also preached in Florida and has served as a public school administrator in Tennessee and Florida.

Charles Gresham is professor of Bible and Christian education at Kentucky Christian College, Grayson, Kentucky. His academic background includes an A.B. from Manhattan Christian College, and the M.R.E. and Ed.D. degrees from Southwestern Baptist Theological Seminary. He has preached and has served on the faculties of Midwest Christian College, Dallas Christian College, Manhattan Christian College, and Emmanuel Seminary, in addition to Kentucky Christian College.

Ann Myers is director of the ministry to the mentally handicapped at Lincoln Christian Church, Lincoln, Illinois. She holds the B.S. and M.S. degrees from Illinois State University and is completing Ph.D. studies in educational psychology at the University of Illinois.

Chris Templar is professor of Christian education at Johnson Bible College, Knoxville, Tennessee. Her academic credits include the A.L.B.C., from London Bible College, B.D. from London University, M.A. from Trinity Evangelical Divinity School, and Ed.D. from Southern Baptist Theological Seminary. She has served as a Christian school teacher in the United States, a missionary in Indonesia, and a church worker in England.

John W. Wade is professor of Christian education at Atlanta Christian College, East Point, Georgia. He holds A.B. degrees from Cincinnati Bible College and Butler University and M.A. degrees from Southwest Christian Seminary and the University of Cincinnati. He previously taught at Cincinnati Bible College and served on the editorial staff of the Standard Publishing Company.

Part One

FOUNDATIONS OF CHRISTIAN EDUCATION

Section Outline

1. Beginning With the Church
   A. The Nature of the Church
   B. The Mission of the Church
   C. The Church's Mission and the Teaching Task
   D. The Church's Mission and Its Practical Application

2. The Bible Speaks: Biblical and Theological Foundations
   A. The Nature of the Bible
   B. The Bible and Christian Education
   C. Biblical Theology as Content

3. The Lessons of History
   A. Christian Education in the Early Church
   B. Christian Education in the Medieval Church
   C. Renaissance and Reformation
   D. Christian Education in America
   E. The Current Scene

4. Toward a Philosophy of Christian Education
   A. A Word About Philosophy
   B. Components of a Philosophy of Christian Education
   C. A Philosophy of Christian Education
   D. Christian Education and the Areas of Philosophy
   E. Implications of a Philosophy of Christian Education

5. Objectives in Christian Education
   A. Meaning, Function, and Application
   B. A Historical View
   C. A Practical View

Christian education is not just the use of methods. Nor is it limited to the Sunday morning Bible school. It is "the school of the church," giving careful consideration to all phases of the church's life and work. Even more, Christian education is "education for Christian living." As such, it should provide the necessary guidance for the total lifestyle of the Christian.

Since Christian education is crucially related to both the ministry of the church and the life of the individual Christian, it must be built upon secure foundations. These foundations not only undergird educational procedures, but they also provide the content and perspective of the total educational process.

The first section of this book explores the foundations that guide current educational programs and practices. The section begins with a discussion of the nature and mission of the church—the context of Christian education. It explores the Biblical and historical information that relates to Christian education. The final chapters set forth a philosophy of Christian education and state those basic objectives that provide specific guidance for the educational process.

Those who would give serious consideration to various phases of Christian education should realize that Christian education is more than *education*—that is, a process by which learning takes place. It is *Christian*—the process serves some greater purpose that is caught up in the meaning of the word "Christian." *Christian education* must be viewed from a particular perspective. This perspective is gained only from a study of these foundational areas.

1

Beginning With
the Church

As you read, think about these questions:
—What is meant by *church education*?
—What is the Biblical understanding of the church's nature and purpose?
—How does our understanding of the church's nature and purpose help us in Christian nurture?
—What is meant by *institutionalization*?

Christian education is church education—that is, education that takes place in the church.

This important fact has often been overlooked. Institutions other than the church (for example, public schools) were expected to do what only the church can do—educate for Christian living. Many parachurch organizations and other agencies that were established to nurture Christians (Sunday school and Christian Endeavor, for example) have tended to detract from the full significance of the church. "Church work" was given over to separate agencies rather than seen as the work of the church through these agencies.

Under the influence of the theological liberalism of the early twentieth century, religious educational leaders came to feel more closely related to secular education than to the church. Religious education came to have little relationship to the his-

toric Christian faith, and its literature lacked sufficient Biblical
and theological emphasis. Such religious education bore little
relation to the church and was "uninterested in exploring the
Biblical evidence for the rootage of teaching in the nature of the
church."[1]

But the Bible is clear on education in the church. It presents
Jesus as the head of the church, and both the builder and foundation of the church. This Jesus, after His death and resurrection (by which He made the church possible), sent the apostles
into the world to preach and teach. Preaching would bring
about obedient response and commitment, and teaching would
ensure that obedient response and commitment might lead to
spiritual maturity and growth. These two ministries became
the effective means of the church's rapid growth throughout
the inhabited world. "They never stopped teaching and proclaiming the good news that Jesus is the Christ," records Luke,
the first church historian.[2]

If Christians are to be faithful to God, then they must recognize that Christian education is a vital ministry of the church.
But to take this educational ministry seriously, they must understand the nature and mission of the church as revealed
through Scripture.

The Nature of the Church

Popular concepts of the church often have little relationship
to what the New Testament reveals. Many think of the church
as a physical building where certain meetings are held, but the
New Testament doesn't even mention church buildings. When
it does equate building to church, as Paul does in 1 Corinthians
3, it speaks figuratively. The church is God's building for
which certain leaders have laid the foundation (in gospel
preaching and missionary outreach) and others have built on it
(in continued preaching and teaching).

The popular concept of the church as hierarchical—that is,
that its essence is seen in its ordained leadership—is just as
erroneous. The idea that "where the bishop is, there is the
church" is not found in the New Testament. This idea reached
its zenith in the papacy of the Middle Ages, saddling the
church with tradition and corruption that necessitated its reform.

Even the Reformation of the sixteenth century was not complete. Though certain Biblical insights were recovered, the acceptance of existing church-state relationships and other erroneous ideas led Protestantism to view the church in denominational terms. Though the church was no longer ruled over by the Roman bishop, it was now the Reformed Church of Switzerland or some other entity of a geographical or sectarian nature. The church was divided according to geography or adherence to certain religious tenets.

Over and against these concepts of the church's nature is that found in the New Testament Scriptures. The church is Christ's: He is its Head, Founder, and Authority. "On this rock [the truth of Jesus' messiahship and deity, confessed by Peter], I will build my church," Jesus proclaimed.[3] Paul, that great preacher and church-planter, acknowledges this fact: "And he [Christ] is the head of the body, the church: he is the beginning and the firstborn from among the dead, so that in everything he might have the supremacy."[4] The church centers in Christ, not in human leadership or sectarian creed.

But the church is made up of people. Peter, who first confessed Jesus to be the Christ and heard His answer, understood this. He wrote, "You also, like living stones, are being built into a spiritual house to be a holy priesthood, offering spiritual sacrifices acceptable to God through Jesus Christ. . . . But you are a chosen people a royal priesthood, a holy nation, a people belonging to God, that you may declare the praises of him who called you out of darkness into his wonderful light. Once you were not a people, but now you are the people of God."[5] The church is people. It is *personal*, not hierarchical or denominational. The Greek word *ecclesia*, translated "church," means an assembly of people, of "called-out-ones." The church is a community of persons who have submitted to the authority of Jesus Christ.

The New Testament also sees the church as people in *relationship*. When the church began in Jerusalem, Peter presented Jesus as Savior and Lord. When individuals obeyed Jesus Christ in baptism, they were "added to their number." This body of people continued in fellowship, as well as in the apostles' teaching, the breaking of bread and prayers.[6]

Fellowship means "partnership." The relationship is first vertical—"Our fellowship is with the Father and with his Son, Jesus Christ"—and then horizontal—"We proclaim to you what we have seen and heard, so that you also may have fellowship with us."[7] Paul wrote that all Christians are members of the one body and should have "equal concern for each other."[8] This relationship of caring and concern transcends all distinctions—racial, social, and sexual—"There is neither Jew nor Greek, slave nor free, male nor female, for you are all one in Christ Jesus."[9]

The Mission of the Church

The church is the body of Christ. It continues the servant-hood of Jesus in this world. It responds to His direction for function and purpose. What Jesus Christ began to do, His church continues to do.

Jesus Christ, God's only Son, came in human flesh to accomplish what sinful man could never achieve for himself—redemption and reconciliation. The resurrection of His physical body is evidence of the reality of that atoning work. The church was created by outpouring and inspired direction of the Holy Spirit. It exists in order to "continue to do and teach" that which Jesus began. In response to Jesus Christ, the church carries forth His mission "to the ends of the earth" and "to the very end of the age."[10]

The risen Lord was quite specific about the nature and extent of that mission. In His appointment with the eleven disciples on a mountain in Galilee He spoke in unequivocal terms:

> All authority in heaven and on earth has been given to me. Therefore go and make disciples of all nations, baptizing them in the name of the Father and of the Son and of the Holy Spirit, and teaching them to obey everything I have commanded you. And surely I will be with you always, to the very end of the age.[11]

The mission of the church is to make disciples of all nations. "Discipling"—as the process is carried out in the book of Acts—involved both preaching and teaching. The gospel was preached, and that "good news" was centered on Christ's redeeming work. Response was immediate. The inspired message brought conviction of sin, awakened and focused faith in Christ, and led to active obedience in baptism. Upon such faith and obedience, these disciples were "added to the church" and became partners with other believers in the community of faith.[12]

Within the fellowship of the Christian community the believ-

ers devoted themselves to the apostles' teaching, which con-
veyed the Lord's commandments. When a person becomes a
disciple of Christ, he enters into a new relationship as a son or
daughter of the living God, a joint-heir with Jesus Christ.[13] The
disciple also becomes a willing, dutiful student who not only
learns God's will, but also does God's will.[14]

The Church's Mission and the Teaching Task

The "Great Commission," by emphasizing teaching and nurture, sets the pattern for Christian education. It establishes the
authority of the risen Jesus that underlies all Christian activity,
and sets forth a program of enlistment and discipleship that
emphasizes initial commitment and continued learning. The
scope of Christian teaching is outlined by the statement,
"teaching them to obey everything I have commanded you."
Christian education is to include "the sum total of Christ's
commandments concerning man's duty both to God and to
man, and is to secure Christian action."[15]

The church's mission can be further seen by noting how the
apostles carried it out. From the first they recognized teaching
as an important function. Jerusalem disciples continued in the
apostles' teaching, and the apostles were accused by the
Sanhedrin as filling Jerusalem with their teachings. Peter and
John were teaching people in the temple and were commanded
"not to speak or teach at all in the name of Jesus."[16] In spite of
such warnings and threats, the apostles continued to teach:
"Day after day, in the temple courts and from house to house,
they never stopped teaching and proclaiming the good news
that Jesus is the Christ."[17]

The apostle Paul also applied the term "teacher" to his calling.[18] Paul is shown to be teaching eleven times in the book of
Acts, and he presents himself as a teacher four times in his
epistles. He and Barnabas taught at Antioch for a year, and they
are mentioned in a group of "prophets and teachers" of the
local church.[19] On his second missionary journey Paul remained in Corinth "a year and a half, teaching them the word
of God."[20] He continued teaching for two years in the school of
Tyrannus in Ephesus.[21] In his closing ministry in Rome, Paul
lived for two years in a rented house, "and welcomed all who
came to see him. Boldly and without hindrance he preached
the kingdom of God and taught about the Lord Jesus Christ."[22]

The apostles themselves clearly stated how important teaching is. Paul lists pastors and teachers among the "gifts" given to the church by the risen Lord in order "to prepare God's people for works of service, so that the body of Christ may be built up."[23] A spiritual leader (an elder) must be "able to teach" and must "hold firmly to the trustworthy message as it has been taught, so that he can encourage others by sound doctrine and refute those who oppose it."[24] The spiritual leader must know the correct doctrine and be skillful in teaching it. Those who have proven their teaching ability are to be especially honored.[25]

As Paul's representative, Timothy was told to teach those in Ephesus. Timothy was to take "the things you have heard me say" from Paul, and entrust them to faithful men who "will also be qualified to teach others."[26] Such directives showed the place of teaching in the early church and also ensured that the task would be continued by future generations.

The Church's Mission and Its Practical Application

An understanding of the mission of the church is relevant to a study of the church's teaching function. Over the centuries, the church has tried various methods of carrying out this essential task.

At any given time in history, Christians fulfill essential tasks by developing certain programs and activities. These are often relevant, meaningful, and successful for a while, but historical and cultural changes occur and the programs become irrelevant and non-productive. But by this time the programs have also become familiar and even cherished. Many are not willing to change or eliminate them—they are considered "sacred" and treated not as expedients, but as essentials. As a result, what sociologists call institutionalization occurs.

Institutionalization generally develops in four stages. The first stage is that period when people are searching for a solution to the demands and needs of the moment. Once they can agree upon a solution, the institution (the techniques, program, or organization that will solve the problem) is established. The second stage is the "efficiency stage," in which the potential values of the institution are realized. Steps are taken to preserve the original pattern intended by the group that established the institution. The third stage is formalism. Rules are established, chains of command developed, set forms or rituals developed, and material structures built to implement and maintain the institution. The fourth stage is one of disorganization, occurring when the mechanisms of the institution no longer work as originally intended. Individuals are little impressed by the ideals of the institution; they become indifferent and uncooperative. The original goals are no longer fulfilled, and the institution is discarded or radically altered.

One can easily relate this overall pattern to the church. But while the church is transcultural and timeless, its institutions are not. At any given time and in any given culture, the church produces certain agencies, programs, and techniques (institutions) to accomplish its universal and eternal tasks. These institutions should never become ends in themselves or be confused with the nature of the church. Since they are all man made and culturally determined (whether Sunday school or evangelistic techniques), they should always be "subjected to continuous rigorous sociological and theological analysis to determine their effectiveness as instruments of the church."[27] In this way, the church's nature is not confused with a particular method of fulfilling its purpose within a given cultural and historical context. The church itself, the fellowship of God's people, must be the norm by which all expedients are judged, according to Snyder:

> In the final analysis, church structure is a question of the community of God's people using their God-given intelligence and creativity to manufacture useful tools to help extend the Church's witness, while always remembering that these manmade tools stand under God's judgment and must never be worshiped.[28]

An understanding of the nature and mission of the church is essential for the development of relevant strategies and the avoidance of institutionalization. The church is God's instrument for bringing His world back under His sovereignty. It was meant to penetrate every society, throw down every evil stronghold, and bring people spiritually captive to the Lord of Hosts. The church must strive to employ a strategy that He will honor and bless by productive results.

Gene Getz suggests that such strategy can be developed only when the strategy is founded on sound principle. Three "lenses" are suggested to correct the blurred vision of the present church's ministry. One is the "lens of history," which reveals the past efforts of Christendom and the tragic failures of institutionalization. Another is the "lens of contemporary culture," which provides understanding of the today's world and implications for the church's ministry in it. The third and most important lens is the "lens of Scripture," which sets forth the nature of the church, its mission in the world, and basic principles governing the essential tasks of the church's mission. Getz concludes:

> Once we develop a proper perspective biblically, historically, and culturally, we must develop a contemporary strategy based particularly on New Testament principles; we must determine current needs in our own local church, formulate relevant objectives and goals, devise contemporary forms and structures, and use every legitimate resource to be a New Testament church in contemporary culture.[29]

Summary

Christian education is the teaching function of the church. It can be understood only within the context of the church. It has validity only if the church is a nurturing community. The church is that kind of community. It must teach, just as it must preach, if it is to be like the church revealed in the New Testament. Any church that neglects teaching has lost something indispensable to its nature as a church. However, the church is also defective when it allows the structures and methods by which it attempts to teach to become institutional idols. The church is people, not programs. Such people, however, must use their God-given talent to devise programs in order to achieve the divine purposes for which they exist. This is the proper order—divine purpose, committed people, practical and relevant programs.

Christian education begins with the church!

Selected Bibliography

Allen, Roland. *The Spontaneous Expansion of the Church*. Grand Rapids, Michigan: Eerdmans, 1962.

Costas, Orlando. *The Church and Its Mission: A Shattering Critique From the Third World*. Wheaton, Illinois: Tyndale, 1974.

Ellis, David J. and W. Ward Gasque. *In God's Community: Essays on the Church and Its Ministry*. Wheaton, Illinois: Harold Shaw, 1978.

Fallaw, Wesner. *Church Education for Tomorrow*. Philadelphia: Westminster Press, 1960.

Getz, Gene. *Sharpening the Focus of the Church*. Chicago: Moody Press, 1974.

Grimes, Howard. *The Church Redemptive*. Nashville: Abingdon, 1958.

Murch, James. D. *Christian Education in the Local Church*. Cincinnati: Standard Publishing, 1943.

Richards, Lawrence. *A New Face for the Church*. Grand Rapids, Michigan: Zondervan, 1970.

Smart, James D. *The Teaching Ministry of the Church*. Philadelphia: Westminster Press, 1954.

Snyder, Howard. *The Community of the King*. Downers Grove, Illinois: Inter-Varsity Press, 1977.

---

[1] Smart, p. 12

[2] Acts 5:42

[3] Matthew 16:18

[4] Colossians 1:18

[5] 1 Peter 2:5, 9, 10

[6] Acts 2:41, 42

[7] 1 John 1:3

[8] 1 Corinthians 12:25

[9] Galatians 3:28

[10] Acts 1:8; Matthew 28:20

[11] Matthew 28:18-20

[12] See Acts 2:24-42, and other examples throughout the book of Acts

[13] Galatians 3:26-28; John 1:12

[14] Matthew 7:24-27; James 1:22-27

[15] Murch, p. 39

[16] Acts 4:18

[17] Acts 5:42

[18] 2 Timothy 1:11

[19] Acts 11:26, 27; 13:1

[20] Acts 18:11

[21] Acts 19:9, 10

[22] Acts 28:30, 31

[23] Ephesians 4:11, 12

[24] 1 Timothy 3:2; Titus 1:9

[25] 1 Timothy 5:17

[26] 2 Timothy 2:2

[27] Taken from *The Community of the King* by Howard A. Snyder. © 1977 by Inter-Varsity Christian Fellowship of the USA and used by permission of Inter-Varsity Press.

[28] *Ibid.*, p. 168

[29] From *Sharpening the Focus of the Church*, by Gene Getz. Copyright 1974. Moody Press, Moody Bible Institute of Chicago. p. 18. Used by permission.

CHAPTER

2

The Bible Speaks: Biblical and Theological Foundations

As you read, think about these questions:
—What is the nature of the Bible?
—What is meant by the statement, "the Bible is a revelation of reality"?
—How is the Bible revelative, normative, and foundational to Christian education?
—How is the Bible significant for educational content?

The personal nature of the church and its authority can only be understood through the Bible. James D. Smart has shown how the Bible is essential to understanding the nature of the church:

> The Scriptures are the record preserved by the Church of how God revealed himself to it and so called it into being, also of how, by continuing to reveal himself to it, he sustained it in being. It is the record of the Word of God that created the Church; and that is able to create the Church ever afresh when it is rightly heard and obeyed. Thus the Word of God and the Church are inseparable.[1]

The Bible alone reveals the Word of God—living in Jesus and proclaimed in the witness of His apostles. The Bible, then, is the Word of God written or "inscripturated." It is crucial to

24

every task involved in the church's mission, especially its educational task!

The Nature of the Bible

The Bible and Revelation

All revelation can be described by the Biblical phrase "the Word of God." Even what is termed "natural revelation" is a result of the Word of God, for when God initiated the creative process He did so by His Word. In the beginning, God said, "Let there be light;" God said, "Let the earth bring forth living creatures." The psalmist poetically described God's creation as speaking about God:

> The heavens declare the glory of God;
> the skies proclaim the work of his hands.
> Day after day they pour forth speech;
> night after night they display knowledge. . . .
> Their voice goes out into all the earth,
> their words to the ends of the world.[2]

The apostle Paul maintained that the world of nature clearly reveals God to mankind: "Since the creation of the world God's invisible qualities—his eternal power and divine nature—have been clearly seen, being understood from what has been made, so that men are without excuse."[3]

God has spoken not only in what has been created for man, but in man himself. The word of decision was spoken: "Let us make man in our image, in our likeness." Then God created man, "and man became a living being."[4]

Jesus Christ is the key even to this revelation through nature, for He is that Word who "was with God and who was God, through whom all things were made."[5] "He is the image of the invisible God, . . . By him all things were created: things in heaven and on earth, visible and invisible, whether thrones or powers or rulers or authorities; all things were created by him and for him."[6]

But it is God's special revelation that is focused in Jesus Christ. In the Old Testament Scriptures we see God speaking "to our forefathers through the prophets at many times and in various ways," but in the New Testament Scriptures, He is speaking "by his Son."[7] The message of the Bible is God's

drama of redemption. It begins with Adam, who acted disobe-
diently, and concludes with the new Adam, whose obedient act
removed the penalty of the first Adam's disobedience. God
called a people (certain descendants of a man of faith, Abraham) to produce a community of faith through the oft-promised
Son who would be born of these people. Later God entered into
a covenant with this people through the mediation of Moses.
When they violated the covenant, He promised a new covenant
to be mediated through one greater than Moses. In this drama
of redemption, God set forth a law that included both moral
and ceremonial aspects, to show how sinful man really is, but
"when the time had fully come" He sent forth His own Son,
"born of woman, born under law"[8] so that He might redeem all
men by a sacrifice given once for all—not upon a stone altar,
but upon a Roman cross.

This drama, set forth on the stage of human history, is revealed in the Bible. The Bible is a record of God's revelation,
His self-disclosure. As such, the Bible is a trustworthy and
adequate bearer of His revelation. Apart from the Bible we
would not know that this special disclosure had occurred. The
Bible is, therefore, the *indispensable* means of special revelation. (The Bible cannot be identified with all special revelation.
As John says of his Gospel, "Jesus did many other miraculous
signs in the presence of his disciples, which are not recorded in
this book."[9] The same could be said of the Bible.)

The Bible is the special revelation of God put in permanent
form. It records both God's deeds and God's words in understandable human words. The Word is there in the words of
Scripture. Carl F.H. Henry writes:

> In the sense that Scripture sets before us both God's acts and
> words, saving events together with their meaning, special revelation
> becomes equivalent to the Bible. . . . This identification of written
> sentences and propositions with the special divine revelation—the
> recognition, that is, of the Word in the form of words—evangelical
> Christianity holds to be not merely the historic Christian view, but
> an indispensable element in a proper Biblical theology.[10]

There is no contradiction between the Word as written and
the Word as personal. Though a book is not a person, a book
often expresses a person's will, nature, or purpose. In a written
record the history of persons and events are captured and held,
thus making the record both indispensable and authoritative.

The Bible and Inspiration

Revelation has to do with disclosure of content. Inspiration has to do with the guidance of those who are used by God in the revelatory process. "Men spoke from God as they were carried along by the Holy Spirit" is the way Peter describes this process.[11] Paul declares that "all Scripture is God-breathed and is useful for teaching, rebuking, correcting and training in righteousness, so that the man of God may be thoroughly equipped for every good work."[12] Here, Paul relates divine guidance ("God-breathedness") to the product—Scripture! Such guidance guarantees the authority and the benefit of these sacred writings. The writings are trustworthy because the content is disclosed by God and because the method of disclosure is peculiarly guided by the Spirit of God.

Both Peter and Paul referred to the Old Testament when they wrote about the authority of Scripture. Evidence points to the same kind of divine guidance for the New Testament. Jesus promised the apostles the Spirit of truth who would guide them into all truth.[13] The book of Acts presents the apostles as being guided in word and action by the Spirit. Paul was aware that he wrote by the power of the Spirit: "We have not received the spirit of the world but the Spirit who is from God, that we may understand what God has freely given us. This is what we speak, not in words taught us by human wisdom but in words taught by the Spirit."[14]

The Bible is the inspired Word of God. It reveals God's redemptive purpose for man as worked out in human history. Great redemptive acts, such as the exodus of Israel from Egypt, and the achievements of Israel are related and explained. This history reveals God's relationship first to a family (Abraham's), then to a nation (Israel), and finally to a person coming from that family and nation, Jesus of Nazareth, who is revealed as God incarnate. But the Bible is more than history, for it shows that the Lord of history has broken into history to manifest His power and purpose. This divinely disclosed content is our basis for understanding what God's people are to be and do in this present age.

The Bible and Christian Education

Christian education, as Sara Little asserts, "is a servant and not a master of revelation." Biblical revelation determines the educational task and guides the educational process. Since the Bible functions as the primary source and the only inerrant criterion for truth, all presumed facts and opinions must be tested by the inspired writings.

The Bible reveals reality, not mere abstract ideas. This reality demands a response. Lawrence O. Richards writes that God's truth must be heard as more than a message requiring only assent; when God's Word is seen as "a revelation of reality," human beings must come to terms with that reality. When an issue "involves a reconstruction of our understanding of reality, our way of living must also change."[15] Reality-orientation determines one's actions, as Richards illustrates:

> It is because of our reality-orientation that we look for doors to enter buildings rather than try to walk through walls. It is because of our reality-orientation that we hesitate to cross the street in the face of onrushing traffic. Our perception of reality tells us that we cannot walk into walls without bruising and that a mistake in gauging the speed and distance on an oncoming automobile is likely to be our last mistake. *When we are fully convinced that something is rooted in reality, we modify our behavior to harmonize with it.*[16]

The truth of this view is apparent in the social and moral realm as well. Adoption of the "playboy philosophy" regarding sexual behavior follows one's assumption that man is mere animal. The use of falsehood, deception, or other purely manipulative devices in human relations is the result of perceiving human beings as things, or means to ends, not as persons who are ends in themselves. Richards is right: "Our response to people, to situations, to all of life, is based ultimately on our whole-person (conceptual and affectual) orientation to reality."[17]

If the Biblical revelation has come from God who created and ordered all things, then that revelation is by nature a revelation of reality. Reality is not the result of man's construction, but of God's creation. The most accurate perceptions of reality, then, come as man's attempts at understanding are guided by the revealed Word of God. Such perceptions demand decision. The Christian who perceives reality guided by the revelation of God must live in harmony with it.

An understanding of the nature of Biblical revelation has tremendous implications for the Christian educator. Biblical revelation is normative and foundational; that is, it sets the standards and provides a basis for all Christian education, including both the content that is taught and the methods by which it is taught. All educational factors must be in keeping with the reality presented in the Bible.

The Bible must be seen as a reality picture, not just as true information. Scripture must be presented as a revelation of reality that confronts one with choices in response to it.

This approach to Scripture can be summarized as follows:[18]

1. God's Word in Scripture must always be understood as a revelation of reality.

2. God's Word must be taught requiring a decision, to produce action that is in harmony with the reality it reveals.

Secular education (and too often, what has gone under the title of religious or Christian education) is designed to communicate information as "truth to be believed," not as a reality demanding decision. This information-oriented teaching/learning process does not deal with *values*, the "what is important to me" issue on which most accept or reject various points of view. The reality-oriented process does raise such issues.

Only an approach to teaching/learning that seeks to deal with learners' values in a context of open, honest, and loving personal relationships (as are provided in the Christian home and the fellowship of the church) is likely to bring learners to accept and live by the reality revealed in Scripture.

Biblical Theology as Content

The Bible is the standard for the approach taken in Christian education and the content of Christian education. In the Bible we find factual information that becomes the content of Christian teaching, but this information is not presented in systematic form. To collect, collate, systematize, understand, and apply Biblical data is the task of the Biblical theologian. Biblical theology is the result. These Biblical concepts, thus arranged, become the basic content from which a curriculum for Christian education is developed.

Biblical revelation begins with God as Creator—perfect, self-revealing, loving, and saving. It involves man, created in God's image, but fallen from that perfect state and in need of redemption and reorientation of his life and thought. The Bible further reveals *Jesus, the incarnate Son of God*, come into the world of reality to provide a real way out of man's predicament by His own atoning life, death, and resurrection. It reveals the church, a family of families, in which worship, fellowship, nurture, and outreach are the essential tasks and relationships of this new community of faith set in the world to accomplish God's purposes.

The Biblical Concept of God

God is revealed in Scripture as Creator, Lord, and Redeemer. His triune nature as Father, Son, and Spirit is seen, not as the basis of speculative philosophy, but in His actions towards man, the crown of His creation. The Father created man in love and for fellowship, but His creation rebelled and sinned against Him. The Son came into the world as a man, as a servant, to redeem and reconcile mankind by His own sacrificial death. The Son was raised from the dead; through the Holy Spirit, He created the church, through which the ultimate purpose of God is to be accomplished. The Spirit led apostolic witnesses into all truth, inspired authentic gospel preaching and Christian teaching; He indwells and energizes individual believers in the body of Christ, the church.

This triune God created man, redeemed man, provided revelation for man, and became an example and substitute for man so that sin may be overcome in man's life. God commands His people to teach and nurture their children so that they may live obediently in relation to Him. He has created the nurturing contexts of family and church wherein this process is to be carried out.

The Biblical Concept of Man

Man is revealed in Scripture as separate from all other created beings because he alone is created in God's image. Man is created to subdue and rule his world. Man is created male and female. Human sexuality is part of that goodness pronounced by God upon His work. Man is created for fellowship—the human fellowship of family and society and divine fellowship with God.

But man has succumbed to temptation, sinned against God, and fallen from his high position. Such sin, through prideful autonomy, has affected all of humanity and the material world as well. Alienation and separation, has become the universal experience both in relation to God and in relation to others. As sinner, man stands in need of a Redeemer. As flawed from

God's original intention, man is in need of a perfect example.

In the perfect manhood of Jesus, the incarnate Son of God, man's need is met, man's sin atoned for, and man's broken fellowship restored. It is in Jesus that flawed humanity sees its perfect pattern and goal. Christian teaching is designed to bring prodigals "to themselves" and speed them on the way home to the Father to live as redeemed sons.

The Biblical Concept of Salvation

Salvation is the theme of the Biblical drama. Sin has ruined the human race. It must be overcome. But man, the sinner, cannot save himself; salvation can only come from that gracious God of love. The initiative was taken by God through the election of a family, a race, a nation. God set in motion the series of historical events we read of in the Old Testament. A covenant of law and works bound the nation of Israel to God.

But the covenant was only temporary. A new covenant of grace, forgiveness, and loving relationship was promised. That new relationship was made possible by a Savior, Christ the Lord, coming into the world as the Incarnate Son of God, born of a virgin. This person grew to manhood, gave himself to a Messianic ministry of healing and service, and voluntarily went to His death on a cross, to bear the sins of all who would accept Him as Savior and Lord. The resurrection of this dead Jesus gave assurance that His atoning work has been accepted by the Father. With His ascension into Heaven, Jesus began His mediatorial and intercessory work as high priest, "able to save completely those who come to God through Him."[19] This same Jesus will come a second time and gather His own from the four corners of the earth—the resurrected dead and the living who will be instantly changed[20]—to enjoy eternity in the presence of God.

But such salvation is not "cheap grace." The life of the Christian is a sanctified life in which holiness is demanded. Within the church, by means of the indwelling Spirit, the saved individual is to be a servant, a minister using the gifts he has to witness about this great salvation to others in word and deed.

Christian ethics is more than do-goodism. Smart is right in his keen criticism of Christian education programs that perpetuate a "suffocating fog of moralism:"

The Christian standard of conduct is not a natural possibility for any person; it is a supernatural possibility, to be realized only through the redemptive power of Jesus Christ working in human persons through the gospel. Therefore, to impress upon a child or youth or adult his duty to fulfill the Christian standard, and to leave him ignorant of the truth of the gospel which alone makes him aware how that standard is to be fulfilled, is as absurd and exasperating as to order a man to shovel two feet of snow from a hundred feet of sidewalk and give him no shovel with which to do it. Moralism bores us because it confronts us with an impossibility. By the very nature of things, ethics are always insecure until they are firmly rooted in our understanding of truth.[21]

The Biblical Concept of the Church and Its Ministry

The church is revealed in the New Testament Scriptures as the community of the disciples of Jesus Christ, who have found peace and pardon from their sins. Entered by obedience to Jesus Christ, the partnership with God demands gratitude expressed in worship and service. It is a "gathered fellowship" to worship, learn, and grow in grace; it is a "scattered fellowship" to preach, teach, and serve.

Each Christian must minister in Christ's stead. The foundational ministry of the church includes all of God's people. But this ministry of the church is also functional. It involves various tasks—preaching, teaching, serving. Every Christian is not equipped to do all these tasks. A variety of service gifts have been given by the one Spirit.[22] Each Christian is to minister, discovering and using his gift to glorify God and help the church grow. And there is a formal ministry, an equipping ministry, revealed in the Scriptures. The Lord gave apostles and prophets in apostolic days to provide the authoritative word of witness. He also gave evangelists, pastors, teachers in every age to share that Word with those without and within the fellowship.[23]

Summary

Through Christian teaching, God's revelation of reality is grasped, and lives are changed to conform to reality. Through the teaching ministry of the church, lives are enriched and individuals are equipped to further the church's ministry in the world. Through Christian nurture, both within Christian families and the greater family of God, young people are led to faithful commitment to Jesus Christ and introduced into an ever-continuing cycle of outreach and growth. The Biblical revelation of reality is the indispensable source and authoritative guide by which such Christian nurture occurs.

Selected Bibliography

Cully, Iris V. *Imparting the Word*. Philadelphia: Westminster Press, 1963.

Gaebelein, Frank. *The Pattern of God's Truth*. New York: Oxford University Press, 1954.

Henry, Carl F. H. (ed.) *Revelation and the Bible*. Grand Rapids, Michigan: Baker, 1958.

LeBar, Lois E. *Education That Is Christian*. Westwood, New Jersey: Revell, 1958.

Richards, Lawrence. *Youth Ministry*. Grand Rapids, Michigan: Zondervan, 1972.

Smart, James D. *The Teaching Ministry of the Church*. Philadelphia: Westminster Press, 1958.

Walker, Dean E. *The Authority of the Word*. Milligan College, 1950.

Walvoord, John W. (ed.) *Inspiration and Interpretation*. Grand Rapids, Michigan: Eerdmans, 1957.

---

[1]From *The Teaching Ministry of the Church,* by James D. Smart. Copyright © MCMLIV, by Walter L. Jenkins. Used by permission of The Westminster Press.

[2]Psalm 19:1, 2, 4
[3]Romans 1:20
[4]Genesis 1:26; 2:7
[5]John 1:1-3
[6]Colossians 1:15-18
[7]Hebrews 1:1, 2
[8]Galatians 4:4
[9]John 20:30
[10]Walvoord, p. 256
[11]2 Peter 1:21
[12]2 Timothy 3:16, 17
[13]John 16:13
[14]1 Corinthians 2:12, 13
[15]YOUTH MINISTRY: ITS RENEWAL IN THE LOCAL CHURCH by Lawrence O. Richards. Copyright © 1972 by The Zondervan Corporation. p. 177. Used by permission.
[16]*Ibid.*, p. 178
[17]*Ibid.*
[18]*Ibid.*, p. 182
[19]Hebrews 7:25
[20]1 Thessalonians 4:13; 1 Corinthians 15:51, 52

[21]Smart, p. 79 (see reference #1)
[22]See Romans 12 and 1 Corinthians 12
[23]Ephesians 4:7-13

CHAPTER

3

The Lessons of History

As you read, think about these questions:
—What are the three important institutions for Christian teaching in the early church?
—Why are the Renaissance and Reformation so important to Christian education?
—Describe the strong religious emphasis in early American education.
—How influential was the Sunday-school movement upon Christian education in the nineteenth century?
—What is meant by the *church school?*

Wherever there is a vital, dynamic religion, there is religious education. Such a religion establishes types of "schools" by which it can teach its basic beliefs and expected behaviors. The Christian community was and is a living religion. It demanded an educational ministry in the first century, and when it has been truest to its basic principles, it has demanded education throughout its history.

An historical study of Christian education provides a perspective for understanding the nature and practice of church education. It shows how, throughout history, the leaders of the Christian religion responded to the need for education in a way suitable to both their religion and their culture. One can learn what the men and women of different periods of Christian history felt was essential to perpetuate the faith. One can distill from their words and actions what objectives governed their teaching. Glaring needs for more effective nurture become apparent as the study progresses.

Christian Education in the Early Church

The Biblical mandate to teach has been essential to the Judeo-Christian heritage since the time of Abraham. Such teaching was centered in the family. When other educational emphases were added through the specific provisions of Covenant-Law, the family continued to be the center. The temple, priests, rituals, symbolic feasts and fasts, and other matters were supplemental. Even after the exile and the dispersion of Jews throughout the Mediterranean world, the family continued to be the supreme educator. The family was the driving force of such new agencies as the synagogue and the late-developing synagogue school of the first century B.C.

This strong emphasis upon religious education, carried on generation after generation in family synagogue and school, is a significant part of the historical and religious context of Jesus and the apostles. Jesus himself was a teacher. He was more, of course; but He was known to his contemporaries as *Rabbi*, Teacher. His methods were educational, not oratorical. His final command to His apostles was to "go and make disciples of all nations, . . . teaching them to obey everything that I have commanded you."[1] The apostles taught as well as preached. Spiritual leaders were to be "able to teach,"[2] so that the instruction would be continued from generation to generation.

A second institution was the *worship service* in which the entire community participated. Patterned after the synagogue service, the apostolic church strongly emphasized teaching and prayer. The apostles understood worship in teaching terms, not aesthetic terms. Even the Lord's Supper contributed to this teaching emphasis. The observance of the Lord's Supper was a teaching tool, a memorial, to spur remembrance and continued understanding of Jesus' redemptive work.

The service of worship grew in length and complexity throughout the early Christian centuries. From the second century on it had two clearly differentiated segments. The first of these was known as the *missa catechumenous*, or the mass of the catechumens. This was a teaching service patterned after the synagogue service of Judaism. Persons who were receiving instruction prior to baptism, known as *catechumens*, were allowed to participate in this portion of the service. It included the reading and interpretation of Scripture. These catechumens were known as "hearers." After this segment of the worship service, the "hearers" were dismissed and the baptized believers remained for the *missa fidelium*, the mass of the faithful. Here the Sacrament of the Lord's Supper was celebrated.

The third institution, necessitated by a growing pagan influx, was the *catechumenate* that flourished in the early church from the second to the fifth centuries. Great numbers of adults from pagan backgrounds were attracted to the church by what they heard and saw. They were prepared neither morally nor intellectually for the demands of the Christian faith that membership in the church entailed. The catechumenate, an adult education program, was devised to meet this need. There seems to have been a threefold purpose of this rather informal educational program: "to provide a period of moral probation during which the candidate's sincerity could be tested; to give instruction on the Bible and the doctrines of the church; and to admit the candidate into a limited but genuine Christian fellowship while he was preparing for baptism."[3] This program was related to the worship service, but careful instruction often was given at other times, either individually or in groups. (Pantaeus, the great Alexandrian teacher, speaks of coming to his Christian faith at "the rude bench of the catechumen."

The plan of such a program that Origen knew (in Alexandria, about A.D. 250) seems to have followed these steps: (1) a preliminary examination of the candidate's moral character and occupation (many occupations were forbidden to Christians); (2) private instruction given to each candidate as seemed necessary; (3) admittance to and participation in the service of worship as a "hearer;" (4) additional instruction outside the worship services in informal classes; (5) further inquiry into the growth and development of the candidate, intellectually and morally; and, (6) intensive instruction prior to baptism and church membership. Such programs varied from area to area.

Christian Education in the Medieval Church

From the middle of the fifth century until the beginning of the sixteenth century, Christian education languished. Several factors contributed to this dearth. The clergy began to dominate more and more, and little individual responsibility of the laity was stressed. Along with the growing practice of infant baptism, this trend cut the foundation from under such an educational program as the catechumenate. The union of state and church tended to eliminate high moral and intellectual standards, since it erased any important differences between believers and unbelievers. Then, too, the dissolution of the Roman empire under the deluge of barbarianism created an instability detrimental to educational development both in church and in society. The institutional church continued to exist and even to "Christianize" the barbaric tribes, but Christian education suffered enormously.

But the light of learning was not completely extinguished during those Dark Ages. Pockets of concern for education still existed in various parts of Europe. Charles the Great of Frankland and, later, Alfred of England attempted educational reforms that had beneficial effect, though mostly for the religious and civic leadership of the day. But even the laity received some informal Christian education. They observed and participated in worship, learning some parts of the service such as the creed, the Lord's Prayer, and the Ave Maria. Beginning in the tenth century, they watched religious drama that portrayed certain Biblical and theological themes. As a result, a sort of popular theology developed that combined Christian doctrine and superstition.

These types of informal popular Christian education did not contribute greatly to the spiritual growth of Christendom, but there was unprecedented institutional and hierarchical growth during this period.

For the nobility there were formal schools. Monastic orders established schools to prepare novices for monastic life. In certain areas, these schools were opened to the sons and daughters of nobility. Cathedral schools developed at the center of the diocese primarily for the training of priests, though these were often open to sons of noblemen as well. The curriculum in these schools centered around the traditional seven liberal arts: grammar, rhetoric, and logic making up the trivium; and arithmetic, music, geometry, and astronomy comprising the quadrivium. To these were added theology and, in some instances, canon and civil law, and medicine.

Toward the close of the twelfth century, certain of the cathedral schools developed into medieval universities as they freed themselves from diocesan control through a guild-like organization of teachers and students. Such universities as Paris, Bologna, Oxford, and Cambridge gave birth to many other similar institutions during the later Renaissance period. Many of the students at these universities were of the clergy, thus higher education became part of the great tradition in Christian education.

Renaissance and Reformation

The Renaissance, beginning the latter part of the thirteenth century, left an indelible mark on education in general. This "revival" or "rebirth" laid the foundation for the humanistic tradition in education. It exalted the individual, quickened interest in this world as well as the next, and recovered the ancient languages and the classical literature of Greece and Rome. It was a secular movement, in the main, "stressing the delights of living, the ideal of liberty, the free exercise of criticism, and, among those who found Christian morality too binding, a freedom from moral restraints."[4]

Along with the Reformation movement, the Renaissance caused great ferment in continental Europe, which penetrated every phase of life. The monolithic power of the Roman Church was broken, nationalism became the order of the day, and individualism grew quickly. The Reformation was distinctly religious, though certainly influenced by the Renaissance (particularly the Christian Renaissance of the North associated with Richard Groote and the Brothers of Common Life). Educationally, the Renaissance and Reformation established the humanistic tradition: Christian education must be concerned with human life, its past development and present opportunities, as well as with theology and ecclesiastical concerns.

The Reformation set forth three basic principles that have had far-reaching consequences in education. The first was the replacement of papal authority with the authority of the Scriptures. The second was the doctrine of "the priesthood of every believer," which stressed individual responsibility before God. The third principle, derived from the first two, demanded universal education. If each individual is responsible to God, he must understand that responsibility in terms of the Word. The Word could be understood only by one who was educated.

Martin Luther, Ulrich Zwingli, John Calvin, and other Reformation leaders encouraged civic leaders to establish schools for both boys and girls. In 1524 Luther addressed a letter to the Mayors and Councillors of all the German cities, urging the establishment of such schools both for the edification of the church and the advancement of civic life. John Bugenhagen, a colleague of Luther, led in the establishment of vernacular primary schools (schools conducted in the native language, not Latin) in northern German parishes. Phillipp Melanchthon, who served with Luther on the faculty of the University of Wittenberg, was instrumental in the establishment and upgrading of secondary education at the grammar school and university levels, where Christian humanism became the content of the curriculum.

In Switzerland, John Calvin was moving along the same lines as the Lutherans. In 1538, he proposed a plan for the school system of Geneva that began with elementary vernacular schools open to all. Secondary schools, called "colleges," were to be established; in these, humanistic and religious studies could be combined so that leaders for both state and church could be trained. John Knox, following Calvin's lead, encouraged the establishment of schools in Scotland based upon this plan. Comparable programs developed in the Netherlands, where Calvinism was also prominent. Thus the two great branches of the Protestant Reformation—Lutheranism and Calvinism—stressed the importance of Christian education.

Not only did the Reformation demand and develop a system of universal Christian education, but it also aided education by translating the Scriptures into the vernacular and distributing these as widely as possible. Such translations were read in church, used in the home, and studied in the schools. The reformers recovered the lost art of preaching with the Bible as the basic content. They also began preaching in the language of the people. Such preaching brought revival and renewal to a church dying in formalism.

The recovery of Biblical Christianity also led to a reestablishment of the home as a center of education, as it has been in apostolic times. Here the Bible and catechisms based upon the Bible (like Luther's Shorter Catechism) were used to instruct children and youth in the basic tenets of the faith. Such home teaching was especially strong among the Dutch, the Scots, and the English Puritans.

Christian Education in America

American Colonial Education

The dominant educational theory and practice of the American colonialism was transplanted from Europe. The English cavaliers of the southern American colonies brought the pattern of Anglicanism, which centered education in the family. Families provided for their children in tuition schools or by a tutor in the home, if they could; children of poorer families received little educational opportunities.

In New England, Calvinistic Puritanism led to the establishment of elementary schools in every township, after the Calvinistic pattern. In addition, secondary education was also established with Latin grammar schools in the larger towns and the establishment of Harvard College in 1636. In New England the religious impulse was strong, and there was church-state cooperation in bringing the schools into existence.

In the middle colonies, the diversity of the religious groups limited the provisions. Each religious group (many with different ethnic and language backgrounds—Dutch, Swedish, Moravian, English Catholic, English Quaker) provided whatever education it could in a parochial pattern. Since there was no impetus by the state or civil governments, as in New England, such provisions were frequently minimal.

Post-Revolutionary Developments

Independence from England and the formation of a new nation brought changes to the patterns of education that had developed among the colonies. The principle of the separation of church and state in the first amendment of the Constitution (especially as the principle was later espoused in state constitutions) eliminated the government support of a particular religious group. This principle was to have far-reaching consequences for American education, particularly Christian education.

Beginning in New England, where universal education was already an established pattern, the states one by one developed a system of public schools. But since these schools were open to all, the elimination of sectarian teaching (teaching that would favor one church group over another) resulted in "secularization," which meant "the withdrawal of the support from private and church schools and the elimination of religious controls over the public schools."[5] State after state wrote provisions into their constitutions prohibiting the use of tax funds for private or parochial schools.

Thus the churches could no longer depend upon the public schools to teach their particular religious tenets. The alternative was to continue to maintain a system of parochial schools supported by church funds (as the Roman Catholics, many Lutheran groups, and other smaller groups did), or to find some way to provide for the teaching of religion and the instilling of their specific beliefs and practices. Fortunately, the Sunday school had been introduced into American life, and these schools became the formal instrument by which most American Protestant groups were able to continue their religious instruction.

The Sunday-School Movement

The origin of the Sunday school is attributed to Robert Raikes, a reform-minded journalist of Gloucester, England, who became concerned about the plight of poor children who had no educational opportunities. In 1780 he began to collect these youngsters on Sunday (the only day they were free from work responsibilities) in order to give them general instruction. His "noble experiment" proved successful, and soon was repeated throughout Great Britain with tremendous results. Sunday-school societies were established to aid these schools by paying the teachers and providing funds for curriculum materials. These early schools were conducted throughout the day on Sunday, with time out to participate in religious services. Instruction in reading, writing, and arithmetic were combined with study of the Bible and the catechism.

Because of a comparable need in colonial America, the Sunday school was introduced as early as 1785. By 1790, the Methodist Conference endorsed such educational ventures and encouraged Methodist preachers to promote them. In 1816, the Philadelphia Union was established to promote Sunday schools in that geographical area. By 1824, several of these city unions merged to form the American Sunday School Union. This union, serving as a non-denominational missionary agency, began to establish Sunday schools wherever there were people, particularly in pioneer and neglected areas.

By the time secularization was developing rapidly within the public schools, the Sunday school was a recognized agency for religious instruction. The churches in the 1830's and 1840's began to embrace the Sunday school as the means to provide religious instruction. Because of this specific use by the various denominations, the Sunday-school movement grew rapidly in the following decades.

After the Civil War, the Sunday-school movement began to find interdenominational cohesion through nationwide Sunday-school conventions and associations. National conventions, first held in 1832, were resumed and met regularly. A world convention was held in 1889. Through these conventions, county, state, and eventually national Sunday school associations developed. These associations, interdenominational and largely lay-dominated, attempted to promote Sunday school interest and develop policies.

Two areas in which these conventions and associations were deeply concerned were the training of teachers and the development of curriculum. Most Sunday school teachers were volunteers recruited from local churches. Few had any specific training. Various proposals for Sunday-school teacher training were set forth, inspired by the methods for training public school teachers. These ranged from reading courses to extensive city institutes for religious instruction.

Along with the need for trained teachers, the need for a curricular system was also felt. In 1872, the International Sunday School Convention adopted a uniform lesson plan and established a lesson committee to develop this plan. Though some denominational boards and publishers opposed the plan, it soon won general favor. An improved and modified uniform lesson plan is still used widely today. This plan provided one lesson graded for all ages in all schools. Such a systematic study of the Bible gave an opportunity for any publishers to provide expositions and helps for the teacher. Though the plan greatly aided volunteer teachers and tended to standardize content, it has been under critical scrutiny for a number of years. Many denominations no longer use this system, preferring alternate approaches that they believe are more educationally sound.

From Sunday School to Church School

In the latter part of the nineteenth century, other needs became apparent that the Sunday school could not meet. Attempts were made to meet the expressional needs of youth through young people's societies, of which Christian Endeavor was the forerunner. This movement began in 1881 in the Williston Congregational Church, Portland, Maine, under the leadership of Francis Clark. Christian Endeavor, appealing to Christian youth's needs for combining study, expression, and service, grew rapidly across denominational lines and stimulated various denominations to begin their own youth programs.

Other youth-related educational programs began in the late nineteenth century, including Christian camping and the campus ministry. The church followed its students to the colleges, first through the interdenominational YMCA begun in the 1840's, then through the efforts of the individual denominations. Christian camping grew out of the camp meeting tradition of the nineteenth century and provided a means of Christian nurture and growth for youth. Organizations like the Salvation Army, YMCA, and the International Sunday School Association established camping programs that stimulated denominational programs.

After the turn of the century, such programs as daily vacation Bible school and weekday religious education were established to supplement and expand the churches' educational program. Vacation Bible school began in 1901 in New York City under the leadership of Dr. Robert Boville. The movement grew so rapidly that within twenty years, every Protestant denomination was sponsoring such schools. The movement that promoted weekday religious education began in Gary, Indiana, where the council of churches and the public school officials developed a "released-time plan" so that children could participate in religious instruction on a weekly basis. This program, guided by Myron Settles, soon spread throughout the nation.

At about this time many leading religious educators were rediscovering Horace Bushnell's emphasis on the Christian family set out in his work *Christian Nurture* as early as 1847. In this classic work Bushnell pleaded for recognition of the Christian family as the chief agency for both evangelism and education. The rise of the child psychology movement after the turn of the century vindicated much of Bushnell's emphasis. It promoted better teaching methods in the formal programs of Christian education, and also elevated the home to an important role in Christian education.

All of these educational emphases (and others such as the adult Sunday-school class emphasis) arose independently of one another. The need for correlation and unification became apparent. The Religious Education Association (established in 1903 under the leadership of Dr. William Rainey Harper, president of the University of Chicago) appointed a committee to address this need. Dr. W. S. Athearn, professor of education at Drake University, headed this committee and authored the results of their deliberations under the title The Church School. This work, published in 1914, suggested that all the different facets of Christian education be correlated under a board or department of Christian education. This board would give oversight and supervision to a total program of education for the church. Thus, the religious education movement in America had evolved from a Sunday school to a church school. The Sunday school no longer carried the total weight of Christian nurture for the churches. Now a number of educational agencies and emphases were correlated to fulfill the church's mandate to teach and nurture.

The Current Scene

Two trends in the first quarter of the twentieth century greatly affected the religious education movement. The first of these was the influence of theological liberalism that spread to America from Europe. Almost every Protestant denomination was affected. Invariably, the liberal segment captured the colleges and seminaries, mission boards, and educational boards of the denomination. The liberal position is difficult to pinpoint, for liberalism was more an attitude than a position. This liberal attitude (some called it the scientific attitude or the attitude of the open mind) tended to embrace the dogma of evolution, radical Biblical criticism, and the social gospel, leading to some fairly general positions:

1. God was seen either as impersonal (as a social concept), or as a sentimental Father of love in whom there was no wrath or judgment.

2. The Bible was looked upon as a sourcebook of religious inspiration, containing legend, myth, and folklore that emphasize a basic morality but not a supernatural absolute.

3. Christ was confessed as a great man, a wonderful moral teacher, but not deity in any unique sense. His death was not

sacrificial or substitionary, and His resurrection was often denied or explained as a mythical indication of some kind of human immortality.

4. The kingdom of God was not the supernatural role of God in the hearts of sinful men saved by Christ's vicarious atonement, but an earthly kingdom to be achieved by educational and legislative reform. The concept of sin was often ignored entirely.

Many of the leaders of the religious education movement accepted the liberal position in part or totally. This affected both the philosophy and the procedures of religious education. Methods were borrowed from the progressive education movement, associated with John Dewey, with its interest in child-centeredness and the "social project." This progressive movement shared with religious liberalism its emphasis upon divine eminence, the inevitability of religious growth, the innate goodness of man, and the concept of the historical Jesus as only an ethical teacher and martyred prophet. Only an occasional voice was raised against this trend.

Liberalism's influence in religious education may be seen statistically. When liberalism became entrenched in the religous education movement, Sunday-school growth declined. From 1906 to 1916 there had been a thirty-five percent increase in Sunday-school membership compared to a 19.5 percent increase in church membership and approximately 17.5 percent increase in population. The next ten years (1916-1926) saw only a six percent increase in Sunday-school membership. From 1926 to 1936 there was an eleven percent loss compared to a 2.2 percent gain in church membership and ten percent gain in population. The individual denominational statistics are even more revealing. Some of the larger denominations that had accepted the general liberal position decreased as much as thirty-four percent. Most of the smaller conservative groups, however, were making tremendous gains at the same time. The Assemblies of God had an increase of more than 300 percent during this decade. Undoubtedly, there were other causes for the decline in Sunday-school membership, but the influence of theological liberalism had much to do with it.

A second trend was what could be called a growing ecclesiastical sectarianism. The nineteenth-century Sunday-school movement was interdenominational and largely lay-controlled. Denominational boards and publishers were opposed to such control. To offset the influence of the International Sunday School Association and capture control for individual denominations, these leaders formed the Sunday School Council of Evangelical Denominations in 1906. When fighting between this organization and the International Sunday School Association reached a peak, a truce was declared and a joint committee was established looking toward merger. W. S. Athearn, a leader in the International Sunday School Association, led the two organizations to merge. The merger plans allowed for greater control by the denominational boards, but also maintained the older concepts of lay activity and control by local authority.

But when these two organizations merged into a new organization (known as the International Council of Religious Education), the denominational publishing agents set themselves to secure control of the new organization. A professional spirit replaced the zealous humility that characterized the voluntarism of the lay leaders of the International Sunday School Association. This council has now, by merger, become the Division of Christian Education of the National Council of Churches of Christ in America, and is further alienated from formerly supportive evangelicals.

With liberalism and professionalism dominating the organization that had historically given direction to American religious education, Bible-believing groups were left without guidance. Some of these, like the Southern Baptists, were large enough to develop an excellent program of their own. Others depended upon whatever direction the older independent publishers such as Standard Publishing Company, David C. Cook, and Union Gospel Press could provide. New publishing ventures, such as Scripture Press, Gospel Light Publications, and R. B. Sweet Company were begun to meet some of these needs.

New interdenominational evangelical agencies were also established to meet some of these challenges. These parachurch organizations provided yeomen service during the years of disappointment and confusion. In 1942, the National Association of Evangelicals came into being as an interdenominational evangelical organization in which "cooperation without compromise" could be secured for Bible-believing individuals, churches, and denominations. Leaders of this organization proposed the reestablishment of a National Sunday School Association. This was accomplished in 1946. This agency, and its associated city, area, and state agencies, have helped to re-emphasize Christian education among evangelical groups.

Summary

What does the future hold for Christian education? One can only suggest certain trends. Even among those mainline denominations that have historic association with the Division of Christian Education of the National Council of Churches, there is a healthier approach to the Bible and theology. Much has been written by such leaders as R. C. Miller, James D. Smart, L. J. Sherrill, and others that point toward a renewal of Biblical relevance for Christian education. In evangelical circles this relevance is taken even more seriously, for evangelical Christian educators such as Lawrence O. Richards, Gene Getz, Edward Hayes, and many others are committed to the full authority of the Bible, and are attempting to restate what this Biblical authority means for the church's educational task.

New methods have also been stressed. The behavioral sciences have helped in the development of new methods. Audiovisuals, group methods, and role-play are some of the newer methods used in vital programs of Christian teaching.

With the growing secularism and other problems in the public schools, many Christian families are opting for Christian day school education for their children. This movement is growing rapidly. Such schools not only provide general education from a thoroughly Christian perspective, but also stress the study of the Bible, which cannot be done in the secular public school.

Millions are not involved in any kind of Christian education. The challenge they present is ever before us. Workers must be trained, teachers inspired, students recruited, and the best methods and programs employed. The church must reach and teach those in need of the salvation provided by the Father through His Son Jesus Christ.

Selected Bibliography

Barclay, William. *Train Up a Child: Educational Ideals in the Ancient World*. Philadelphia: Westminster Press, 1960.

Benson, Clarence H. *A Popular History of Christian Education*. Chicago: Moody Press, 1943.

Castle, E. B. *Moral Education in Christian Times.* New York: Macmillan, 1958.

Cully, K. B. (ed.) *Basic Writings in Christian Education.* Philadelphia: Westminster Press, 1960.

Eavey, C. B. *History of Christian Education.* Chicago: Moody Press, 1964.

Kennedy, William B. *The Shaping of Protestant Education.* New York: Associated Press, 1964.

Lynn, Robert W. *Protestant Strategies in Education.* New York: Associated Press, 1964.

Miller, R. C. *Education for Christian Living.* Englewood Cliffs, New Jersey: Prentice-Hall, 1963.

Sherrill, Lewis J. *The Rise of Christian Education.* New York: Macmillan, 1944.

---

[1]Matthew 28:19, 20
[2]1 Timothy 3:2; 2 Timothy 2:2
[3]Sherrill, p. 66
[4]Miller, p. 22
[5]Sherrill, p. 20

CHAPTER

4

Toward a Philosophy of Christian Education

As you read, think about these questions:
—What is meant by *philosophy*?
—What are some of the elements of a philosophy of Christian education?
—How are the traditional areas of philosophy related to Christian education?
—What are some of the implications of the philosophy of Christian education for educational practices and procedures?

A philosophy of Christian education can help us understand Christian action as it relates to the revealed Word. The following is an attempt to explore such a philosophy.

A Word About Philosophy

The term *philosophy*, which literally means "love of wisdom," has been used in different ways. Its classical use was to refer to the products of thought, the attempts at developing a comprehensive interpretation of the universe. More recently, philosophy has been seen as a means of clarifying meanings and relationships, rather than in developing systems of interpreting reality.

The term is used in a less sophisticated way in the phrase "philosophy of life." Everyone is, in this sense, a philosopher, since each person makes choices and assumes certain values in terms of those beliefs (positive or negative) that guide his life. However uncritical or inconsistent these beliefs may be, they determine thought and action.

Philosophy as a method is concerned with careful thought. It is an attempt to see things as a whole and to interpret the data presented by all aspects of reality. As content, philosophy attempts to set forth a comprehensive answer to the ultimate questions: What is the nature of reality? What is the origin of the universe, and man? What is the nature of knowledge, and how is it possible? What is the ultimate destiny of man and the world?

One immediately sees the interrelationship of philosophy and religion. They are not identical, but they overlap each other. Through the centuries attempts have been made to wed the two. Others have seen such attempts as a dubious and dangerous flirtation. In the second and third centuries of the Christian era, Justin Martyr (c100-165), Clement of Alexandria (c150-215), and others assured their readers "that many a pagan had been led to true religion through philosophy and that philosophy was to the ancient Greeks what the Old Testament was to the Jews."[1] But at the same time, others such as Tertullian (c160-220) were speaking vociferously against any such alliance.

Philosophy's value has been apparent only when it has become the servant of religion. All too often throughout Christian history, these roles have been reversed: religion was tailored to the prevailing philosophical viewpoint and that which Paul warned against in his letter to the Colossians occurred: "See to it that no one takes you captive through hollow and deceptive philosophy, which depends on human tradition and the basic principles of this world rather than on Christ."[2] But the use of man's redeemed mind to think clearly about reality is a worthy pursuit—not only in itself, but in its practical apologetic value, so that the confusion of unclear thinking and its results might be swept away to make room for faith. Such reasonable faith can help convince Christianity's cultured despisers.

In modern times philosophy is no longer the pretentious and all-inclusive subject it had been to the ancients. The philosopher's method was applied to various specific areas of human thought and activity. Hence, there developed the philosophy of history, the philosophy of religion, the philosophy of science, the philosophy of law, and other "professionalized" philosophies. These were attempts to think carefully and critically about specific areas of knowledge and develop a more pragmatic approach to understanding and performing in them. The philosophy of education is seen in this sense.

The philosophy of Christian education is the application of critical thinking to the educational enterprise of the church. It is "the analysis of the underlying principles or presuppositions implied in the religious community's effort to teach its faith."[3] Whence come these principles and presuppositions? This crucial question becomes the watershed of current theoretical statements of Christian educational philosophy.

Components of a Philosophy of Christian Education

Beginning Point

Any philosophical approach must have a beginning point. In current attempts to develop a philosophy of Christian education, one must begin with a thorough commitment to that "revelation of reality" seen in Scripture; the alternative is to begin with man's ability to select concepts to provide a basis for the church's educational task. There is no other option. The philosopher of Christian education must stand not only on the Word, but under the Word. He must bring his thinking into submission to the "mind of Christ" as seen in the Word of truth, the Scriptures. The Scriptural revelation of reality provides the framework for a Christian world view that is the presuppositional base for any educational enterprise.

Frank E. Gaebelein has listed some of the elements of that world view set out in the Bible.

> The living God, Creator of all things, Source of all being, Sovereign of the universe; man created in the divine image, an image ruined through sin beyond human power to repair but not beyond God's power to regenerate; the incarnation of the Son of God, and His atoning and renewing work through His death and resurrection; the activity of the Holy Spirit in the outcalling of Christ's Body, the Church; and the consummation of earthly history through the

"glorious appearing of the Great God, and our Savior Jesus Christ"—these are the spacious context of a Christian philosophy not only of education but also of any other area of human knowledge and concern.[4]

Gaebelein adds: "Nor is there anything sectarian or cultic about this framework; the truths comprising it are in the best sense ecumenical. Although they are and have been clouded by tradition and dogma or weakened by rationalistic concessions, such truths as these remain the essential frame of reference for a Christian world view."[5]

Such a Christian world view, derived from the reality revealed in the Bible, is the touchstone of all other areas of knowledge. Whatever physical science says it has discovered about the universe in which we live, whatever biological science claims about the essential aspects of life, whatever psychology says about human behavior, whatever sociology may posit about human relationships, group and society cultures—these must all be evaluated in terms of this Christian point of view.

Behavioral Research

Since Christian education is particularly concerned with people (teachers and students), careful scrutiny must be given to the behavioral sciences—anthropology, sociology, and psychology.

There is no unanimity among these scientists. Some of the views developed in these fields are compatible with a Christian world view; others are diametrically opposed. Many behavioral scientists operate on naturalistic assumptions that would eliminate human freedom and responsibility. They see man as material, not spiritual, with no relation to a sovereign Creator who made man in His own image. Such a view is incompatible with the Christian view of man, notes Lawrence Bixler: "To attempt to teach the Christian faith by a method that rests upon a psychology that is mechanistic and humanistic is to defeat the very purpose of Christian teaching."[6]

While secular insights into man's behavior should always be tested against the Scriptural view of man, they should not be ignored totally. Facts about human personality may be discovered that are "usable concepts even in those systems which have an inadequate world view or frame of reference. It is the frame of reference that distorts the meaning of the facts. The facts remain regardless of the meaning that is attached to them."[7] [8]

A Philosophy of Christian Education

In the past, any philosophy of education has frequently been identified in terms of four basic types or systems of philosophy in general. These four are Naturalism, Idealism, Realism, and Pragmatism. When these systems are analyzed in order to formulate a philosophy of Christian education, they are either rejected or certain elements are chosen from one or more of the systems compatible with the analyst's position. Another system is suggested here, one that allows for no competitors, that may be called "revelational theism" or "Christian realism."[9] A tentative philosophy of Christian education can be set forth in terms of this system in two different ways: (1) to state one's philosophy in terms of the various content areas of the philosophical enterprise; (2) to present certain educational implications that commitment to "Christian realism" demands.

Christian Education and the Areas of Philosophy

Metaphysics is that area of philosophical thought that seeks to understand ultimate reality. It is concerned about the origin of all things and the center of existence. The term, coined by the Greek philosopher Aristotle, literally means "after nature."

The Christian educator begins with a metaphysical commitment to the personal God who has disclosed himself in Scripture. He is the "ground of being," the Creator and originator of the material universe. This is the basic starting point—the presupposition—of all Christian thought and action. Christian education must begin, continue, and end with thorough commitment to the concept of the personal God.

Cultured despisers may consider such presuppositions (taken on faith) simplistic, but there must be some similar beginning point for any system of thought or process of action. The Christian educator believes in the great affirmations of Scripture: "In the beginning God created. . . ." "In the beginning was the Word, and the Word was with God, and the Word was God. . . . The Word became flesh and lived for a while among us."[10] This position is not simplistic, but profound. It provides the foundation upon which the whole of reality can best be explored by man.

Epistemology is the area of the philosophy concerned with the nature and validity of human knowledge. Whence comes knowledge? How certain is knowledge? How are knowledge and faith related? Can truth be known? What are the tests of truth if it can be known? These are the epistemological questions. In the history of thought, two competing epistemological orientations have developed. *Rationalism* stresses the role of reason in providing certainty of knowledge. *Empiricism* stresses the role of sense perception and experience in arriving at truth.

The Christian philosopher takes a higher vantage point than do the rationalists or empiricists. Since he begins with the Creator-God who discloses himself to man, he understands knowledge as not only possible but grounded in the Sovereign Lord who speaks and the eternal Word, made flesh, who says, "I am the Truth."[11] It follows, then, that all truth is God's truth. The human ways to knowledge have been opened by the Creator, who has made man competent to explore and understand his material environment and has created the kind of universe that can be explored and understood.

But the truth man discovers in "God's picture-book" (as the German preacher and theologian Helmut Thielicke terms the universe) must always be evaluated in terms of the revealed truth of special revelation. Man needs the guidance of Scripture because God's creation is vast and complicated, only slowly yielding its secrets to man, and also because man is a sinner—sin has affected his mind, will, and soul. Paul makes this statement in his epistle to the Romans:

> ... What may be known about God is plain to them, because God has made it plain to them. For since the creation of the world God's invisible qualities—his eternal power and divine nature—have been clearly seen, being understood from what has been made, so that men are without excuse.
>
> For although they knew God, they neither glorified him as God nor gave thanks to him, but their thinking became futile and their foolish hearts were darkened.[12]

Men, properly chastened and humbled by the fact that they are sinners, can know! They can know God, through faith in His incarnate Son, "the Word made flesh." They know themselves and the universe through empirical observation, critical reason, intuitive insight, and scientific investigation, and judged by the revelation of reality found in Scripture. The "assured results" of science are not "assured" if they run counter to that which is clearly revealed in Scripture—they do not conform to reality!

The philosophy of Christian education must take seriously this "revelational epistemology." Since Christ desires His people to be "sanctified in the truth,"[13] Christian education must give attention to epistemological concerns.

From a philosophical perspective, anthropology is that area in which the nature of man is explored. The psalmist asks the crucial question: "What is man that you are mindful of him?" He asks that question within two contexts—the immensity of the universe and the greatness of the Creator. The answer comes: You made him a little lower than the heavenly beings and crowned him with glory and honor. You made him ruler over the works of your hands; you put everything under his feet:"[14]

But here is the paradox: Man was created king of the universe and crowned with glory; but he has sinned, and "falls short of the glory of God."[15] The Christian educator must deal seriously with this Biblical paradox. Man is not intrinsically good, for he has sinned; yet he has great value, for the living God came in the person of His own Son to die for him and redeem him. Through God's grace, by means of the gospel, man can be saved from his lost condition and restored to fellowship with God.

This Biblical anthropology speaks volumes to the practice of church education. It must be redemptive and restorative, relying upon the Word of grace to sanctify the learner. Teachers must be agents of God's grace, not overestimating the goodness of students, nor underestimating the power of God's love, but joining together with students as redeemed sinners on the way to deeper commitment and greater service.

Axiology is that branch of philosophy that investigates values. Among the ancient Greeks the axiological quest was to discover what is ultimately good and beautiful. Studies in ethics (good and bad behavior) and aesthetics (the nature of beauty) developed. In more recent years, the general term axiology has been used because it can cover all the main questions that ethics and aesthetics raised. The term encompasses political, personal, economic, and aesthetic values.

In this day values are too often perceived in terms of pleasure, immediate satisfaction, utility, or adjustment to change. Seldom are they related to an absolute standard that transcends changing social custom. But the Christian's commitment to the God of revealed truth is a commitment to ultimate good. "No one is good—except God alone," Jesus said to the rich young ruler.[16] That One who is goodness itself has set forth standards of conduct and value for all of man's relationships.

Redeemed man is to determine right and wrong behavior, and proper attitudes and appreciations. His God has given a moral law, manifested the highest value in self-giving love, and presented the goal of all life in eternity. The Christian, then, behaves according to these beliefs.

Kenneth Gangel stresses the church's responsibility to point out absolute standards for values:

> In the midst of a materialistic society, the church must attempt to inculcate a value system that takes its roots from complete commitment to citizenship in heaven rather than a cabin at the lake. It must touch these values in its classrooms, preach them from its pulpits, and enable its parents to communicate them in day-by-day family living.
>
> The value of the cross and the eternal city are not relative values. They rest in Him who transcends time and bids all men, like Paul, to count all things but loss in order to gain the excellency which is Christ.[17]

Implications of a Philosophy of Christian Education

Certain implications must be considered in developing a consistent philosophy of Christian education. These implications grow out of the Christian educator's commitment to those "first principles" that have been explored in this chapter.

Curriculum

Curriculum is a word that originally meant "circle;" it was a name given to the circular course where chariot races were held. The term, in its original setting, suggested a goal, a race to be won, a course to be followed, preparation and intense activity leading the participant to his destination. When applied to education, the term can be used to denote printed materials, but in a wider sense, the curriculum of an educational enterprise is the sum total of all learning experiences designed to accomplish the goals of that enterprise. In this comprehensive sense, curriculum is the total program.

The Biblical revelation must be at the very heart of this curriculum if there is to be the integration of all knowledge according to a Christian world view. As Gangel says, "If God is ultimate reality, if truth is inseparably related to His revelation, and if the objective of church education is to make people like Jesus Christ, then the centrality of the Bible in the church's curriculum is a foregone conclusion."[18]

There need not be a lack of creativity and adaptation in curricular construction, however. If the curriculum is truly based on Biblical revelation, then there is room for wide exploration of relevant themes and practical approaches in leading students to a deeper commitment of their whole lives to Jesus Christ.

Teachers

The practice of Christian education must be in the hands of Christian practitioners. Both those who administer the program and those who teach must be committed Christians. Such practitioners must be people of deep, abiding faith, who have allowed that faith to dominate *and* stimulate their intellect, and who are allowing that faith "to work through love" when they teach others. Such practitioners should be students of the Word of truth who are always seeking to explore its implications for the life and growth of their charges.

A negative aspect must also be considered. Paul warns in Ephesians against the "cunning and craftiness of men in their deceitful scheming."[19] The Christian teacher will be on guard against not only the open opposition of errant doctrines, but also the insidious, persuasive secularism of present-day thinking and practice.

A demand for excellence faces each Christian involved in the educational ministry of the church. The teacher must realize that such excellence is never realized through human effort or ingenuity alone. Such excellence is achieved only when the Christian teacher or leader has responded seriously to God's call. He realizes that he is effective only as God works through him, but he constantly seeks to become a more usable instrument through the expansion of his understanding and the development of his abilities and skills.

Methodological Approach

The behavioral sciences have provided valuable insights into the communicative process. Some of the modern methodological emphases can be used successfully in Christian teaching when they are cut away from their humanistic context and integrated into a Christian framework. Pupil activity, social relevance, concern for the individual, and problem solving techniques are valuable in the Christian approach to education. Any method that is in harmony with a Biblical understanding of man's nature can be used if expedient and effective.

The key to acceptable methodology is *love*. Man by nature desires fellowship, interaction, and sharing. But man's sin causes him to be alienated and isolated. Christian educators will attempt to overcome this isolation by allowing the love God has poured out into their hearts by the Holy Spirit[20] to beget such love within their students.

Evaluation

Evaluation is not something outside the educational experience, an essential part of effective education. The learning experience itself must be studied to determine if goals have been achieved. Evaluation is essential to improvement.

Evaluation of Christian education must always be implemented in terms of the church's goals. Our goal should be to "reach unity in the faith and in the knowledge of the Son of God and become mature, attaining to the whole measure of the fullness of Christ."[21] If this is our goal, then evaluation is not merely mechanistic technique, but an observable analysis of growth patterns. Such growth is more than intellectual, for mature Christian persons know, love, and serve God.

Purpose

The circle is completed. The practice of Christian education by Christian teachers, using Biblical materials and acceptable methods, is evaluated in terms of the purpose of Christian education. Such purpose can be understood only in terms of the Biblical revelation of God's purpose for man and the church.

Summary

A Christian education program is guided by a philosophy, whether it is formally stated or not, for the practices of every educator emerge from certain beliefs and presuppositions. The framework of that philosophy begins with God who revealed himself through creation and in the Bible. He can be known by those whom He created for companionship with Him. That philosophy becomes practical as it affects the selection of curriculum content, teachers, methods, and goals. A philosophy of Christian education is the glue that holds an educational program together.

Selected Bibliography

Athearn, Walter S. The Minister and Teacher. New York: Century Press, 1930.

Bixler, Lawrence. How to Teach. Cincinnati: Standard, 1964.

Brown, Colin. Philosophy and Christian Faith. London: Tyndale Press, 1969.

Brubacher, John S. (ed.) Modern Philosophies of Education, second edition. New York: McGraw-Hill, 1950.

Burgess, Harold W. An Invitation to Christian Education. Birmingham, Alabama: Religious Education Press, 1975.

Butler, J. Donald. Four Philosophies and Their Practice in Education and Religion. New York: Harper and Row, 1957.

Byrne, Herbert W. A Christian Approach to Education. Grand Rapids, Michigan: Zondervan, 1961.

Clark, Gordon. A Christian Philosophy of Education. Grand Rapids, Michigan: Eerdmans, 1946.

Cully, K. B. The Search for a Christian Education Since 1940. Philadelphia: Westminster Press, 1965.

Gaebelein, Frank. (ed.) Christian Education in a Democracy. New York: Oxford University Press, 1951.

Gangel, Kenneth. Leadership for Church Education. Chicago: Moody Press, 1970.

LeBar, Lois. Education That Is Christian. Westwood, New Jersey: Revell, 1958.

Lee, James Michael. (ed.) The Religious Education We Need: Toward the Renewal of Christian Education. Birmingham, Alabama: Religious Education Press, 1977.

Little, Lawrence. Foundation for a Philosophy of Christian Education. Nashville: Abingdon Press, 1957.

---

[1]Brown, p. 7
[2]Colossians 2:8
[3]Cully, p. 502
[4]Gaebelein, p. 42

[5]*Ibid.*

[6]Bixler, pp. 31, 32

[7]*Ibid.*, p. 32

[8]For example, the insights of Erik Erikson on the stages of psychosocial development (see his *Childhood and Society*, 1963), particularly the adolescent "identity crisis," are helpful to the Christian educator. The same can be said for Robert L. Havighurst's concepts of "developmental tasks" (see his *Developmental Tasks and Education*, 1952), and Jean Piaget's emphasis upon the "stages of cognitive development" in childhood and early adolescence (see his *Science of Education and the Psychology of the Child*, 1970).

[9]The term, "Christian realism" is preferred by Warren C. Young in his *A Christian Approach to Philosophy*, Baker Book House, 1958.

[10]John 1:1, 14

[11]John 14:6

[12]Romans 1:19-21

[13]John 17:17

[14]Psalm 8:4-6

[15]Romans 3:23

[16]Mark 10:18

[17]*Leadership for Church Education* by Kenneth Gangel. Copyright 1970, Moody Press, Moody Bible Institute of Chicago. p.35. Used by permission.

[18]*Ibid.*, p. 37

[19]Ephesians 4:14

[20]Romans 5:5

[21]Ephesians 4:13

5

Objectives in Christian Education

As you read, think about these questions:
—What is meant by *objectives*?
—How do objectives function?
—What is the objective for Christian education?
—Distinguish between levels and kinds of objectives.

The terms *aims, objectives,* and *goals* are synonymous. They imply direction and purpose. Specific objectives for any program are determined by the purpose of that program. The Biblical, historical, and philosophical foundations of Christian education govern the development of its goals.

Those who are committed to the Biblical revelation have had much to gain by setting forth clear comprehensive statements of educational objectives. But, tragically, they have often failed to do so. Even when they have given attention to objectives, they have used a simplistic set of goals that fail to denote theological intent or educational methodology. Because of this failure, evangelical Christian education has been victimized by sloganeering. Slogans such as "reach, win, teach, train, send" or "bring, build, and send" have been substituted for carefully stated behavioral objectives spelled out in terms of Biblical purpose. Careful attention must be given to educational objectives—their nature, source, function, and application.

Meaning, Function, and Application

Objectives are the desired outcomes of a given process. They may be comprehensive or specific; they may relate to one lesson, one unit, or a total program of instruction. Comprehensive objectives are formulated according to the total purpose of Christian education. Specific objectives adapt and apply these comprehensive objectives for a unit of study conducted with a particular group having its specific age-level and other characteristics.

C. B. Eavey suggests that the educational process may be viewed as a succession of flights of stairs that one climbs to reach the top of a building: "To arrive at this destination is the ultimate or final goal, but it can be attained only as the first, second, and perhaps other flights of stairs have been ascended."[1] Objectives must be viewed in this broad manner. They must include every level and every facet of Christian education.

Objectives for Christian education are derived from Biblical revelation and human need, *in that order*. The Bible alone provides much of the information we need for determining objectives. In the light of the Bible and in view of contemporary human needs the objectives of Christian education are determined.

Objectives should satisfy the following demands:[2]

1. They should apply to practical daily life.
2. They should cover the religious, social, and personal needs of the individual.
3. They should be true to the revelation of divine truth.
4. They should be true to human experience.

Clearly stated objectives can be valuable to the Christian education process, for the following reasons:

1. They help the pupil to know what is expected of him if he is to successfully complete a course of study. + teacher
2. They guide the curriculum planner to decide what content to include and what to omit.
3. They also help the teacher to decide how to organize content, what methods and activities to use, and what materials to choose for a given lesson or unit.
4. They provide a basis for evaluation. A pupil can evaluate his progress. Teachers can determine the progress of pupils. Program planners can use data provided by students and

teachers to determine, in part, the effectiveness of specific programs.

A Historical View

Wherever there has been Christian teaching, goals or objectives have been present. They are not always stated, but they underlie the process. Historical studies[3] have pointed out the objectives of the teaching activity of the apostolic and post-apostolic church. Similar studies of the educational philosophies of Luther, Calvin, Zinzendorf, Wesley, and Campbell reveal the educational objectives (though not consciously stated as such) accepted by these great religious leaders. Goals are also stated in the literature of the Sunday-school movement, although these goals have been modified over the years.

Attempts to formulate and clarify objectives of Christian education did not occur until the twentieth century. In 1922, a list of 22 character traits was published as a guideline to educational activity. In 1929, Paul H. Vieth, director of research of the International Council of Religious Educators, completed a study of comprehensive objectives of religious education. This study was presented to the faculty of Yale University as a doctoral dissertation. It was published in 1930 under the title *Objectives in Religious Education*. It remains a valuable work in the field of religious educational goals.

Vieth arrived at seven comprehensive objectives in his study (to these an objective on the Christian family has been added). These were accepted by the educational forces aligned with the Division of Christian Education of the National Council of Churches of Christ in America. They are as follows:

1. God

Christian education seeks to foster in growing persons a consciousness of *God* as a reality in human experience, and a sense of personal relationship to Him.

2. Jesus Christ

Christian education seeks to develop in growing persons such an understanding and application of the personality, life, and teachings of *Jesus* as will lead to experience of Him as Saviour and Lord, loyalty to Him and His cause, and will manifest itself in daily life and conduct.

3. Christlike character

Christian education seeks to foster in growing persons a progressive and continuous development of *Christlike character*.

4. Christian social order

Christian education seeks to develop in growing persons the ability and disposition to participate in and contribute constructively to the building of a *social order* throughout the world, embodying the ideal of the Fatherhood of God and the brotherhood of man.

5. Churchmanship

Christian education seeks to develop in growing persons the ability and disposition to participate in the organized society of Christians—the *Church*.

6. Christian family

Christian education seeks to develop in growing persons an appreciation of the meaning and importance of the *Christian family*, and the ability and disposition to participate in and contribute constructively to the life of this primary social group.

7. Christian life philosophy

Christian education seeks to lead growing persons into a Christian interpretation of life and the universe; the ability to see in it God's purpose and plan; a *life philosophy* built on this interpretation.

8. Bible and other materials

Christian education seeks to affect in growing persons the assimilation of the best religious experience of the race, preeminently that recorded in the *Bible*, as effective guidance to present experience.

But even among the ecumenically oriented leaders represented in the Division of Christian Education of the National Council of Churches, this formulation of objectives seemed less than satisfactory. A committee was formed, with Lawrence C. Little as chairman, which over a period of five years produced a document on objectives. In this document a new statement of purpose was presented, accompanied by five general objectives to achieve this purpose:

The supreme purpose of Christian education is to enable persons to become aware of the seeking love of God as revealed in Jesus Christ and to respond in faith to this love in ways that will help them grow as children of God, live in accordance with the will of God, and sustain a vital relationship to the Christian Community.

To achieve this purpose Christian Education, under the guidance of the Holy Spirit, endeavors:

To assist persons, at each state of development, to realize the highest potentialities of the self as divinely created, to commit themselves to Christ, and to grow toward maturity as Christian persons;

To help persons establish and maintain Christian relationships with their families, their churches, and with other individuals and groups, taking responsible roles in society, and seeing in every human being an object of the love of God;

To aid persons in gaining a better understanding and awareness of the natural world as God's creation and accepting responsibility for conserving its values and using them in the service of God and of mankind;

To lead persons to an increasing understanding and appreciation of the Bible, whereby they may hear and obey the Word of God; to help them appreciate and use effectively other elements in the historic Christian heritage;

To enable persons to discover and fulfill responsible roles in the Christian fellowship through faithful participation in the local and world mission of the church.[4]

During that same five-year period, another group was working on a single objective for senior high young people. The commission noted that it did not conceive objectives of Christian education "as a list of tasks to be performed or relationships to be dealt with or areas of content to be covered, but as one end toward which the whole process is directed."[5] The following is their statement of this one objective that determines all else that takes place in the education process:

The objective of Christian education is to help persons to be aware of God's self-disclosure and seeking love in Jesus Christ and to respond in faith and love—to the end that they may know who they are and what their human situation means, grow as sons of God rooted in the Christian community, live in the Spirit of God in every relationship, fulfill their common discipleship in the world, and abide in the Christian hope.[6]

Along with this objective, five instrumental learning tasks are arranged to show how the objective provides the basis for both teaching and evaluation:

(1) Listening with growing alertness to the gospel and responding to it in faith and love.

② Exploring the whole field of relationships in light of the gospel.
③ Discovering meaning and value in the field of relationships in the light of the gospel.
④ Personally appropriating that meaning and value.
⑤ Assuming personal and social responsibility in light of the gospel.[7]

The two committees met together and resolved the differences between their approaches. The senior high objective was agreed upon. It is included in the 1965 publication, *The Church's Educational Ministry: A Curriculum Plan*—the result of an ecumenical cooperative curriculum project sponsored by the National Council of Churches. This weighty volume (848 pages and five pounds) was designed to be useful to curriculum planners in the educational ministry. In this work, the objective is related not only to the learning tasks listed above, but also to five content or experience areas: life and its setting, revelation, redemption, vocation, and the church. The objective, the tasks, and the areas are carefully related and applied to various age groups, from nursery to adults.

Many Christian communions are not represented by the National Council of Churches. For them, these objectives are not acceptable, for theological as well as political reasons. The Southern Baptist Convention has been one of the few conservative groups that has given careful and continuous attention to objectives for their educational programs. Some years ago, their Sunday School Board produced a pamphlet entitled *Unto a Full Grown Man*. This resembled the Vieth approach, listing seven major objectives, but the direction and approach was different. These seven objectives were set out in relation to seven areas of experience. The implications of each objective for each age group were also included. The seven areas were: (1) in relation to the Bible (note the primacy given to this goal), (2) in relation to God, (3) in relation to Jesus, (4) in relation to the church, (5) in relation to self, (6) in relation to others, and (7) in relation to the home. In more recent years, the Sunday School Board has issued an annual *Curriculum Guide* in which revised objectives are stated.

Southern Baptists have also seen the value of a single encompassing goal for their program of teaching and training:

The overarching objective is to help persons become aware of God as revealed in Jesus Christ, respond to Him in a personal commitment of faith, strive to follow Him in the full meaning of Christian discipleship, live in conscious recognition of the guidance and power of the Holy Spirit, and grow toward Christian maturity.[8]

This objective is then applied to certain experience areas such as Christian conversion, church membership, worship, knowledge and conviction, attitudes and appreciations, living, and service. Some suggestions are given as to ways of achieving this objective.

Most other Biblically-oriented conservative groups have done little to work out comprehensive goals. Some have depended upon publishers of Christian literature—such as Standard Publishing, Scripture Press, Gospel Light, and David C. Cook—to devise objectives for their curriculum, and have adopted and applied these generally to their total educational program. Others have just assumed that their programs are purposeful, and have gone merrily on their way doing what they have always done. But such "activity without clearly defined purposes is no substitute for quality instruction and purposeful learning."[9]

A Practical View

This historical overview shows how important objectives in Christian education have been thought to be. Objectives serve not only to help promote better teaching and learning, but they become a standard for the total program of Christian education. Such a standard is an evaluative tool that can be applied to every program and age level by church leaders.

A statement of comprehensive objectives can also be adapted to each age group. Teachers and leaders can decide what programming can best meet the needs of a given age group. They can learn to capitalize on people's interests and needs to help achieve educational goals. They can decide what level of learning is essential in the light of already-stated goals, before a person or group of persons can go on to additional educational experiences.

The following application to adults, adapted from the pamphlet *Unto a Full Grown Man*, points out the practical value of objectives.

1. *The Bible.* The Christian education of adults seeks to lead them to know, appreciate, and acknowledge the Bible as the

authoritative and sufficient source of God's will, and to achieve skill in personal study of the Bible and in the application of Biblical truth to daily life.

2. *God.* Christian education seeks to lead adults to recognize God as Creator and Lord of all life, to develop an awareness of God as a living personality, and to help create a personal relationship with Him.

3. *Jesus Christ.* Christian education seeks to lead adults to understand and appreciate the life and teachings of Jesus Christ, to find in Jesus God's greatest revelation of himself, and to surrender their lives in complete dedication to Jesus as Savior and Lord.

4. *Church.* Christian education seeks to foster in adults an understanding of the nature and mission of the church that Christ established, to become a responsible member of the local congregation by actively supporting the total church program, and to serve Christ through His church with increasing effectiveness.

5. *Self.* Christian education seeks to develop in adults an understanding of the sacredness of human personality, to grow consciously in Christlikeness, to develop a concept of truth, life, and the universe in harmony with the Biblical revelation, to use the presence, power, and leadership of the Holy Spirit in daily living, to accept the full responsibility of the Christian stewardship of all their possessions, and to appreciate and use the best in their religious heritage, experience, and culture.

6. *Others.* Christian education seeks to develop in adults an unselfish disposition toward others that seeks to promote their welfare; first, by attempting to bring them to acknowledge Jesus as Savior, and second, by working to promote a Christian society throughout the world.

7. *Home.* Christian education seeks to develop in adults an understanding of God's will for the home and the ability and disposition to build a Christian home and provide for the spiritual nurture of their children.

On the basis of these objectives, adapted to adults and related to various experience areas, a program of adult education could be set up to meet the specific needs of adults in any situation. This program could include various kinds of formal study—in the Sunday school, Sunday evening training programs, vacation Bible school for adults, and home Bible studies—that would be aimed at achieving these goals. The total program could also include various kinds of experience, formal and informal, to help adults sanctify the home and make it a center of Christian nurture. There would need to be training programs in evangelism and church leadership in order to fulfill these objectives. Careful plans would also be laid for evangelism among adults, so that more adults could be won to discipleship.

More specifically, these objectives would serve in the process of curriculum production of materials to be used with adults in formal Christian teaching. Biblical material would be arranged carefully and sequentially in order to achieve the objectives. Each lesson would also have suggested aims that would be in harmony with the more general objectives.

Summary

A statement of objectives is an attempt to put into usable form the philosophy of Christian education derived from the Biblical revelation of reality. The Biblical philosophy of Christian education commits the educational forces of the church to the development of new persons in Jesus Christ.

The achievement of this overall goal demands clearly stated objectives that can provide direction for learning tasks and educational experiences. Methods and materials, buildings and equipment, educational administration, and programming within and beyond the local church must all fulfill the objectives of Christian education. Committees of Christian education in local churches must be keenly aware of their objectives, studying them, clarifying them, and setting them out to guide the educational work of the church. Far from being what some modern theologians see as but a "methodological addendum," Christian education is at the very center of a vital church's ministry to its world.

Selected Bibliography

Allen, Clifton V. and W. L. House (eds.) The Curriculum Guide. Nashville: Convention Press, 1961.

Byrne, Herbert W. A Christian Approach to Education (revised edition). Milford, Michigan: Mott Media, 1977.

The Church's Educational Ministry: A Curriculum Plan. St. Louis: Bethany Press, 1965.

Haberman, Milton. "Behavioral Objectives: Bandwagon or Breakthrough?" Journal of Teacher Education 19 (Spring 1968), pp. 91-94.

Hakes, J. Edward (ed.) *An Introduction to Evangelical Christian Education*. Chicago: Moody Press.

Jaarsma, Cornelius. *Fundamentals in Christian Education*. Grand Rapids, Michigan: Eerdmans, 1953.

Miller, Randolph C. *Christian Nurture and the Church*. New York: Charles Scribner's Sons, 1961.

The Objectives of Christian Education. New York: National Council of Churches, 1958.

The Objectives of Christian Education for Senior High Youth. New York: National Council of Churches, 1958.

Price, J. M. (ed.) *Survey of Religious Education*. New York: Ronald Press, 1940.

Sherrill, Lewis J. *The Gift of Power*. New York: Macmillan, 1955.

Vieth, Paul H. *Objectives in Religious Education*. New York: Harper and Brothers, 1930.

Whitehead, Alfred N. *The Aims of Education*. New York: Macmillan, 1929.

---

[1] p. 56, An Introduction to Evangelical Christian Education by J. Edward Hakes. Copyright 1969. Moody Press, Moody Bible Institute of Chicago. Used by permission.

[2] Price, p. 112

[3] For example, Kent's *The Great Teachers of Judaism and Christianity* and L. J. Sherrill's *The Rise of Christian Education*

[4] *The Objectives of Christian Education*, pp. 21, 22

[5] *The Objectives of Christian Education for Senior High Young People*, pp. 12, 13

[6] *Ibid.*, p. 14

[7] Ibid., p. 34

[8] Allen and House, *The Curriculum Guide* (Nashville: Convention Press, 1961) pp. 14, 15. Used by permission.

[9] Hakes, p. 13 (See reference #1)

Part Two

MATERIALS AND METHODS FOR CHRISTIAN EDUCATION

Section Outline

6. A Curriculum for Christian Education
   A. What Is Curriculum?
   B. Prerequisites for an Effective Curriculum
   C. Principles for an Effective Curriculum
   D. Selection of Curriculum Materials

7. The Teaching/Learning Encounter
   A. Jesus the Teacher
   B. The Role of the Christian Teacher
   C. The Nature of the Learner
   D. Communicating the Word to the Learner

8. Helping Preschoolers Learn
   A. Understanding the Preschool Learner
   B. Goals for Early Childhood Education
   C. Organizing the Preschool Department
   D. Choosing Effective Teaching Methods

9. Helping Elementary Children Learn
   A. Understanding Elementary Children
   B. Goals for Teaching Children
   C. Organizing the Elementary Children's Department
   D. Effective Methods for Teaching Elementary Children

10. Helping Youth Learn
    A. Understanding the Adolescent
    B. Goals for Teaching Youth

C. Organizing the Youth Department
D. Effective Methods for Teaching Youth

11. Helping Adults Learn
    A. Understanding Adults
    B. Goals for Teaching Adults
    C. Organizing to Teach Adults
    D. Effective Methods for Teaching Adults

12. Helping Exceptional Persons Learn
    A. Traditional Categories of Special Education: Aids in Defining Potential
    B. Principles in Educating the Exceptional Person

13. Audiovisual Methods
    A. A Biblical Basis for Using Visuals
    B. Values of Audiovisual Aids
    C. Types of Audiovisuals
    D. Evaluating Audiovisual Material
    E. Organizing Audiovisual Materials

14. Helping the Family Teach
    A. The Family in the Bible
    B. Biblical Guidelines for the Family
    C. Contemporary Problems Facing the Family
    D. The Church and the Family

15. Building and Equipping for Christian Education
    A. Current Trends in Building
    B. Planning for Building and Equipment
    C. The Needs of Each Age Group
    D. Adaptation of Existing Space

Christian education involves a specific point of view that rests upon the Biblical, historical, and psychological foundations. These foundations are crucial if Christian education is to remain *Christian*.

From foundations grows the actual practice of Christian teaching. Every congregation and teacher proceeds with some kind of method, planned or not. All select and use materials that rest upon some kind of assumptions for the practice of teaching. Those methods and materials should be in harmony with Biblical principles.

The second section of this book explores principles to guide the selection and use of methods and materials. The section begins with an examination of the principles that guide curriculum design. Then it explores the basic principles involved in the teaching/learning encounter. The next five chapters examine various groups of learners—their characteristics, organization of their classes, and possible teaching methods. The final three chapters present principles that apply to three special areas—audiovisual materials, the family, and buildings and equipment.

6

A Curriculum for Christian Education

As you read, think about these questions:
—What is curriculum?
—What are three prerequisites for a curriculum?
—What are four principles for curriculum planning?
—Who should select curriculum materials for a congregation?

What Is Curriculum?

The word *curriculum* can be used in a variety of ways, as the following quotations illustrate. Look for the key word or phrase in each:

1. "Our curriculum prepares ministers and directors of Christian education. Look at the courses required."

2. "The music curriculum has been developed by adding classes in theory, history, and choral conducting."

3. "We buy our curriculum from X Publishing Company."

4. "Our curriculum prepares ministers and Christian educators. The Christian education major requires twenty-eight course hours in Christian education, each designed to build upon the previous course. It also requires field work and finally an internship. Each course relates to the objective of preparing a functioning Christian educator."

Review the definitions. In the first example, curriculum equals courses. In the second, it is used to designate subject matter. In the third, it means materials. The last example includes courses, but it is more comprehensive. It assumes a goal, courses, experiences, materials, and a design for fitting those courses, experiences, and materials together to achieve the goal.

The word curriculum literally means "race course" or "race track." It may be used to include everything that happens in an educational setting, but that definition is too broad for our use in the church. A minister, Christian educator, or superintendent can neither foresee nor control everything that happens educationally to those in the church. However, they can plan and implement some experiences that affect the life of the learner.

Curriculum may be defined in this way: "A curriculum is a plan by which the teaching/learning process may be systematically undertaken."[1] This definition demands that the following conditions be met:

1. Curriculum is planned.
2. It is planned with specific goals in mind.
3. It is designed—it begins at point A and proceeds in an orderly fashion to point B.
4. Its content is selected to achieve goals.
5. It uses materials designed to achieve goals.
6. It requires the presence and influence of a teacher.
7. Its methods are chosen so as to achieve the goals.

Curriculum: goals, plan, design, materials, teachers, methods. A good curriculum doesn't just happen. It requires understanding and application of basic principles.

Prerequisites for an Effective Curriculum

Based on the Bible

The most important question about a curriculum is what will be taught. For Christian education to be genuinely Christian, the curriculum must be based upon the Word of God. That does not mean that extra-Biblical content cannot be used, but it does demand that any extra-Biblical material be used in harmony with the purpose and message of the Bible. The Bible is the chief textbook for Christian education. It controls the curriculum.

To say that curriculum is Bible-based is to imply more than mere transmission of facts. Memorization of information or recital by rote, as beneficial as both may be to provide a basis for knowledge, are inadequate by themselves. The word *knowledge*, as it is used in the Bible, assumes that information is always coupled with behavior.

A Bible-based curriculum accepts the inspiration of the Bible and uses the Word itself to guide what is taught. It keeps Christ and the pupil's response to Him in clear focus. It teaches the Bible from the perspective of faith and calls for a definite response from the learner.

2. Related to Pupil Needs

An effective curriculum also meets the needs of the pupil. It takes the learner into account: how old he is, what he already knows, what his capabilities are, and how he learns best. A curriculum for preschoolers would be quite different than one for adults—if not in sections of Scripture covered, then certainly in goals and methods.

To plan an effective curriculum, the planner must answer some basic questions about each age level:

1. What of the Bible can be understood by this age group?
2. What of the Bible is most important for this group of learners?
3. How do these learners learn most effectively?
4. What shall we teach to them? In what order? How?

Characteristics of the various age levels are detailed in Chapters 8-12.

Utilizes Sound Teaching Principles

An effective curriculum is based on sound teaching/learning principles. Learning is most effective when the lesson and the material used are related to the learner's experience. Learning is most efficient when the pupil learns by actively participating. The basic principles of effective learning will be developed in further detail in the next chapter.

Principles for an Effective Curriculum

G. Campbell Wyckoff outlines four principles for constructing an effective curriculum. These four principles will serve as the outline for this section.

Principle of Context

Where does Christian education take place? The principle of context takes into account where people are when they are confronted with the Word of God.

The first place for many to be introduced to the Word of God is in the home. Children observe the ways parents demonstrate their faith. They absorb attitudes toward God, Jesus Christ, and the church. Although the home may teach specific Bible information, its chief function is to transmit attitudes, responses, values, and lifestyle.

Christian education also occurs in one-to-one situations. Two friends discuss the Bible over lunch. A caller presents the terms of salvation to a non-Christian in his home. A mother answers her child's questions. All of these are Christian education.

But the local congregation is also responsible for Christian education. Two centuries ago, formal Christian education happened in a public school in which the preacher was the teacher. But the public school has long since stopped providing Christian education. Therefore, the church has developed a variety of formal teaching programs to fill the gap. Sunday school, children's church, youth groups, vacation Bible school, and weekday classes are examples of such programs.

A congregation that takes seriously its commitment to Bible teaching will acknowledge and observe the principle of context. Although it cannot control what happens within the walls of each home, it can provide information, materials, and programs to support and strengthen parents. Neither can a congregation plan and control every one-to-one contact made by its members. But just as with the family the church can provide materials, information, and programs to equip the individual for fruitful one-to-one contacts.

Despite these limitations, a congregation can plan and design the formal learning experiences that occur within its corporate life. The principle of context demands that curriculum not be left to chance. Curriculum must be chosen according to plan for each teaching program, and then those programs must be coordinated with each other. The plan should take into account what is taught in Sunday school, and how that subject matter is complemented or supplemented by what is taught in youth meetings, vacation Bible school, children's church, and midweek classes.

Month	Sunday School	Graded Worship
Sept.	Going to God's House (4 weeks)	We Talk With God We Worship God We Work With God We Obey God
Oct.	Going to God's House (1) Giving for God's House (4)	We Love Our Parents We Love Our Friends We Tell Others About God's Love We Send God's Helpers Far Away We Help at God's House
Nov.	Thanking God for His House (4)	We Thank God—Homes We Thank God—Food We Thank God—Water We Thank God—Care
Dec.	The Baby Jesus (4)	God Sent His Son Jesus Was Born People Visit Baby Jesus God Watches Over Jesus
Jan.	The Baby Jesus (2) The Boy Jesus (3)	Jesus Is God's Son Jesus Is Kind Jesus Helps People Jesus Forgives Jesus Loves Everyone
Feb.	The Boy Jesus (1) The Man Jesus (3)	Jesus Teaches About God Jesus Teaches to Pray Jesus Teaches Us to Love God's House Jesus' Disciples Help Him Do God's Work

Figure 6-1. Curriculum for 2's and 3's, September—February

For example, a curriculum for preschoolers might use the same theme (perhaps even the same content) for Sunday school, children's church, and youth meetings, because this age level benefits more from repetition of concepts than it does from a large volume of information. Figure 6-1 illustrates such a curriculum.

At the youth level, a Bible book study for Sunday school and topical studies for youth meetings may be planned. To assure coordination, the topical studies could be developed from themes from the book being studied for Sunday school. Or supplementary topics, not covered elsewhere in the youth curriculum, could be chosen.

A family enrichment calendar can also help to coordinate the different parts of the curriculum. The calendar would suggest family activities designed to complement and reinforce the Biblical material being used in the church's formal teaching programs.

However it is implemented, the principle of context demands that a curriculum take into account all agencies of teaching, not just the Sunday school.

Principle of Scope

The principle of scope refers to the choice of what content to include for each age level. An effective curriculum will seek to acquaint the pupil with God's will. The curriculum planner must decide what specific portions of the Bible are understandable to and teachable for a particular age group. A well-planned curriculum must also plan in what order Biblical portions will be studied—not only in a given year, but from age level to age level.

W. Kent Gilbert, in *The Functional Objectives for Christian Education*, explores what subject matter is appropriate for each age level. He divides Biblical content into six categories—God, Bible, church, fellow man, world, and self—and suggests content and goals for each category and each age group. This resource provides valuable assistance for the curriculum planner.

The principle of scope is taken into account by each publishing company as it plans a total curriculum for babies through adults. A congregation must be especially careful to take this principle into account when curriculum materials from several different sources are used. The principle also helps to avoid overlap from one teaching program to the next.

The principle of scope requires that at least three other decisions be made:

1. How much time will be given to various portions of

Scripture? An effective curriculum should not teach entirely from the Old Testament or from the New Testament. Some balance must be maintained.

2. In what order will the Bible content be studied? This needs to be planned so that the Bible will make sense to the learner.

3. What needs are evident in the lives of the learners? Content should be life-related.

The principle of scope, then, refers to what is studied and in what order it is pursued.

Principle of Process

The principle of process refers to the way in which content is communicated. It deals with the question of methodology. A curriculum cannot be considered complete until thought is given to the most effective method for teaching specific age levels.

The teacher is the key to effective communication of the Bible. First of all, he is a model of the power of God's transforming grace. He demonstrates what he teaches with his own life—if he teaches well. He also plans for a certain classroom atmosphere as well as lesson structure and presentation.

Curriculum materials are designed to help the teacher with process. Curriculum writers assist by suggesting ways to set up the classroom, build the lesson, and present the content. Materials are resources for the teacher; they are never substitutes for his personal example and creativity.

Principle of Design

The principle of design refers to the manner in which learning experiences are woven together. A variety of designs is possible. Four are most common.

1. _Uniform._ Everyone in the church studies the same Bible content at the same time. The advantage is that everyone in the family studies the same thing, and the content can later serve as the basis for family worship and discussion. However, some content is too difficult for some age levels (for example, Romans for preschoolers). At the same time, the content most appropriate for preschoolers may not best meet the needs of teenagers. Few publishers continue to pursue this design.

2. _Cycle-graded, or group-graded._ In this design, a cycle of

lessons is designed for particular age levels, usually a two-, three-, four-, or six-year cycle. For example, there may be a four-year cycle of lessons for preschoolers. All preschoolers deal with the same material on the same Sunday. Over a four-year period, the entire cycle will be covered. A different cycle is then used for elementary school children, another for youth, and another for adults. This way, the content that is most appropriate for each age level and learning ability can be chosen. On the other hand, group-grading eliminates the advantage of a common theme for family worship and discussion. Several publishers follow this pattern.

3. *Closely graded.* This design provides different content for each age level. It is an attempt to plan Bible curriculum much as a public school curriculum is planned. Fifth grade classwork builds upon fourth grade skills that rest upon third grade content. Such a design focuses upon the needs of a narrow age level, but in this advantage also lies its main weakness. Not all people begin their Christian education at the same age level, or progress at the same rate. Some publishing companies use this plan.

4. *Electives.* In an elective system, each person chooses his own course of study from a list of studies available each quarter. Sometimes a class selects its own study topic (another type of elective). This system is commonly used for adults, and sometimes for senior highs.

The curriculum planner must decide which approach he will use.

Selection of Curriculum Materials

Who Selects Materials?

Every church must settle the issue of who is to select curriculum content and materials. Shall the teachers? The learners? Or someone else?

The teacher could make the choice. He is the key to effective communication of Biblical material. He should teach what he wants to teach and feels comfortable sharing. However, such an arrangement permits little coordination among teachers, classes, and other teaching agencies. Nor does it provide a needed check and balance system to assure that Biblically sound materials are chosen.

A case can also be made for allowing the learner to select

his own curriculum. Curriculum must be need-related, and the pupil should know his needs better than anyone else. His interest would be increased if he were to select his own course of study. Yet, the biggest danger to this approach is that sometimes real needs are not felt. The average learner also has a tendency not to push himself into new areas of content, attitudes, and behaviors, unless he is guided or highly motivated to do so.

How should content and materials be selected? The overseers of a congregation are the likely candidates for the job. One task of an overseer is to model the Christian lifestyle.[2] A second, as a shepherd of his people, is to feed the flock and to protect it.[3] The overseers may (and probably should) seek the counsel of teachers, parents, learners, educational planners, and developmental psychologists. They may commission the minister or Christian education director or other qualified persons to design the curriculum. But the final approval of content and resources should be left to the overseers, whose job it is to feed and protect the flock of God.

How Are Materials Chosen?

The final selection of materials must be founded upon criteria that take into account both content and methodology. Four criteria will guide the selection process.

1. *Biblical.* Do the materials regard the Bible as the inspired Word of God? Is the Bible taught as historically true? Is the Bible taught in such a way that the students learn more of Jesus Christ?

2. *Pedagogical.* Are the materials suitable for the age group being taught? Are illustrations and applications suitable for the age group? Are sound learning principles used? Are visuals suitable for the age group? Do the materials use a variety of teaching methods?

3. *Ease of use.* Do the materials contain a step-by-step plan that is easy to follow? Are visuals available? Are the visuals of good quality? Do pupils' books contribute to lesson development? Could an inexperienced teacher use the materials without confusion?

4. *Attractiveness.* Are materials colorful? Are they easily read? Are pictures and print the proper size for the age level? Is the paper of good quality?

Summary

Curriculum is a plan by which the teaching/learning process may be systematically undertaken. An effective curriculum must be based on the Bible, related to the pupil's needs, and utilize sound teaching principles. Four principles guide the curriculum—context, scope, process, and design. Selection of curriculum materials is the responsibility of the overseers of the church.

Projects

1. Interview an elder from your congregation. Find out what content and materials are used for each age group in the church, and why they are used. Determine who makes the final decisions about curriculum.
2. Evaluate two or three samples of curriculum materials for one age group. Use the criteria outlined above. Decide which sample best demonstrates the principles outlined in this chapter. According to which design is it organized?

Selected Bibliography

Gilbert, W. Kent. The Functional Objectives for Christian Education. St. Louis: Lutheran Board of Parish Education, 1959.

Hass, Glen, Joseph Bond, and Jon Wiles. Curriculum Planning: A New Approach. Boston: Allyn and Bacon, 1974.

Miller, Randolph Crump. Biblical Theology and Christian Education. New York: Charles Scribner's Sons, 1956.

_____. The Clue to Christian Education. New York: Charles Scribner's Sons, 1950.

Miller, T. Franklin, Beverly Welton, Harold Johnson, and James Blair Miller. Basics for Teaching. Anderson, Indiana: Warner Press, 1968.

Wyckoff, D. Campbell. Theory and Design of Christian Education Curriculum. Philadelphia: Westminster Press, 1961.

---

[1]Theory and Design of Christian Education Curriculum, by D. Campbell Wyckoff. Copyright © MCMLXI by W. L. Jenkins. p. 17. Used by permission of The Westminster Press.

[2]1 Timothy 3:1-7

[3]Acts 20:28

CHAPTER

7

The Teaching/ Learning Encounter

As you read, think about these questions:
—What qualities in Jesus' life made Him an effective teacher?
—What are the qualities of an effective Bible teacher?
—What unique qualities does a learner possess?
—What are the parts of an effective Bible lesson?

_____

"When Jesus had finished saying these things, the crowds were amazed at his teaching, because He taught as one who had authority, and not as their teachers of the law."[1] What teacher has not dreamed of a response like that? Who wouldn't want to teach as persuasively and powerfully as Jesus?

He who teaches God's Word is in the business of communication. How is he to communicate effectively? The place to begin analysis is with the master teacher, Jesus. A study of Jesus' teaching reveals that the following elements are involved: (1) a teacher, (2) a pupil, (3) an environment, (4) a curriculum, (5) a goal, and (6) a method.

Jesus the Teacher[2]

The Samaritan Woman

John 4:1-42 outlines Jesus' contact with a sinful Samaritan woman at the well of Sychar. Look carefully at the situation and find each of the six elements of a teaching encounter.

The teacher was Jesus. He initiated conversation (4:7, 10). He directed thinking (4:13, 14, 21-24). He presented information (4:16, 18). He revealed who He was, but allowed the woman the freedom to choose how she would respond to Him (4:26).

The pupil was the sinful Samaritan woman whom Jesus met at the well. She was argumentative (4:11, 12) and tried to evade the objective of His teaching (4:19, 20). She reasoned (4:25) and expressed eagerness to learn (4:15). And when she finally learned the lesson that Jesus was the Christ, she responded by doing something about what she had learned (4:28-30).

The environment was informal—a well outside a Samaritan village. A prepared teacher and a receptive pupil turned it into a classroom.

The curriculum was a message from God himself. It was communicated by an able teacher.

The goal was clear as the lesson began to unfold. All along Jesus intended for the woman not merely to know facts, but to use those facts to know that He was the Messiah (4:26).

The method was interactive. Jesus spoke. She responded. Jesus spoke again. She responded again. Both teacher and learner were active participants in the process.

On the Road to Emmaus

Luke 24:13-35 relates another teaching incident in the life of Jesus. It too can be analyzed in order to discover basic principles of Jesus' teaching.

Again the teacher was Jesus, who initiated the conversation (24:17) and asked questions (24:17, 19, 25, 26). He listened to find out what the learners knew (24:18-24), and He explained the Scripture to them (24:27). In a variety of ways, He presented information, stimulated thinking, and elicited response.

The pupils were two of Jesus' followers, now disappointed and discouraged by the events of Calvary. They already knew the Old Testament Scriptures, but they needed to be reminded. As they learned, they discussed what had happened (24:15), answered questions (24:18-24), and listened (24:27). They completed the learning process by believing that Jesus is the Messiah (24:32-35).

The environment was informal—a dusty roadway between Jerusalem and Emmaus. An alert teacher transformed it into a classroom.

The *curriculum* was primarily the Old Testament Scriptures (24:27), always pointing to the Christ (24:25, 26).

The *goal* seems to have been for the disciples to believe that Christ was risen (24:25, 26). Indeed that was the outcome (24:34).

The *method* was interactive. Jesus listened while the pupils spoke. The pupils answered questions. Jesus lectured. The pupils related information. Both teacher and learners were active participants in the learning process.

The Role of the Christian Teacher

Who Is an Effective Teacher?

Researchers have tried for years to isolate the characteristics and practices of effective teachers. Their conclusions have failed to identify any particular teaching methodology or specific traits possessed only by effective teachers.

Ryans conducted a comprehensive study on the characteristics of teachers who had been rated "good" or "poor" by trained observers. The observers evaluated twenty-two dimensions of classroom behavior. Despite the expected individuality in personal traits, Ryans found certain traits common among the teachers rated "good:" they tended to see the good side of other people; they enjoyed social relationships, including those with their pupils; they possessed superior verbal intelligence and a strong interest in reading; they tended to let the pupil learn for himself rather than directing his learning; and they were well-adjusted emotionally.

Arthur Combs summarizes the evidence from studies about effective teachers in this way:

> As we have seen, research on the competencies have been unable to isolate any common trait or practice of good teachers. But the unanimous failure in itself demonstrates an important fact: a good teacher is primarily a unique personality. . . . *A good teacher is first and foremost a person* and this fact is the most important and determining thing about him. He has competence, to be sure, but not a common set of competencies like everyone else."[3]

Like Combs, Morse and Wingo conclude that the teacher is the key to good teaching: "The characteristics which are important to good teaching involve the ability to relate to and work with pupils and the ability to organize the learning experiences in some systematic manner."[4] Jesus had demonstrated that long before researchers began their exploration.

Qualities of the Effective Teacher

What qualities are part of that unique personality that makes an effective teacher? The following acrostic suggests some of the necessary qualities.

T—*teachability*. An effective teacher is willing to learn. He seeks new information, tries new methods, and continues to grow in his personal spiritual life.

E—*example*. An effective teacher, especially in the Sunday school, must be a worthy example of what he is teaching. He is fully aware of the truth of Jesus' statement, "Can one blind man be guide to another? Will they not both fall into the ditch? A pupil is not superior to his teacher; but everyone, when his training is complete, will reach his teacher's level."[5] The teacher models the process of Christian growth. He can say with Paul, "You know yourselves how you ought to copy our example."[6]

A—*attitude*. An effective teacher is positive. He believes in his pupils. He believes that he is doing God's work. He really wants to teach.

C—*commitment*. An effective teacher is committed first to the Lord Jesus Christ, to His Word, the Bible, and to the ministry of sharing Jesus with people. He is committed even in the face of difficulties that he will most certainly encounter.

H—*sense of humor*. An effective teacher possesses a healthy sense of humor. Although he need not be an extremely witty person, he appreciates the humor of his students and circumstances.

E—*enthusiasm*. An effective teacher has a zest for living, a joy in the Christian life, and the enthusiasm to share his joy with the individuals who make up his class.

R—*good relationships with people*. An effective teacher understands that his goal is to help individuals to know the Lord. Therefore, he loves people and builds personal relationships with them. He is interested in people and is sensitive to their needs. He never forgets that his message is to people and for people. In short, he knows that:

For truth to have its transforming impact on the human personality, love is utterly essential! It is truth that is communicated in the context of a close and loving relationship that will be used by God to remold and renew the believer's personality toward God.[7]

Responsibilities of the Teacher

What are the responsibilities of an effective Christian teacher? The Bible explicitly states those duties.

1. *Study God's Word carefully and consistently.* "Try hard to show yourself worthy of God's approval, as a labourer who need not be ashamed; be straightforward in your proclamation of the truth."[8] The reason is evident—that pupils will be introduced to Jesus Christ. The curriculum is God's Word, brought alive by a growing, developing Christian teacher.

2. *Be willing to do whatever is necessary to be an effective teacher.* "Take your share of hardship, like a good soldier of Jesus Christ. A soldier on active service will not let himself be involved in civilian affairs; he must be wholly at his commanding officer's disposal. Again, no athlete can win a prize unless he has kept the rules."[9] No teacher worth his call attempts to get by with as little as possible.

3. *Be an example.* "In everything set them an example by doing what is good. In your teaching show integrity, seriousness and soundness of speech that cannot be condemned."[10] The effective teacher's words and behavior are in harmony.

4. *Be prepared.* "Hold the Lord Christ in reverence in your hearts. Be always ready with your defense whenever you are called to account for the hope that is in you, but make that defense with modesty and respect."[11]

5. *Know your pupils.* Take the time to get to know each person in your class, so that you can teach him what he really needs to learn.

6. *Teach with purpose and for a decision.* Bible teaching is more than mere impartation of facts. In the New Testament, teaching is always the presentation of information in a way that requires people to make a decision about it. Jesus called for a response from the learner; an effective teacher does the same.

The Nature of the Learner

The teacher's understanding of human nature clearly affects his teaching behavior. It is important, then, for his theory of personality to be formulated on Biblical principles.

Created by God

> Then God said, 'Let us make man in our image, in our likeness, and let them rule over the fish of the sea and the birds of the air, over all the livestock, over all the earth, and over all the creatures that move along the ground.' So God created man in his own image, in the image of God he created him; male and female he created them . . . God saw all that he had made, and it was very good. . . . And the Lord God formed man from the dust of the ground and breathed into his nostrils the breath of life, and man became a living being.[12]

Man is different from any of the rest of God's creation. God fashioned man from the substance of creation that preceded him, yet man is differentiated from and superior to what preceded him. Man's life-giving essence is the breath of God, and he shares in the very likeness of God.

Man is like God in his *rational* processes. Man can think and reason and remember. He is more than a robot who responds simply because stimuli are present. He can assimilate data, arrange it, and use it in ways that have not been used before. No creature other than man can think, reason, and create.

Man is like God in his *emotional* processes. Man can love and be loved. He can become angry or feel and express tenderness. His emotional responses are not dependent only upon stimulus-response reactions. He experiences the full range of human emotions and can choose under what circumstances he will express them.

Man is like God in his ability to *choose*. Although his environment does exert a powerful influence upon him, man is more than a product of his environment. Made with freedom to choose, man is capable of acting in God's likeness or of behaving contrary to divine mandate. Neither God nor the devil nor man's environment predestines man's behavior—he chooses.

Man is like God in his *moral* nature. He may share in God's purposes and plans. Built into man is a conscience that can be developed to share God's values with Him. Man experiences guilt, and he can discern between good and evil. But because man has the freedom to choose, his conscience can be misdeveloped, or violated, or hardened.

Man is like God in that he has an *immortal spirit*. Physical existence is not man's end. A man's physical body will die, but his spirit will live for eternity.

Man is like God—not in physical appearance, but in the totality of his personality, which we call the "self." It is the "self" that chooses to sin; that is, to use rational, emotional, and moral processes as he chooses rather than to bring glory to his maker. Evil, then, proceeds from the self. In a state of righteousness, all of man's capabilities find harmonious expression, but in a state of unrighteousness his capabilities are abused and distorted.

Conversion reestablishes a basis for righteousness. Because Jesus Christ changes a person from the inside out, he is once again able to grow toward harmony with God.

The Christian teacher is acutely aware of the nature and potential of those whom he teaches. He is sharing with rational, feeling, moral creatures who can choose to be like God or to rebel against Him. His job has eternal implications.

Born to Grow

Made in the image of God, man grows and develops from the day he is conceived. Physically, he increases in size from the moment of conception. Rationally, he grows from a non-reasoning, non-thinking creature to become a creative, abstract thinker. Emotionally, he develops from mere response to stimuli, until he shares in the full range of human emotions. Morally, he learns right from wrong, and he gains experience and skill in making choices.

Man's growth may be summarized as follows:

1. It is purposeful.
2. Each individual actively develops according to his own rate.
3. The goal of development is independent maturity.
4. Education is the process by which guidance is provided for that inherent forward impetus called growth.
5. The whole personality is involved in growth, which occurs from the interaction of physical, emotional, rational, and moral needs and functions.

The Christian teacher must be aware of this impetus for growth and be prepared to stimulate and motivate the learner. His goal is changed lives—growth toward Godlikeness. He will actively involve the learner, utilizing every facet of his personality. Larry Richards summarizes the process well:

> Christian education is not to be designed to produce a product. It is to be designed to supply what is needed for the process of growth to proceed healthily and normally . . . Christian education is con-

cerned with the progressive transformation of the believer toward the character, values, motives, and understandings of God Himself.[13]

Communicating the Word to the Learner

Communicating the Word to the pupil is the crux of Bible teaching. Some interpret this to mean an intellectual process of imparting facts. Others see it as a "do as I do" process that emphasizes modeling and relationships to the neglect of information. Effective communication involves both of those processes, designed to stimulate the learner to grow.

The teacher's life and example are the starting point. But the teacher needs a guide for structuring a teaching/learning encounter.

Effective communication begins with a *goal*. Jesus had a goal in the two situations examined earlier in this chapter. So must today's Bible teacher. The teacher wrestles with the Biblical content long enough for it to work in his own life. But he must then focus on one truth appropriate for the needs of his class members. Then he identifies the changes of behavior he will seek in the lives of his pupils. As Lois LeBar observes: "A pupil's growth is determined not by what he hears, but what he does about what he hears."[14]

We may describe the communication process by four words: hook, book, look, and took.[15]

The teacher first decides how to gain the pupil's attention. This is the *hook*. How will he whet the pupils' appetites for Biblical material?

Next the teacher will guide the pupils in a Bible study. This is the *book* section. Not only does the teacher determine what truth should be discovered, but also how he will involve the pupil in the process of discovering it for himself.

The next step is to examine implications for today's living that are suggested by the Bible material. This is the *look* section. Again the teacher must decide how he will guide the pupils to active exploration of life implications.

The teacher completes the learning cycle by guiding the pupil to decide how he will respond to the material he has studied. Although the teacher cannot follow each class member around in the ensuing week, he can send the Bible material and implications with the learner by providing a *took* in each lesson. He does so by eliciting a specific response that the student agrees to make as a result of the lesson.

The teacher is a resource person, a planner, a guide, a fellow learner. He designs goals and accomplishes them by building a sound lesson that begins with a need, proceeds to information, examines implications, and stimulates decision-making.

Summary

Jesus provides the example for Christian teaching, both formal and informal. His goal was changed lives, and His method was interactive.

The effective teacher is someone who models Christlikeness, provides needed information, relates to the learners, and plans for active pupil involvement in the learning process.

The learner, whatever his age, is created in the image of God, sharing His rational, emotional, moral, and choosing nature. He violates that nature with sin, but the goal of Christian education is to restore him to a harmonious relationship with God.

To be effective, Bible teaching proceeds according to a design: a goal, an attention getter, Bible exploration, life exploration, and decision-making.

Projects

1. Observe a Bible teacher in action. How well does the teacher demonstrate the qualities of an effective teacher? Does he evidence understanding of the learner? Does he communicate well?
2. Using the material in this chapter, write a two-page evaluation of your own potential as a teacher of God's Word. Cite areas of strength. Where do you need to improve?

Selected Bibliography

Brown, Lowell. *Grow, Your Sunday School Can Grow.* Glendale, California: ICL, 1975.

Combs, Arthur W. *The Professional Education of Teachers.* Boston: Allyn and Bacon, 1965.

LeBar, Lois. *Education That Is Christian,* Westwood, New Jersey: Revell, 1958.

Morse, William C. and G. Max Wingo. *Psychology and Learning.* Chicago: Scott-Foresman, 1962.

Richards, Lawrence O. *A Theology of Christian Education.* Grand Rapids, Michigan: Zondervan, 1975.

_____, *Creative Bible Teaching.* Chicago: Moody Press, 1970.

---

[1]Matthew 7:28, 29

[2]Since this section specifically presents two of the Biblical accounts of Jesus teaching people, the Scripture references will remain in the text. Otherwise, Scripture references will be footnoted as all other references are.

[3]Combs, pp. 6, 8

[4]Morse and Wingo, p. 9

[5]Luke 6:39, 40, *NEB*

[6]2 Thessalonians 3:7, *NEB*

[7]Richards, *A Theology of Christian Education,* p. 45

[8]2 Timothy 2:15, *NEB*

[9]2 Timothy 2:3-6, *NEB*

[10]Titus 2:7, 8

[11]1 Peter 3:15, *NEB*

[12]Genesis 1:26, 27, 31a; 2:7

[13]Richards, *op. cit.,* p. 22

[14]LeBar, p. 136

[15]Richards, *Creative Bible Teaching,* pp. 108-112

CHAPTER

8

Helping
Preschoolers Learn

As you read, think about these questions:
—What are the chief characteristics of a preschooler?
—What effects do a preschooler's characteristics have on the way he is
   taught?
—What are the goals for teaching preschoolers?
—How should preschool classes be organized?
—What are at least five methods for teaching preschoolers?

Todd is five years old. He was born only a short time ago, a
helpless little fellow who could neither remember nor respond
beyond basic needs. But five years have passed quickly; he is
now a sturdy, at times independent, learning personality. He
has learned much in language, attitudes, skills, and facts during these five years—more than he will learn in any comparable period of time during the rest of his lifetime.

How has Todd developed? How will the principles and facts
of his development contribute to the determination of preschool teaching goals and methods?

Understanding the Preschool Learner

Physical Development

The preschool years are years of almost continual physical

97

growth and change. Small and helpless as he is, the newborn infant possesses that which is essential for him to grow and develop physically. It is his God-made nature to grow and mature, even if the rate is slow. Every individual has his own rate and pattern of development.

Physical growth is initially rapid. During the first year an infant will triple his weight. By the time a child is two, he is approximately one-half of his eventual adult height. From the age of two until six, a child grows a total of approximately nine inches and gains an average of five pounds per year.

Motor development accounts for significant physical growth during the preschool years. During the two or three years following the rapid physical growth of the first eighteen months, the dominant physical change is large muscle development. The pattern of development proceeds from large muscles to small muscles. Small muscle development will not be finished during the preschool years.

A child first learns to grasp objects and to follow them with his eyes. He rolls over and lifts his head. He learns to walk perhaps as early as nine or ten months of age; almost always by fifteen to eighteen months old. Then he explores by touching and handling objects. His preschool years are spent in adding, then refining, a variety of physical skills: jumping, skipping, running, and manipulating. A major achievement is toilet training, which is dependent upon adequate muscle development so that the child can control urination and elimination.

The latter part of the preschool years shift to small muscle development, although that continues into the elementary school years. Small muscle development allows for the handling of pencils and scissors, for example, and eventually increased visual acuity.

Because of his rapid growth and continuing development of motor skills, activity is a chief characteristic of a preschooler. He cannot be expected to sit still for long periods of time without a change of focus to keep attention. He likes to move and learns through activity when it is planned and guided. His attention span is roughly one minute per year of age.

The teacher should take into account these principles to better accommodate a preschool child physically:

1. Use equipment geared to the child's size. In most cases, it will be more effective to have children sit on the floor rather than in chairs.

2. Avoid small muscle activities such as intricate coloring and cutting. Use large crayons and pencils.

3. Change activities often in order to maintain attention.

Intellectual Development

A child is more than a physical being. He can express himself with language. His intellectual nature distinguishes him from any other member of the animal kingdom. How does it develop?

Intellectual development is affected both by heredity and environment. It once was thought that intelligence was entirely attributable to genetic inheritance. Although intelligence does depend on genes, early care and early intellectual and language stimulation are major factors as well. Some research suggests that those environmental factors may mean as many as fifty to seventy-five points on later intelligence scales.

What is measured as intelligence in Western culture is dependent largely upon language development. Acquiring language is perhaps one of the most important learning tasks of the preschool years. When a child can finally speak and express himself, he becomes more than a bundle of physical needs. He has the tools to express thought and to develop measurable intelligence.

Language development follows an orderly pattern, not only in Western culture, but in other parts of the world as well. Babies begin the journey toward language by cooing and crying during their first five months. These seemingly meaningless sounds are essential for future language development. Then at about six months, the infant begins to babble. Various sounds are distinguishable, but nothing is yet understandable. Finally, when the baby is about ten months old, he begins to imitate sounds. By the time he reaches a year, he is finally able to say two or three words.

Five factors contribute to language development. The first is grammatical structure, which is well developed by age six and fully adult by the middle elementary years. At age one, a child uses one-word sentences. By the time he reaches eighteen months, he uses two-word sentences. He begins to use three-word sentences by the time he is two. Finally, by the time he is four, he is capable of composing full, complex sentences. Children usually use nouns first, then add interjections, verbs, adjectives, pronouns, and adverbs in that order.

A second factor is pronunciation. Many children experience difficulty with *st, str, dr, fl,* and *th* sounds, sometimes due to hearing problems. Usually patient teaching and careful pronunciation will overcome such problems. Speech models are particularly important for a child to learn to pronounce words correctly.

Stuttering may also occur during the preschool years, often because the child thinks more rapidly than he is able to express himself. A child usually outgrows this problem unless undue pressure and attention is directed toward it. It also helps to encourage the child to slow down when he speaks.

A third factor in language development is vocabulary. It develops slowly during the child's first eighteen months, although he will recognize many more words than he says. By the time a child is two, he has a working vocabulary of about 272 words. His vocabulary increases to 846 words by age three, 1,540 by age four, 2,072 by age five, and 2,562 by age six—rapid growth indeed.

The fourth factor in language development is *rate of speaking.* The fifth is *communication style,* which is a combination of the other four factors. Both depend upon the models to which a child is exposed.

Language development is a complex process that affects a child's ability to express himself and his thoughts. He is born with the innate qualities from which language develops. How well it develops depends upon his language models, how much language stimulation he receives, the amount of reinforcement given to him, and his own rate of development.

Intellectual growth occurs in an orderly sequence, just as language development does. Jean Piaget, a Swiss psychologist, has studied intellectual development in children and youth. He has concluded that there are definite stages of thought through which a child progresses.

Before the age of two, a child is preoccupied with sensory experiences and motor activities. Piaget calls this the *sensorimotor stage.* During this period, a child does not usually develop new ways of dealing with unique situations, but resorts to responses that worked in similar earlier situations.

The remainder of the preschool years is spent in what Piaget calls the *preoperational* stage. While the sensorimotor child is restricted to direct interactions with his environment, the preoperational child can manipulate symbols (like words) that represent the environment. This is closely related to vocabulary development.

Although language symbols are used, the period from two to seven differs from later periods. One difference is concreteness. An adult can analyze and synthesize information, but a preschooler cannot. His thinking is limited to objects actually present or those he has experienced directly.

Preschool thought is also marked by *irreversibility*. Reversible thought is the basis for logical thinking. For example:

$$3 + 5 = 8 \qquad \text{and} \qquad 8 - 5 = 3$$
$$\text{or}$$
$$\text{All men and all women} = \text{all adults}$$
$$\text{and}$$
$$\text{All adults except all women} = \text{all men}$$

In each case, one thinks his way from one place to another and then back again. A preschooler cannot do that. Ask a four-year-old girl, "Do you have a sister?" She answers, "Yes."

"What is her name?"

"Carrie."

"Does Carrie have a sister?"

The reply is, "No." She is not ready for logical thinking.

Preschoolers also center their attention on one detail of an event and do not shift attention to other aspects. Show a preschooler two clay balls of equal size and ask, "Are they the same size?" and he will say that they are. Then right before his eyes, roll one ball into a sausage shape. He will insist that one is now bigger than the other. That happens because he centers on only one detail. (If he centers on height, he will think the round ball is larger. If he centers on length, he will believe the sausage to be larger.)

This information about the intellectual development of preschoolers has some important implications for Bible teachers:

1. Choose concrete words in communicating to preschoolers.

2. Center on one theme or concept for a Bible lesson. Avoid too many details in stories or pictures.

3. Use a wide variety of sensory experiences in teaching.

4. Avoid detailed, logical explanations.

5. Use visual aids to illustrate and reinforce words and ideas.

Psychosocial Development

A preschooler is a physical being and a thinking, intelligent individual. But he is more than that. He is also a feeling personality.

A newborn infant is limited in his range of emotional response. He can express distress (mostly vocally) and delight. When a baby is distressed, he is very, very distressed, and lets it be known in no uncertain terms. But when he is happy, he is all smiles and gurgles and cooing. Before many months, perhaps by five or six months, he experiences and expresses anger. By the time he reaches his ninth month, he experiences anxiety of strangers. Fear appears between twelve and eighteen months of age. Those fears are nearly always of tangible objects or circumstances: large animals, new places, and new people, for example.

At best, emotional responses of young children are unstable. They react strongly to frustrating or rewarding experiences. It is an arduous journey from the first appearance of emotional responses to the ability to control emotional behavior.

A second facet of psychosocial development is socialization, or the ability to live in a social setting. A child brings into the world his unique genetic inheritance, which affects his social development as surely as it does physical and intellectual growth. But living in society is also a matter of learning. Parents serve as key persons, although teachers and other caregivers also contribute to social learning.

Play behavior provides a fascinating view of social development. Before eighteen months, children react to each other only as objects, not as playmates. Between eighteen and thirty-six months, true social interest emerges, but children still do not play *with* each other; they engage in parallel play. But from three years on, peers become increasingly important. Play progresses from associative play with no organization at age three to self-organized, cooperative play at four. Such progress assumes adequate social interaction with peers.

Play is a child's work. Adults play to escape the routines of life, but children play to imitate life. They are great pretenders who use ideas, information, and behavior from "real life" in their play. By so doing they develop and reinforce their ideas.

Development of self is another facet of psychosocial behavior. Self-concept is an individual's awareness of his own characteristics and attributes. It begins to emerge by age two or three. Closely akin is self-esteem—the value a child puts on himself. Self-esteem emerges before kindergarten.

Identity is the next step in the development of self. Identity may be defined as awareness of group membership and the expectations, privileges, restraints, and responsibilities that accompany membership in the group. The foundations are laid during the preschool years when a child learns acceptable social behavior.

Self is developed most adequately when certain factors are present. One is parental acceptance of the child, which is demonstrated by affection and a comfortable family life. A second is discipline—clear rules consistently and firmly enforced. Physical abnormalities and maturation rate also contribute to development of the self.

Another aspect of psychosocial behavior is sexual development. Sex-related behavior appears first at ages three to five. Sex interest and sex play are common among preschoolers. They are curious about the difference between boys and girls.

Although children must be taught modesty and proper sexual behavior, their interactions with adults about sex should be based on honesty, truth, and acceptance. Healthy psychosexual development depends upon models of self-acceptance and observation of physical affection between parents. A loving father is particularly important for a child to see and imitate in order to learn appropriate male and female behavior.

This information about psychosocial development has the following implications for the teacher of preschoolers:

1. Be prepared for fluctuations in emotional response.

2. Be prepared to repeat rules for behavior and to correct misbehavior over and over again. Self-directed social behavior does not emerge overnight.

3. Use guided play experiences in teaching.

4. Praise the child for what he does well. A good rule is to say something good about every child during every class session. Be sure that praise is genuine and about items the child can control. For example, say, "You did a good job of picking up the blocks. That is very helpful," rather than responding to the same incident with, "You are the best boy." Such a response will allow him to repeat acceptable actions and to change unacceptable ones.

5. Establish clear boundaries for behavior in the classroom. Enforce them consistently and firmly.

Moral and Spiritual Development

Man is moral because he is spiritual, rational, and able to choose. What is moral-spiritual development? Cornelius Jaarsma offers an insightful explanation:

> It is nothing less than development of the whole person in all dimensions of personality such that consecration of the spirit to the service of God and moral righteousness find expression in the fulness of life . . . Moral-spiritual values of the Christian flow from a restored relationship to God in faith and a humble obedience to His will as He makes it known in His Word.[1]

Moral behavior includes two facets. The first is development of intention and conscience (which is internal), and the second is adherence to social norms and responsibilities. Indicators of moral behavior are (1) resistance to temptation, (2) guilt, (3) independence of action from external sanctions, and (4) confession and assumption of responsibility for actions. Not all of these are fully developed during the preschool years.

Conscience begins to emerge during the preschool years. Home conditions are vitally important for healthy conscience development. Parental warmth plus firmly enforced rules tend to produce well-behaved children who are able to accept responsibility for their behavior and who internalize behavior expectations. A warm, loving father is especially important in conscience development for both boys and girls.

A young child is growing morally. His morality is determined largely by the rules laid down by others (usually his parents). He judges things and events as either black or white. At first he behaves properly because of fear of punishment; later he behaves properly in order to please. Not before the middle of his elementary school years does he consistently behave properly because of his own decision.

At the same time, the preschooler can be taught to love Jesus and to want to please a loving God. His attitudes toward God will reflect the concrete relationship he experiences with his own father (or father substitute). The major area of spiritual growth is the shaping of attitudes toward God, the Bible, and the church.

A teacher of young children should take into account the following principles:

1. Work with simple spiritual concepts related to the experiences of the child.

2. Build basic attitudes toward God, Jesus, the church, the world, the Bible, the family, and self.

Goals for Early Childhood Education

The basic goal for all Bible teaching is summed up in Ephesians 4:13: ". . . until we all reach unity in the faith and in the knowledge of the Son of God and become mature, attaining the full measure of perfection found in Christ." The foundations are laid in the early childhood years through relationships with loving adults.

Much preschool Bible teaching time is spent in laying foundations. Basic Bible stories are presented to build a love for the Bible and an acquaintance with God, Jesus, and those who loved Him. Conversion will not come for some time yet, but ideas and attitudes begin to sprout in the early years.

Bible material is presented in a loving environment in order to build basic attitudes. The child hears Bible facts and responds to them in a well-planned Bible teaching classroom. Attitudes and values are modeled and reinforced.

Goals for preschoolers may be summarized in this way:

1. Each child will associate God, Jesus, the natural world, and the Bible with the love of people around him.

2. Each child will gain basic knowledge of God, Jesus, the natural world, and the Bible.

3. Each child will have satisfying experiences with adults and children at church, where he hears adults talk about God and Jesus.

4. Each child will feel that he is important and know that he is made by God.

5. Each child will want to love and help others.

Organizing the Preschool Department

Determine Groups Needed

Each separate room for preschoolers should be considered a department. Each department has a leader and teachers.

How does one determine how many departments are needed? Several factors should be considered: number of children enrolled, number of prospects available, amount of space, and number of potential workers. This information should be collected and analyzed each year prior to promotion. Children should be assigned to their groups according to a consistently applied basis. For example, a church may require that a child be two by October 1 to enter a preschool class. It is suggested that churches use the date used by local schools to determine eligibility for first grade.

These guidelines may be used for determining department size:

Babies	12	2's	15-18	4's	18-20
Toddlers	...12	3's	15-18	5's	18-20

Age groups may be combined if there are only one or two children of any age. However, babies and toddlers should always be in a separate room from 2's through 5's. Whenever it is possible, provide a separate department for each age level.

Recruit Workers

Once the number of departments has been determined, list the number of workers needed for each department. Use these guidelines:

Babies and Toddlers—one worker for every four children, but no less than two in any department.

2's and 3's—one worker for every five children, but no less than two in any department.

4's and 5's—one worker for every six children, but no less than two in any department.

Select workers carefully. Teachers mold children's attitudes more by personal qualities than in any other way. Seek men and women who have a growing relationship with Jesus, who genuinely love children, who are healthy and energetic, and who can work on a team.

Look for men as well as women. Many children do not have a father at home, and the presence of a man will meet some of their special needs. For the most part, avoid high school students. Although they are willing, few are mature enough to handle preschoolers as they should be handled.

Recruit workers for a ministry. Give them a clear idea of their responsibilities. The department director is responsible for worker enlistment, teachers' meetings, visitation, supplies, and general administration. He may also serve on the teaching

Sunday School	Activity	Children select activities from several options	2's & 3's 35-40 min. 4's & 5's 25-30 min.
	Together	All children together for music and special features	10-15 min.
	Bible Story	One teacher with a small group	2's & 3's 10-15 min. 4's & 5's 15-20 min.

TRANSITION—5 MINUTES

Church Time	Choosing	Choose from activities used in Sunday school	2's & 3's 35-40 min. 4's & 5's 30-35 min.
	Together	Retell story, snack, rest	15-20 min.
	Tell Me	Life-related story, music, finger fun	10-15 min.

Figure 8-1. Sunday morning teaching schedule for a preschool department.

team. Teachers are responsible to attend planning meetings, to prepare thoroughly, to lead learning activities, and to visit in the children's homes.

Arrange Teaching Time

Teaching time should be flexible for preschoolers. The purpose is to provide satisfying learning experiences from the time the child first arrives until he departs for home. It is preferable to develop both the Sunday school and church times into one time block for this age level. One set of curriculum materials can then be used to teach one concept per Sunday.

Figure 8-1 shows a teaching schedule designed for a department in which two or more teachers share together.[2] It is essential for a teacher to be present at each interest center, but the plan can be modified for a Sunday school in which one teacher works with only a few children. Interest centers and activities are set up in various parts of the room, and the entire class then moves from center to center. The following lesson plan illustrates such a modification:

Title: God Made Everything
Scripture: Genesis 1
Goals: 1) Children can name things God made.
        2) Children thank God for things He made.
Activity 1: Picture Center (Foods God made)
Activity 2: Book Center (*How God Gives Us Peanut Butter* and *How God Gives Us Bread*)
Activity 3: Food Center (Eat peanut butter and bread)
Activity 4: Picture Center (Trees, lakes, and plants God made)
Activity 5: Nature Center (Tulip)
Activity 6: Bible Story Time
Activity 7: Nature Center (Plant Seeds)
Activity 8: Music Center

The key to arranging teaching time is to provide for frequent change of activity.

Choosing Effective Teaching Methods

Preschoolers learn primarily through their environment and through the people in that environment. Earlier discussion of the characteristics of preschoolers suggested that children learn from guided play experiences that use ample sensory experiences. Preschool Bible lessons may be built around several kinds of activities.

Block Building may be used during Activity Time or Choosing Time. Use large cardboard blocks for toddlers, even 2's and 3's, but if possible, provide wood blocks for 4's and 5's. A creative teacher will be able to stimulate children to build many Bible-related items with blocks.

God's Wonders is an effective center for either Activity Time or Choosing Time. It may include nature objects, nature books, planting, nature walks, and slides of nature objects and scenes.

Books are also best used for Activity Time and Choosing Time, although they are occasionally useful for Together Time. Collect a variety of books, but on any given Sunday, put out only books relating to the Bible concept for the day.

Puzzles are best used for Activity Time and Choosing Time. A variety of puzzles should be collected, but just as with books, put out only the puzzles relating to the theme for the day.

Home Living activities may be planned for Activity Time and Choosing Time. This center allows the child to practice Bible concepts in everyday situations like those at home. Home living materials may be made or purchased.

Art activities may be used during Activity Time or Choosing Time. Painting, finger painting, working with clay, cutting and pasting, drawing, coloring, and making simple crafts are all useful art activities.

Storytelling may be used at any time, but it is the central method for Bible Story Time, Together Time, and Tell Me Time.

Music may be used throughout the session. It is most widely used during Together Time. Rhythm instruments may be introduced as well as singing. Records can be helpful.

Pictures illustrate concepts mentioned at any point in the day's activities. They are especially useful as an aid to storytelling. Pictures include felt pictures, stand-up figures, flannelgraph figures, dioramas, or filmstrips. Use them often.

Four criteria should be applied to the selection of methods for any given Bible lesson:

1. Will this method present, reinforce, or otherwise relate to today's Bible concept?

2. Is this activity one my class enjoys and is capable of doing?

3. Do I have access to the necessary materials for this method?

4. Is there someone available to guide this activity?

Summary

Teaching Todd the preschooler will be challenging, fun, and rewarding when you remember Todd's physical, intellectual, emotional, and spiritual capabilities and then plan to meet them. Set your goals, recruit your staff, arrange your schedule, and select the best ways to stimulate him to learn. Lay Bible foundations and shape attitudes for those later days when he will make the decision to live his life with Jesus Christ.

Projects

1. Select a preschool child to observe. How is he like the description in this textbook? How is he different?
2. Talk to someone who works in a preschool department. How is it organized? How is the Bible teaching time arranged? Why?
3. Plan a Bible lesson for preschoolers using Jesus' birth as the Bible content. How many methods can you use from the above list?

Selected Bibliography

Boone, Eldon M., Jr. *Working with Preschoolers at Church.* Nashville: Convention Press, 1974.

Harrell, Donna and Wesley Haystead. *Creative Bible Learning for Young Children.* Glendale, California: ICL, 1977.

Jaarsma, Cornelius. *Human Development: Learning and Teaching.* Grand Rapids, Michigan: Eerdmans, 1961.

McCandless, Boyd R. and Ellis D. Evans. *Children and Youth: Psychosocial Development.* Hinsdale, Illinois: Dryden Press, 1973.

Phillips, John, Jr. *The Origins of Intellect: Piaget's Theory.* San Francisco: W. H. Freeman and Co., 1969.

---

[1] Jaarsma, *Human Development: Learning and Teaching,* p. 155.
[2] From CREATIVE BIBLE LEARNING by Donna Harrell and Wesley Haystead, copyright 1977 by G/L Publications.

CHAPTER

9

Helping Elementary
Children Learn

As you read, think about these questions:
—What are the chief characteristics of elementary children?
—How do these characteristics affect how they are taught?
—What are the goals for teaching elementary children?
—How should children's classes be organized?
—What are at least ten ways of teaching children?

Jeffrey is six years old. He faintly resembles what he was as an infant six years ago, but he will hardly be the same child six years from now. At six, he is in the first grade, ready to begin formal education and immense changes. The foundations were laid during his preschool days, but now the superstructure begins to emerge. Jeffrey continues to grow physically and expands and refines the social, emotional, intellectual, and spiritual areas of his life.

Jeffrey is about to experience significant changes during these coming six years. His teacher will do well to understand and respond to those changes.

Understanding Elementary Children

Physical Development

Growth rate slows during the elementary years, perhaps as a

111

prelude to the rapid physical development that will occur during adolescence. Changes in height and weight are steady but slow. Coordination improves dramatically. So does motor development, which approaches adult standards by the end of elementary school.

Perhaps the most dramatic physical transition occurs late in elementary years when prepubertal changes begin. This is especially important for girls who not only undergo prepubertal changes, but are quite likely to experience the onset of puberty itself. Girls will likely experience a growth spurt during the late elementary years, probably outgrowing the boys. Many girls will also begin their menstrual cycles.

The onset of puberty has definite social implications. Early-maturing girls, especially tall ones, may well experience some self-esteem problems related to their sizes. The teacher must be attuned to the child's need for personal affirmation.

A high premium is assigned to motor skills at this age level. This too has profound social implications. Children are selected or passed over for most childhood games on the basis of physical skills and coordination. The child with well-developed skills has an advantage in social relationships, the means by which self-concept is built.

At any stage along the way, the key to physical description of elementary children could accurately be: "Active!" These youngsters can concentrate on a task for a significant amount of time if they are actively involved in it. With their tendency to overdo, they need enforced periods of relaxation or quiet involvement.

Eyes do not fully mature before eight years for most children. Therefore, primary-age children often have difficulty focusing on small print or objects.

The alert teacher will observe physical characteristics by heeding the following principles:

1. Alternate active with quiet times. But at all times, keep the child actively involved in learning.

2. Be alert for concern among early-maturing girls and late-maturing boys. Give them personal affirmation for who they are so they can learn to accept themselves.

3. Use large lettering for primaries so that children may read easily.

4. Give each child recognition and affirmation—not just those who are popular among their peers.

Intellectual Development

Perhaps the most significant achievement of the elementary years is learning to read. The foundations were laid in the preschool days, when the child acquired language. Now language can be used not only for oral communication, but for visual communication as well. Successful reading depends upon five environmental factors:

1. Rich language environment.
2. Significant adults who read a great deal.
3. Attainment of concrete operations intellectual level (see later in this section).
4. Interaction with adults interested in reading.
5. Appropriate social and emotional development.

Elementary age children are curious about nearly everything. During the primary years especially, curiosity and interest may shift from one thing to the next. But by fifth and sixth grades specific interests begin to emerge.

Distinct sex differences can be found in specific abilities and overall academic achievement. For example, girls generally are superior in verbal fluency, spelling, reading, mathematical computation, and overall grades. On the other hand, boys excel in mathematical reasoning and spatial manipulation. These differences may be due to the fact that girls are more intent on pleasing others while boys tend to spend their time doing things that interest them. Males generally achieve at a higher level than females later in life.

A child enters elementary school still thinking in a preoperational manner (as described in the previous chapter). Somewhere near age seven he enters the concrete operations subperiod, which will extend to the end of his elementary years. His thinking begins to develop in several areas.

1. *Conservation of number*. During the preoperational period, even after a child can make one-to-one correspondence between symbols and what they represent, he may be fooled if one set of objects (vases, for example) is placed in a line and the other set (flowers) in a cluster. He will perceive the sets to be no longer equal. However, once he reaches a concrete operations stage, he cannot be fooled.

2. *Conservation of weight, size, and volume*. The preschoolers sees two balls as equal if they are shaped alike, but when the shapes change before his eyes, he will say that they are of different sizes. At about seven, a child will agree that the quan-

tity of the two balls is the same, but will deny that weight is. Later, at about nine years, he will agree that weight is the same, but not volume. Finally, by age eleven, he will say that volume is the same too.

3. *Numbering in a series.* A preoperational child finds it impossible to match one set of objects to another set of different objects while at the same time arranging them in order of size. He can arrange objects in order of size, but when he does, he ignores number. He can count, but when he does, he ignores differences in size. The child at a concrete operations level can do both. We can summarize by saying that the elementary child can begin to reverse thought and also to decenter. (Both concepts were explained in the last chapter.)

The mental activities of a child have moved from sensory experiences (at birth), to perceptions, to intellectual operations. This progression makes it possible for him to understand cause-and-effect relationships, scientific information, and mathematical computation and reasoning. The bases for logical reasoning are established.

Differences in cognitive style also become apparent. "Cognitive style" refers to ways of thinking and responding. Impulsive thinkers are concerned about quickness while reflective thinkers are more concerned about correctness of answers than speed in answering. Children also differ in distractability, ability to memorize, and ability to solve problems.

A teacher of elementary children should take intellectual characteristics into account by observing the following principles:

1. Be alert to individual differences in rate and style of learning.

2. Stimulate natural curiosity. Relate learning to the child's interests.

3. Avoid abstract logical reasoning.

4. Provide a variety of instructional activities and styles in order to appeal to the variety of skills, abilities, and interests in the class.

Psychosocial Development

In elementary school, one's peers are powerfully important. Feelings of competence and a sense of worth depend upon foundations laid in the family, but those foundations of self-concept are tested against the reactions of a social group. A child relates to peers not as a subordinate as he does with adults, but on equal status. To some degree, the quality of those relationships determine his ego strength and behavior. "All the boys do it," is a logical argument for almost any elementary-age boy.

As children reach nine, ten, and eleven, they assert increasing independence. Their newfound independence is evidenced by wandering afield without permission, by less communication with adults, and sometimes by carelessness in appearance. Until then, however, a child is usually eager to please adults.

Boys are more aggressive than girls. With a group of boys together, plenty of wrestling, shoving, and punching can be reasonably expected. Both boys and girls are highly competitive. There is usually competitiveness between boys and girls.

Elementary age children become selective in their choice of friends. They have a best friend and sometimes an "enemy" as well. Friendships are generally with someone of the same sex.

Prejudicial attitudes begin to emerge. These reflect the opinions of older behavior models.

Sexual interest is also prevalent, especially among girls, many of whom reach puberty before they finish elementary school. Children's interactions with adults about sex need to be based on honesty, truth, and openness. Correct terminology should be used. A child's healthy psychosexual development depends upon having an adult who models self-acceptance and who expresses physical affection. The model is usually provided by parents or parent substitutes.

Perhaps the most crucial condition for healthy psychosocial development during this period is the existence of appropriate behavior expectations coupled with firm, consistent enforcement of them. Parents and teachers must not abdicate their leadership and authority before the child is ready for excessive independence.

Observance of these characteristics will make teaching elementary age children a satisfying experience. Take into account the following principles:

1. Be alert to the need of each child for affirmation. Be generous with praise—but offer praise for specific behaviors that the child can choose to control.

2. Arrange your teaching time in such a way as to permit each child to make choices for activities in which he will par-

ticipate. This principle will be developed further later in this chapter.

   3. Capitalize upon competitiveness, but make it a competition in which everyone can be a winner. Set it up so that the child competes against himself.

   4. Be honest and open with children.

   5. Set and enforce reasonable behavior standards.

Moral and Spiritual Development

A child's conscience continues to develop during the elementary years. As it was during the preschool years, models are most important—especially warm, nurturing fathers or father substitutes. The primary child has yet to internalize behavior sanctions—he still determines morality by parental rules and the threat of punishment. But as the elementary years draw to a close, the youngster begins to behave appropriately most of the time because he chooses to. Much of his moral behavior is related to psychosocial maturity as well as to direct moral instruction.

The older child begins to make moral judgments in more than black and white terms. He still is not intellectually capable of abstract reasoning and complex logical thinking, but he begins to see moral decisions in their context. He can assume the other person's point of view, which allows him to consider possible alternatives for action.

A child is sensitive to spiritual teaching, especially when it is presented by caring adults whose lives reflect the teachings they are giving. He is ready for Bible teaching if it is presented in concrete, life-related terms.

Many elementary children make salvation decisions, usually based upon a desire to please Jesus more than from a deep sense of sin. They can define sin, but in terms of specific behavior rather than as a state of rebellion toward God. Such an understanding is an adequate beginning point for Christian life, especially if they are led to the next stage of understanding as adolescents.

The teacher of elementary children should observe these principles:

   1. Teach him to trust God and His Word.

   2. Use concrete Biblical experiences to support Bible concepts.

   3. Practice what you teach.

Goals for Teaching Children

Goal setting is essential. Teachers must know what they want to accomplish when they teach children. At least three objectives determine the kind of teaching given to elementary children.

The most basic goal is to teach Bible facts. By the time a child completes his elementary school years, he should know basic people and events of the Bible, be able to name the books of the Bible, be able to find Bible references, and be able to name and describe the divisions of the Bible. Primaries will continue to work with the simple concepts of the preschool years, adding some detail, but Middlers and Juniors can work with chronological information.

A second goal is to continue to build attitudes toward God, Jesus, the Bible, the church, and self. Although teaching must emphasize Bible facts, it goes beyond mere presentation of information. It must be related to the feelings and behaviors of the children in day-to-day living.

Third, the foundations should be laid for conversion, which may not occur until the early adolescent period. Facts and attitudes contribute to conversion, but sin, forgiveness, and obedience also must be stressed—not as a way to manipulate children to make decisions they are not yet ready to make, but in order to provide a Biblical basis for salvation decisions whenever they do occur. The children who do become Christians also need guidance in Christian living—information, practice, and encouragement.

Organizing the Elementary Children's Department

Determine Groups Needed

Although there are similarities between first graders and fifth graders, there are definite differences in development. It is best to group elementary children into at least three categories, each covering a two-year interval. Churches with too few children to do this could have one group of first and second graders and another of third through sixth graders.

Basic guidelines for department and class sizes are based on the assumption that groups should be small enough for each child to receive individual attention.

Grade	Maximum Class Size	Maximum Department Size
1-2	6-8	30-35
3-4	7-9	35
5-6	8-10	35-40

A department leader must also decide whether to divide classes by sex. The best argument for doing so is the competitiveness between boys and girls, especially at grades five and six. Probably the best reason for not doing so is the fact that boys and girls co-exist very well in public schools. There is no right answer to the question. It depends upon local factors: nature of the children, availability of men to teach, and personal preference.

Recruit Workers
Once the needed departments and classes have been determined, worker needs may be analyzed. A teacher for each class and a supervisor for each department are essential. Add to those, as they are available, assistant teachers, department secretaries, and musicians.

Children's workers are special people and should be carefully chosen. They should be growing Christians who provide a warm, caring example of the Christian life. They must understand children and be able to relate to them. The ability to work on a team is another asset.

Recruit both men and women for all age levels. Couples working together in a class provide a good example of a Christian family and provide both male and female models for children who may lack them at home.

The ministry of the children's worker involves preparation and Bible teaching, but it also calls for participation in the lives of the pupils through visitation, listening, and social activities. An effective teacher teaches well because he ministers both inside and outside the classroom.

Arrange the Teaching Time
The Sunday school for children should allow the children to make choices and provide for normally active children to participate in the learning process. Children's departments operate on the same overall schedule as the rest of the Sunday school. The time block should be arranged in the children's departments to permit children to learn most effectively.

15-20 minutes   Small Groups (Each child chooses a planned introductory activity such as a puzzle, game, or art when he arrives. The activity is related to the Bible content.)

30-35 minutes   Entire Class Group (The Bible materials are presented and life application is made. Activities completed during the small group time may be displayed or reported as they relate to the lesson preparation.)

10-15 minutes   Entire Department (All classes within a department share together with music, prayer, and class activities.)

Adjustments to this schedule may be made for either a greater or lesser time allotment.

Effective Methods for Teaching Elementary Children

The teacher of children may choose from seven basic categories of methods. Each of the seven categories includes several specific activities.

Art

Children enjoy art activities and learn by expressing themselves in that way. What they create visualizes the Bible material for themselves and others in the class. Art methods are especially appropriate for children who find it difficult to express themselves verbally. Here are some easily-used art activities:

Cartooning	Friezes and Murals	Posters
Charts	Maps	Slide Making
Dioramas	Mobiles	Time Lines
Displays	Paper Tearing	

Drama

Creative dramatics allows children to reinforce concepts and facts while also experiencing feelings of those with whom they identify in the drama. A variety of dramatic activities are possible.

Choral Speaking	Monologue	Puppet Plays
Dramatic Interview	Pantomime a Story	Role Playing

Written Communication
Written activities are appealing to many children. They are effective for reporting and recording information, reflecting feelings, and expressing ideas and feelings.

Banner Headlines	Newspaper Writing	Word Games
Diary Writing	Poems	Word Puzzles
Letter Writing	Story Writing	

Oral Communication
Communication probably shall always include oral forms, teacher-to-pupil, pupil-to-teacher, and pupil-to-pupil. Every Bible lesson will depend upon some oral communication forms.

Brainstorming	Lecture
Buzz Groups	Listening Teams
Discussion	Panels
Films and Filmstrips	Question and Answer
Free Association Quiz	

Games
Children explore their world through games. Games are effective ways to present and review information and to teach Bible verses. Use the list below or make up your own.

Bible Verse Games	*Facts Games*	*Review Games*
Connect the Words	Flash Cards	Add-a-Word
Match Picture to Idea	Matching	Baseball, Hockey, Basketball, Football
Match the Halves	Password	Bible Bee
Match the Words	Spinner	Fill in the Blank
Put in Order	TV Formats	Matching

Music
Children enjoy and respond to music. Music is used for worship experiences, but musical activities are also valuable to teach or reinforce facts or concepts and to express response to Biblical material.

Choose Song to Illustrate Concept   Listen to Music
Create Original Songs   Make Rebus Chart of
Illustrate Songs   Words of Song

Research

Research and report methods work well with children, especially if the type of research is varied.

Examining Objects   Guided Study   Reports
Field Trips   Interviews

Summary

The world of an elementary child is an expanding, fascinating one. Teaching Jeffrey is a matter of first understanding his physical, intellectual, psychosocial, and spiritual capabilities and then designing lessons to communicate with him. It is challenging and worthwhile to see children grow in faith and response toward God.

Projects

1. Observe two elementary age children, a second grader and a fifth grader. How are they like each other? How are they different from each other? How do they match the description made in this chapter? How do they differ from it?
2. Interview a worker in a children's department. How is it organized? How is the teaching time arranged? Why?
3. Plan a Bible lesson for children using Jesus' resurrection as the Bible content. How many methods can you use from the list above?

Selected Bibliography

Biehler, Robert F. *Psychology Applied to Teaching.* 3rd ed. Boston: Houghton-Mifflin, 1977.

McCandless, Boyd R. and Ellis D. Evans. *Children and Youth: Psychosocial Development.* Hinsdale, Illinois: Dryden Press, 1973.

Phillips, John, Jr. *The Origins of Intellect: Piaget's Theory.* San Francisco: W. H. Freeman and Co., 1969.

Rives, Elsie, and Margaret Sharp. *Guiding Children.* Nashville: Convention Press, 1969.

Watson, Robert I., and Henry Clay Lindgren. *Psychology of the Child and Adolescent.* (fourth edition). New York: Macmillan, 1979.

Helping Youth Learn

As you read, think about these questions:
—What are the chief characteristics of youth?
—How do the characteristics of youth effect how they are taught?
—What are the goals for teaching youth?
—How are youth classes to be organized?
—What are at least ten ways of teaching youth?

Henrietta Mears, longtime Director of Christian Education at First Presbyterian Church in Hollywood, California, herself an exceptional teacher of youth, used to say, "No one loves junior highs except their mothers—and even they wonder on occasion!" More than a few who have tried their hands at teaching junior highs and senior highs would agree.

Teaching youth is, at best, demanding. It calls for committed teachers who try to understand teenagers and who communicate the Word creatively, speaking to the needs of teens. But teaching youth, when it is done well, is rewarding for both now and the future.

Understanding the Adolescent

Physical Development

Dozens of definitions of adolescence have been offered. None seems to be adequate by itself, for adolescence is a complex interaction of physical, emotional, intellectual, and cultural factors that affect the entire personality. Adolescents are individuals, each developing at his own rate. Besides that, adolescence, as we know it, is not a universal phenomenon.

Adolescence, whenever it begins and ends, and in whatever culture it occurs, involves significant physical changes that are called puberty. Most girls will experience the onset of puberty sometime before they become teenagers, a fact that affects self-image. On the other hand, boys may not experience puberty until eighth or ninth grade, fully two years later than girls. For boys who mature even later than the average, self-image is negatively affected.

A predictable sequence of physical changes occur for both boys and girls. Both begin with a change in hormone balance. But the age at which puberty occurs is unpredictable. The following list shows the sequence of changes:

Girls	Boys
Change in hormone balance	Change in hormone balance
Rapid skeletal growth	Rapid skeletal growth
Breast development	Enlargement of genitals
Appearance of straight pubic hair	Appearance of straight pubic hair
Maximum growth spurt	Voice cracks
Appearance of kinky pubic hair	First wet dream
Onset of menstruation	Appearance of kinky pubic hair
Appearance of underarm hair	Maximum growth spurt
	Appearance of downy facial hair
	Appearance of chest and underarm hair
	Final voice changes
	Appearance of coarse facial hair

The average age for puberty for girls is eleven to twelve, fourteen for boys. The physical process will usually be completed by the end of high school, although some boys add height after their high school graduation.

Both boys and girls may expect a growth spurt. Girls usually experience theirs earlier than do boys. It is not as extreme for them as for boys who sometimes add six inches and twenty-five pounds in a single year. Rapid growth produces awkwardness—and that carries with it profound social implications.

Sexual characteristics, both primary and secondary, are predominant among the physical changes of adolescence. The changes bring about new, intense feelings, which teenagers must learn to identify and handle. The onslaught of these feelings, and how the adolescent handles them, has significant social implications. For example, research indicates that the male sex drive peaks at age seventeen or eighteen—before most men have a socially acceptable means of sexual expression.

Acne is a frequent result of hormone changes. For appearance-conscious teens, it is devastating.

Much of a teen's sense of worth centers around physical characteristics and appearance. He cannot change them (except possibly for skin conditions), so he needs to learn to accept himself as he is. To do so is to take a giant step toward maturity.

The alert Christian teacher observes the following principles to take into account physical characteristics of youth:

1. Avoid calling attention to awkwardness or unusual physical characteristics.

2. Get acquainted with each pupil individually.

3. Deal with sexual matters honestly and without embarrassment. Hold forth a Christian view of sexuality.

4. Provide grooming and hygienic information on an individual basis for those who need it.

Intellectual Development

According to the Swiss psychologist, Jean Piaget, the teen makes the transition from the concrete intellectual operations of childhood to formal, abstract, logical thought. It is no small transformation, for it permits him to think creatively, to test hypotheses, to build and follow logical arguments. The process begins in the late elementary or early junior high years and is usually completed by age fifteen.

Because teens can understand cause and effect and can begin to reason abstractly, they can also begin to plan a long-range course of action. Yet, teens are people of the "here and now," their action much more apt to be dictated by the feelings and pressure of the present than by the hopes of the future. Still they do possess the capacity for future planning.

Three teaching principles should be observed by a teacher of teens:

1. Challenge teens with Biblical material that goes beyond mere restatement of factual material learned during childhood. Deal with the meanings of the Bible and how Biblical material fits into God's overall plan for man.

2. Later teen years are ideal times to deal with doctrinal material.

3. Whatever the nature of the Biblical material, whether factual or doctrinal, be clear and specific in making life applications.

Psychosocial Development

Psychosocial development is probably the most crucial transition of the teen years. Physical changes inevitably happen, but emotional and social changes are not nearly so routine. Somehow a teenager must make the culturally-expected changes from childhood to adulthood. It does not happen without a certain amount of personal struggle.

Teen years are a time of starting a search for personal identity. The crucial questions are: who am I? where am I going? why am I here? Healthy family relationships permit the answers to be found more easily than they would be otherwise.

Identity seeking is done in a variety of ways. Some experience what may be called identity confusion, which is characterized by little trust of others, difficulty with interpersonal relationships, and experimentation with socially inappropriate behavior such as drug usage, misuse of sex, or delinquent behavior.

Others seem to declare a moratorium in the process of finding identity. They choose to experiment and to toy around with extreme behaviors. Their behaviors, short of delinquency, tend to resemble those of confused identity.

Some choose identity foreclosure. They experience little, if any, crisis. They simply adopt the attitudes and behaviors of adults with few, if any, questions asked.

Another group of teens choose the route of achievement. Their behavior is relatively mature and flexible. They experience good interpersonal relationships and tend to be leaders.

Whichever route to identity is chosen, an adolescent must see himself as an individual, apart from his parents. This need for independence, important as it is, is probably the source of more parent-teen conflicts than any other source. Teens often assert themselves merely to test independence, especially when parents are reluctant to grant it or when they grant more than youth need at that time. Teens need a degree of freedom, but at the same time they need solid parental standards to bounce against.

Not the least of the psychosocial struggles is the adoption of appropriate sex roles. Healthy family models and relationships are of great value at this point. Teens tend to adopt the roles they have observed, if what they have seen is positive and if there has been open discussion of sex roles and functions.

Teens must also learn to accept their own physiques. This task is accomplished far better in the presence of loving, supportive adults.

Peer pressure is intense during the teen years. Everybody needs somebody to belong to, and for a teen it is usually his peers. Cliques tend to shape many teenage standards: dress, hair, sexual behavior, political opinions. An intense loyalty exists among clique members, and they fiercely defend each other to adults or to those outside their social set. Not all peer pressure is negative, of course, especially if the social set holds high standards.

Moods are most unpredictable among teens. Much of that is due to physical factors, but solving the question of identity is also very much a factor.

Adolescents spend considerable time falling in and out of love. Early adolescents often have crushes on teachers and counselors. In later adolescent years, crushes occur with teens of the opposite sex. Teenage love is intense and all-absorbing. It also creates jealousy, felt every bit as intensely as love.

Dating begins during adolescence. It is a valuable experience, for it helps a teen to relate to the opposite sex, to learn sex roles, and to achieve a degree of emotional independence. But for those who do not date, it has a distinct negative effect on self-image.

While peers do exert powerful pressure on teens, so do parents—for grades, achievement, college, a "proper" career choice, acceptable friends. Those pressures are generally handled well by teenagers who experience healthy family relationships.

A youth worker cannot ignore the psychosocial characteristics of those whom he teaches. To do so is to invite failure.

Careful observance of the following principles will give a boost toward success:

1. Involve teens in planning for Bible material to be covered, group activities, and expected group behaviors.

2. Hold forth high expectations and standards for your teens. Challenge them.

3. Build the confidence of teens by giving them opportunity to perform tasks and by praising them for genuine effort and achievement.

4. Be prepared for unpredictability in moods and behavior. Do not berate teens for moodiness and erratic behavior. Lead by example.

5. Recognize the importance of peers. Do not try to undermine group loyalty. Rather, work with each teen to encourage his own decision-making. Give him support when he must stand against his peers.

Moral and Spiritual Development

During adolescence, one establishes his own value system. No longer will parents' values and religion be adequate without personal examination and decision. Given the teen's independent nature and search for identity, the quest for a personal value system follows naturally.

Doubts emerge during these years. A teenager, armed only with the facts and faith of childhood, confronts scientific and philosophical material of all kinds—much of which ignores or denies the truth of the Bible. He handles the new material either by reexamining and reconfirming his faith, or by abandoning it. His reevaluation will proceed far more positively if he finds a supportive atmosphere of faith in which to express his doubts and to seek answers.

Although many adolescents reject their childhood faith, evidence indicates that spiritual questions are not set aside. However, teens seem to have little reverence for what the older generation considers sacred, at least until they reach the same conclusions on their own. While an adult reasons logically, a teen, although capable of such reasoning, frequently draws his conclusions on the basis not only of fact, but of peer concerns and personal feelings that have not yet been tested out by fact or experience.

Merton Strommen did a comprehensive study of the values of 2,952 Lutheran youth. He found marked differences between boys and girls. More girls than boys aspire to religious goals, social service, and reflection. Boys, however, were more likely to follow through on their aspirations.

Strommen further discovered a lack of relationship between religious knowledge and values. Indoctrination is not tantamount to communication of values. However, teens are challenged by a religious experience that calls for commitment and loyalty. They respond to Bible study that moves from the mere presentation of facts to the integration of Biblical material with daily behavior. They respond when they are forced to think for themselves, as they are led face to face with Christ.

Strommen draws four conclusions that the Christian teacher of youth would do well to heed:[1]

1. The vitality of a youth ministry varies in direct proportion to the degree of sensitivity and concern that adults hold toward their youth.

2. Adults hold an image of youth that tends to increase the chasm between the two and make communication increasingly difficult.

3. Youth need the dynamic that indoctrination alone cannot give. They require Bible facts coupled with life application presented in an atmosphere that permits questioning and discussion.

4. Youth are reachable by and for the church.

Goals for Teaching Youth

Teachers of youth need a clear sense of direction for their efforts. Three basic goals give needed guidance.

The first goal is to provide for spiritual growth. Growth is made on the basis of Bible information that is more than a mere retelling of stories as they were presented during childhood. The first step is discovery of facts and principles from God's Word, and the second step is exploring how those facts and principles apply to life situations. The final step is to practice using the principles and to share the results. This first goal deals with the thinking, feeling, and doing processes, all of which are essential for spiritual transformation.

The second goal is to activate youth for service. This goal is logically linked to the first. A study of God's Word, as outlined above, results in motivation for service. The teacher provides guidance in choosing and carrying out acts of service.

The third goal is to challenge youth to make decisions on the basis of Bible principles. Moral and ethical conduct, choice of vocation, use of leisure time, and dating behavior are all decisions that should be affected by commitment to Jesus Christ. Every teacher should make it his goal to bring teens to make those decisions in light of God's Word.

Three goals—spiritual growth, service, decision-making—give a clear sense of direction to the teacher of teens. They are attainable and desirable.

Organizing the Youth Department

Determine Groups Needed

Analyze the youth enrollment in your church to decide how many groups to provide. How many youth are there? What is the age and sex of each?

Youth classes should not exceed twelve to fifteen in attendance. A youth class can be conducted successfully for as few as five.

If you have more than twelve to fifteen teens in your church, you must decide how to divide them. One possibility is to divide by age. Junior highs (according to the age definitions of junior high in your community) and senior highs would then be placed in separate classes. This would permit classes to be designed to meet the specific needs of early and late adolescents.

A second possibility is to divide by sex. This division allows the specific needs of boys and girls to be met. Many feel that discipline is also more easily maintained.

If teens are evenly distributed from grade seven through grade twelve, probably the best division to make first would be by age between junior highs and senior highs. The next division could be between boys and girls at each level. Later additions could include classes for boys and girls at even narrower age ranges.

When enrollment calls for creation of more than four youth classes (fifty to sixty enrollment), a second youth department should be added. Additional departments may be added as needed.

Recruit Workers

Leaders are the key to a successful youth department. A fully committed teacher is more important than any amount of facilities or materials.

The effective youth leader is one who models the Christian life. He is one who deeply cares about youth. He is flexible. He is full of life and enthusiasm. He understands youth. He is willing to guide pupils to discover truth on their own, rather than tell them everything himself.

Each class needs a teacher, and each department requires a department leader. Usually men will teach boys' classes, and women will teach girls. The department leader can be either a man or a woman—the major requirement is organizational ability. Assistant teachers may be recruited as they are needed and available.

Arrange the Teaching Time

A variety of patterns may be used to organize the time block assigned to the youth department. On rare occasions it may be desirable to have the entire department together for the total teaching time. Such an arrangement would be appropriate for guest speakers and films.

At other times, the entire department could gather for a brief assembly time and then divide into small permanent class units. Or they could meet in permanent class units followed by a department assembly. The normal pattern, however, is for each small permanent class group to spend the Sunday school time together. The teacher must then plan and use the time block to the greatest advantage.

A Bible session should be built around the pattern outlined in Chapter 8. The teacher focuses on a life-related theme from the Bible material for the day, formulates appropriate objectives, and then plans the hook, book, look, and took to accomplish the objectives. The diagram below pictures a suggested time allotment within three possible time blocks.

Lesson Section	60 min.	45 min.	30 min.
Hook (Attention)	10	5	5
Book (Bible Study)	25	20	15
Look (Life Application)	20	15	5
Took (Decision)	5	5	5

Time allotments may be altered, depending upon the subject matter and objectives.

Whichever pattern is chosen, the entire session should be developed to focus on the objectives for the day. Films, lectures, music, and any other large-group activities should be chosen because they contribute to the lesson objectives.

Effective Methods for Teaching Youth

Methods are the means by which God's Word is communicated. They are essential, but they are predicated upon four assumptions:[2]

1. The Holy Spirit is the chief agent of Christian nurture. Our purpose is to provide the context in which He can work.

2. The whole Bible is the source of truth.

3. The teacher communicates nonverbally, with body language and example, as much as he does with what he says.

4. The learner learns best when he is actively involved in the learning process.

A wide range of activities are available to stimulate and inspire youth. These may be divided into seven basic categories.

Lecture

Lecture is essentially one-way communication. It is best used to present information in limited time segments. It is the most efficient method for large groups. But lecture can be varied to involve the learners. Try some of these techniques.

Choral Reading	Films	Listening Teams	Symposium
Demonstrations	Interviews	Monologues	

Discussion

Discussion is a deliberate conversation among two or more people. It explores issues and answers and attempts to solve problems. Discussion does not always just happen; it must be planned and stimulated. Techniques such as these can be used to help initiate good discussions:

Agree-Disagree Statements	Interviews
Brainstorming	Listening
Buzz Groups	Panels
Case Studies	Problem Solving
Circle Response	Question-Answer
Debates	Teams

Written Communication

Another means by which youth may be involved is to have them write out their ideas. These activities are especially good for clarifying feelings and stimulating thinking:

Bible Character	Modern Parables	Question Box
Comparison	Newspaper Story	Self-Evaluation
Letter Writing	Paraphrase	Story Writing
Log, Journal, Diary	Poetry	TV Script
Memo Writing	Prayer Writing	Word Puzzles

Drama

Many youth like to dramatize roles, either Biblical or present-day. These activities encourage the learner to identify with the feelings of an individual and to gain insight and understanding of actions:

Formal Drama	Role Play	Slide Show
Pantomime	Skit	TV Program

Art

Any pictorial or graphic expression of Bible material or concepts can be classified as art. Art activities are especially good to visualize and reinforce truth:

Advertisement	Campaign Badges	Graphs
Brochures	Coats of Arms	Maps
Banners	Collage/Montage	Mobiles
Book Covers	Displays	Murals
Bumper Stickers	Graffiti Posters	Rebuses

Music

Music activities are helpful in presenting Bible truth and for expressing thoughts and responses to that truth:

Concept and Song Match	Singing
Hymn Paraphrase	Songwriting
Musical Commercial	Tune Writing

Research

Any activity that involves a learner in consulting various sources may be called Bible research. It provides opportunity for a learner to discover Bible truth for himself:

Book Report   Question Research   Time Line
Field Trip   Reaction Sheet

Criteria for Use of Methods

A teacher must choose from the multitude of methods available to communicate God's Word. What determines his choice of the means by which he will communicate? Six factors serve as criteria:

1. Aim of the lesson.
2. Size of the group.
3. Size of the room.
4. Resources and supplies available.
5. Abilities and interests of students.
6. Time available.

Summary

A visit to the world of adolescents will assist the potential Bible teacher. As with any other age level, teaching adolescents requires an understanding of their physical, intellectual, emotional, social, and spiritual characteristics. Once that understanding is reached, facilities, personnel, and time are organized to communicate to them. The challenge is demanding, but the rewards are abundant.

Projects

1. Observe a junior high student and a junior in high school. How are they like each other? Different? How do they match the descriptions outlined in this chapter? How do they differ?
2. Think back to the youth classes in your home church. How are they organized? How is teaching time arranged? How could the classes be improved?
3. Plan a Bible lesson for youth using Luke 15:11-32 as the Bible basis. How will you use several of the methods listed above?

Selected Bibliography

Dacey, John Steward. *Adolescents Today*. Santa Monica, California: Goodyear Publishing Co., 1979.

Farmer, Franklin. *Working with Youth in the Sunday School*. Nashville: Convention Press, 1974.

Reed, Bobbie, and Rex E. Johnson. *Bible Learning Activities: Grades 7 to 12*. Glendale, California: Gospel Light, 1974.

Seely, Edward D. *Teaching Early Adolescents Creatively.* Philadelphia: Westminster, 1971.
Strommen, Merton P. *Profiles of Church Youth.* St. Louis: Concordia, 1963.

----

[1]From PROFILES OF CHURCH YOUTH © 1963 Concordia Publishing House. Used by permission.
  [2]Seely, p. 11

11

Helping Adults Learn

As you read, think about these questions:
—What are the major characteristics of each level of adulthood?
—What are the goals for teaching adults?
—How are adult classes to be organized?
—What are at least ten ways of teaching adults?

Adult—adults—adulthood. Those words are used often, but they are difficult to define.

An adult can be defined in physiological terms—sexual maturity, for example. But that hardly seems to be adequate. (Consider all the teenage pregnancies—are all of those girls adults?) The definition can also be made by intellectual measures, or financial independence, or legal age, or work, or marriage, or willingness to assume responsibility. Each of these measures by itself is inadequate: each is an important facet of adulthood, but each, when taken alone, excludes some whom we judge to be adults.

In some cultures adulthood is marked by an initiatory rite; an individual moves directly from childhood to adulthood. In Western culture, this is not the case. Instead, an individual experiences a lengthy adolescence that finally blurs into adulthood. As a result, there is little agreement about a precise time

or definition for the beginning of adulthood.When does adulthood begin? Age eighteen is a logical lower limit, because of
the significant marker events that occur at that time: a person
reaches legal age, graduates from high school, and attains some
degree of independence.

Even if the beginning of adulthood can be defined, further
definition is necessary. The adult years cover three-fourths or
more of the average person's life span. Adulthood is not just a
succession of years of dull uniformity. The adult years are
characterized by changes just as significant as those in childhood and adolescence.

Most psychologists divide adulthood into three distinct
periods: young adulthood, middle adulthood, and older adulthood. The dividing lines between these periods are just as difficult to define as the lower limit of adulthood. One cannot be
dogmatic about the ages assigned to each period, but for the
discussion in this chapter, the following definitions will be
assumed: young adulthood extends from eighteen to thirty-
four, middle adulthood from thirty-five to fifty-nine, and older
adulthood from sixty until death.

Understanding Adults

Everything that happens to a person affects him in some
way—graduation, childbirth, getting a job, college. These concrete experiences are called marker events, and much of life
can be evaluated on the basis of them. But not everything that
happens to an individual can be defined or explained by external marker events, for much change comes from within. These
internal changes are called developmental stages.

An adult's life includes both internal and external changes.
Sometimes an adult attributes internal changes to external
events—that is, he believes that internal changes would have
been eased or avoided altogether, if he had experienced different marker events. However, adults will experience predictable
developmental stages whatever the marker events. Far from
causing developmental stages, marker events are often affected
by developmental stages.

Robert J. Havighurst, renowned developmental psychologist
at the University of Chicago, defines a developmental task as "a
task which arises at or about a certain period in the life of the
individual, successful achievement of which leads to his hap-

piness and to success with later tasks, while failure leads to unhappiness in the individual, disapproval by society, and difficulty with later tasks."[1] What are the expected developments at each stage of adulthood?

Young Adults

Young adulthood has been characterized by some as pulling up roots and formulating a personal self-definition not totally dependent upon one's relationships with his parents. Two major tasks confront the young adult on his way to achieving self-definition. One is the completion of identity formation, a task begun during adolescence, and the second is competency in what he does. The young adult may choose from a variety of lifestyles, but whatever his choice, he must come to a clear image of himself as an adult and a feeling of being competent in an adult world.

A variety of marker events accompanies the internal developmental stages. A significant one is selecting a marriage partner—or learning to live as a single adult. Choice of partner and the process of learning to live with him reveal much about a person's self-identity and feelings of competence. Success or failure of the marriage contributes to feelings of competence. Women, especially, tend to derive identity and competency from the marriage relationship itself.

Closely akin to marriage is managing a home and family. Young adults must decide if and when they will have a family, where they will live, and how to manage money. All of these decisions contribute to self-identity and personal competency.

A third event is the beginning of a vocation. To a degree, that is a reflection of personal identity, but it is a key to the search for competency as well. Vocation is especially important to men who must be the breadwinners for a family (career women experience the same needs).

Each of these three marker events require reevaluation during the thirties, when one must modify his expectations for his marriage and job. The seventh year of marriage is critical because of the readjustments demanded. The same is true of the seventh to tenth years in a vocation. The individual must reexamine and recommit himself to the marriage or job. If he does not, the marriage fails, or a job change is negotiated. Either outcome affects identity and competency to some degree. Eventually the thirties take on a more orderly and rational lifestyle.

Middle Adults

Middle adults are caught in the squeeze between two generations. It is not an easy dilemma to resolve. Much of the middle
adult's developmental work is wrapped up with those two generations.

The squeeze comes from parents on the one side. Although
parents are more and more peripheral to the middle adult's
day-to-day routine, he eventually must come to grips with
parental aging and the decisions it demands. In the person
of aging parents, he is also brought face-to-face with his own
mortality.

On the other hand, middle adults are confronted with the
reality that their children are less and less involved in family
life. Children grow up to be adolescents and adults, and they
pull up roots and strike out on their own. Unless middle adults
have a clear sense of the squeeze in which they find themselves, they often resort to excessive control of children in an
effort to maintain a sense of safety and immortality.

Physiological changes are clear signals to middle adults that
they are not immortal after all. Gray hairs, hard-to-lose extra
pounds, tiring more easily, menopause—all are reminders that
the body is aging and will one day die. Friends die of heart
attacks and cancer, another personalization of death, a fact to
be dealt with either positively or negatively.

Marriage requires renegotiation. Children leave home, and
partners are left to deal directly with each other. It is another
critical time for a marriage, calling for patience and sharing.

The adult of thirty to fifty faces a distortion of time: *whatever
is to be done must be done now.* How he handles this is determined by his view of himself.

A middle adult comes to terms with age in one of three ways.

1. The middle-aged kid tries to relive adolescence and free
himself from responsibility.

2. The protector of the status quo grows old before his
time with rigid attitudes and lifestyle.

3. The well-adjusted person seeks to achieve renewal—
realizing physical and vocational limitations and accepting
them without undue regret, coming to terms with age and en-
joying it, redefining attitudes toward money, finding a sense of
meaning in life, accepting death, and approving self.

Usually the middle adult will handle much of his developmental work by age fifty or so, and his pattern will then follow

him through the remainder of life. If he chooses the middle-aged kid route, he will likely move from one self-defeating pattern to another. If he protects the status quo, he becomes old and set in his ways. But if he chooses and achieves renewal, he lives the final decade of the middle years with zest, growing toward old age with the feeling that he has done well in life. He grows into older adulthood gracefully.

Older Adults

Older adulthood has sometimes been called a "period of decline," but it could just as easily be viewed as a time of delight and enjoyment. Which way it is viewed (and lived) by the older adult depends largely upon how well he made the adjustments of middle adulthood. Assuming that one did cope well with the reality of mortality, older adulthood becomes a time for living.

Even so, there are new adjustments to be made, many of them associated with external circumstances. One is the adjustment to the biological facts of aging—decreasing strength and vitality, wrinkled skin, aches and pains. Physical response slows, medical needs arise, and eyesight and hearing begin to fail. The older adult must learn to handle these changes without loss of self-esteem.

Retirement brings with it another set of adjustments, some economic and others psychological. Retirement results in reduced income, which alters lifestyle and, sometimes, living arrangements. Retirement creates idle time that must be handled responsibly and creatively if older adulthood is to remain lively and satisfying. Retirement also relays a message to the retiree: Am I any longer worth anything? Who needs me now? Reassessment of meaning is essential.

Loss of a spouse might have occurred earlier than age sixty, but it will occur in older adulthood if it has not already. Not only will the older adult lose his spouse, but he will lose other loved ones and friends. He must deal with the grief and loneliness. Loss of spouse may also result in economic and residential readjustments.

Older adults must learn to meet civic, social, and spiritual obligations. They can grow old isolated from the rest of society, or they can blossom and contribute the wisdom of their years to those around them.

Older adults, then, have their own growth process. How well they experience this process is determined in middle adulthood, but their maturity is demonstrated in the final set of adjustments before they "step over Jordan" to meet the Lord.

Single Adults

More than seven million single adults live in America, a sizeable segment of the adult population, far too many to be ignored. A single adult is any unmarried adult; having been widowed, divorced, or never-married.

The previous description of adults at each level of development applies to single adults too. But because of their singleness, single adults find some of those needs intensified.

Never-marrieds experience need for intimacy and companionship. They must learn to accept singleness so that they can create healthy relationships with others in order to meet companionship needs. They experience sexual temptations and the temptation to avoid responsibility and ministry to others. They must also resolve the tension between dependence and independence.

Divorced and separated singles experience the same needs as never-marrieds, but also the need to forgive oneself and one's mate for the failure in the marriage. They have difficulty making re-entry into society and the church as a single. They often experience financial and family stresses, especially when children are involved. Both men and women require readjustment in personal support systems (many men may need to learn how to do the laundry, keep house, and cook, while women may know little about caring for the car or the property).

Widows and widowers experience most of what never-marrieds and the divorced do, but they must also deal with grief and loneliness. Their self-concept requires readjustment from being an extension of their partner back to being single.

Extra attention to the unique needs of single adults will help them to use their singleness for ministry, rather than misery.

Distinctives of the Adult Learner

The adult learner is far more than a child to whom grown-up stories are told. He is more than an adolescent with doubts and yearnings for independence. He is an individual seeking maturity, while beset by complex pressures. He cannot be treated as a child or adolescent and be expected to respond.

The teacher of adults must understand the basic distinctives that mark an adult learner:

1. He is a unique person with his own individual history and present needs. Every learner at every age is unique, but not in the same sense as an adult. Although ten-year-olds differ in some ways, they are very much alike in others. But it is almost impossible to make any generalized statement about a forty-year-old (or any other adult, for that matter). There is no physical uniformity, no likeness of thinking style, no uniform procedure in making emotional adjustments.

2. He learns as a total person, not just intellectually. His developmental work—the way he handles his internal changes—will affect his perceptions and reactions.

3. He brings valuable experience, definite ideas, and well-formulated attitudes to the learning situation. These affect the learning situation.

4. He learns best when he is an active participant. Yet involvement is voluntary; careful planning by the teacher is required to motivate him to participate.

5. He learns through interaction with others and identification with groups. Once he trusts and values people and groups, he is open to accepting their attitudes and values, which he begins to emulate.

6. He learns by association with a teacher who models a particular lifestyle. He imitates the lifestyle and seeks the information the teacher has to offer.

7. He has not learned until he translates learning into personal behavior.

Goals for Teaching Adults

Three basic goals give direction to teachers of adults. The first is to provide sound Biblical instruction, which means more than a weekly mini-sermon. Using group participation methods, the teacher will guide students to explore God's Word systematically to find its message for today. The lesson will involve reviewing Bible facts and exploring the meaning of the Biblical material for the lives of the students.

But adult Bible teaching requires more than a mini-college approach. It does not merely present academic material, but explores how that material is usable in daily life. A second goal, then, is the application of Biblical material to contemporary life. Good Bible teaching confronts the learner, and demands that he decide how to use Bible material in real-life situations. This goal forces the teacher to deal with attitudes as well as data.

The third goal for adult Bible teaching is to equip adults for service. Service and outreach should be practical outcomes of effective teaching. Once a person learns God's Word and understands its demands on his life, he will want to become involved in ministry to others. A good adult teacher will be alert for opportunities to minister to others, and will challenge his pupils to take advantage of them.

Organizing to Teach Adults

Determine Groups Needed

Survey the congregation to determine the number of adults and the age of each. This will give some idea of the potential for the adult Sunday school. Then decide how the adults will be assigned to groups. In most cases, age grouping is recommended for Sunday school because it groups those whose interests are similar, because it is easily understood, and because it is easily administered. Some churches further divide men and women, but younger adults do not find this practice appealing. Local custom may guide at that point.

Some churches have introduced an elective system in which adults group themselves. Each quarter each adult chooses his own course of study. The elective system has much to commend it: people are more motivated because they are studying what they want to study. However, this system allows some adults to get lost from Sunday school. There is no permanent class group that shepherds them, or to which they feel loyalty. Electives probably work best in a small congregation (along with some kind of built-in shepherding system) than in a larger congregation where permanent groups meet fellowship needs.

The optimum manageable size for an adult Sunday-school class is thirty in attendance (this does permit more than thirty to be enrolled). Thirty or fewer in a class promotes a good student-teacher relationship, a critical factor if the teacher is to model a growing walk with Christ. It also permits a greater degree of group interaction and allows greater teaching variety.

If possible, plan for at least two adult classes—one for younger adults and one for older adults. This arrangement will provide a more comfortable situation for newcomers. The minimum effective number for a class is an attendance of five.

Recruit Workers

Each class unit requires a teacher. Quality teaching is accomplished by quality people. Look first for those who have a personal relationship with God and can maintain personal relationships with others. He needs to be approachable, open, honest, willing to study, and open to the use of different methods.

An adult class also needs a class leader (sometimes called the president) to whom is delegated the responsibility for coordinating class efforts and activities. A major part of his work should be to lead the class to contact prospects and absentees and to shepherd class members.

An effective method of doing the outreach and shepherding work is to establish caring units. Each unit leader (or couple) would be responsible for six other members (or couples). Members may be assigned to a group, or they may choose. Unit leaders would also be responsible for interaction beyond the classroom, contacting absentees, being alert to needs in the group, and contacting prospects for the class.

Each class needs a secretary who will maintain records and a social chairperson who will coordinate special activities. A good social leader will involve class members in planning and carrying out social functions.

One reason for limiting the size of an adult class is to involve as many people as possible in class activities. Following the plan described in this section involves a large proportion of class members in a variety of leadership activities.

Arrange the Teaching Time

A Sunday-school session for adults should be structured carefully. Everything that happens must contribute to the goal for the day.

A four-step structure for adults is shown in Figure 11-1.[2]

Fellowship activities should be planned to direct people to share with one another. Although serving coffee and donuts can help toward this end, other definite sharing experiences should be planned.

The Hook is critical, for it should be designed to stimulate interest. It serves to whet the appetite of the pupils.

The Book and Look sections direct the adult learner to an exploration of God's Word and its meaning for life. The wise teacher utilizes a variety of methods to involve the learner in the process of discovery.

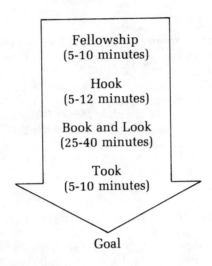

Figure 11-1. Structure for an adult Bible lesson.

The Took section involves the learner in deciding how he will use the Biblical material in his life. These decisions may be shared with others, unless they are too personal to share.

Effective Methods for Teaching Adults

A wide variety of teaching methods and techniques are at the disposal of the teacher of adults. The lists below will stimulate the teacher's imagination.

Discussion

Most adults like to be involved in a class session. However, good discussion requires planning and stimulation. Try some of the techniques listed below:

Agree-Disagree Statements
Brainstorming
Buzz Groups
Case Study
Circle Response
Completion Statements
Debate
Interview

Listening Team
Neighbor Nudge
Panel
Picture Response
Problem Solving
Question-Answer
Word Association

Writing

Adults respond well to writing that summarizes Bible material or reflects upon it. Several techniques are possible:

Acrostic	News Story/Headline	Prayer Writing
Graffiti Poster	Outlining	Puzzles
Letter Writing	Parable Writing	Scrambled Verses/
Log/Diary/Journal	Paraphrase	Statements
Memo	Poetry Writing	

Art

Some adults enjoy expressing Bible truth and application through art forms. Choose from the list below:

Advertisement	Charts	Murals
Banners	Collages	Puppets
Bulletin Boards	Friezes	Slide Making
Bumper Stickers	Magazine Tear	Symbolic Shapes
Cartoon Strips	Mobiles	Word Posters

Drama

Another method is drama, in which the learner portrays the Biblical material and/or application of it:

Choral Reading	Role Play	This Is Your Life
Pantomime	Skit	TV Show

Music

Adults respond well to musical activities to express Bible facts or applications. Consider the possibilities below.

Commercial Jingle	Hymn/Song
Original Hymns/Songs	Paraphrase
Hymn/Scripture	Hymn/Song Rewrite
Comparison	Hymn/Song Response

Oral Communication

Oral communication is a basic form for teaching adults. There are several possibilities for involving class members:

Assignments	Lecture	Memorization	Reports

Summary

Adults experience developmental adjustments, just as learners of any other age. An effective Bible teacher will take careful note of the special needs at each level of adulthood. Wise is the Bible teacher who heeds the guidelines for organization and teaching of adults. His efforts will be blessed!

Projects

1. Interview three adults, one at each level of adulthood. Find out what they perceive their needs to be. Ask them to react to the textbook description. Find out what appeals to them in an adult Bible class.
2. How are the adult classes in your home church organized? Compare those classes with the guidelines for organization described in this chapter.
3. Plan a Bible lesson for adults using 2 Corinthians 5 as the text. How will you use some of the methods listed above?

Selected Bibliography

Cooper, John C. and Rachel Conrad Wahlberg. *Your Exciting Middle Years.* Waco, Texas: Word, 1976.
Gould, Roger. *Transformations.* New York: Simon and Schuster, 1978.
Havighurst, Robert. *Developmental Tasks and Education.* 2nd ed. New York: David McKay Co., 1952.
Huyck, Margaret Hillis. *Growing Older.* Englewood Cliffs, New Jersey: Prentice Hall, 1974.
Marlowe, Monroe and Bobbie Reed. *Creative Bible Learning for Adults.* Glendale, California: ICL, 1977.
Sheehy, Gail. *Passages: Predictable Crises in Adult Life.* New York: Dutton, 1975.

CHAPTER

12

Helping Exceptional
Persons Learn

by Ann Myers

As you read, think about these questions:
—What is the difference between *being* value and *doing* value?
—What are the traditional areas of special education?
—What barriers hinder the development of potential in exceptional persons?
—What general principles can be derived to help discover and develop potential in exceptional persons?

This chapter deals with an educational ministry too often neglected by the local church: the Christian education of the exceptional person. The reasons for this neglect include feelings of fear, lack of confidence in the ability to organize and conduct programs, and the pragmatic questioning of the expenditure of resources for individuals "who are never going to learn, anyway." The aim of this chapter is (1) to replace fear with understanding, (2) to encourage the pursuit of competence in methods and techniques for educating the exceptional person, and (3) to answer the questioning of pragmatists with a different perspective—one that encourages every human being to measure his own spiritual growth and development not in comparison to others, but in relation to his own potential for thinking, feeling, and acting.

The perspective for the Christian education of exceptional persons rests on the distinction between value based on *being* and value based on *doing*. *Being* value is the value that every person has because man is a special creation, made in the image of God. David, in the eighth Psalm, gives us insight into being value. Mankind stands just below the angels and above the rest of creation. The majesty of His creation makes us stand in awe of the value God has bestowed upon us.

Every person has being value, regardless of his circumstance. It is not assigned by man. Others may choose to acknowledge it or to ignore it, but its existence and extent is not determined by others. It is God-given. Being value also carries with it the capacity for value based on *doing*. Psalm 8:6 points out that a part of human nature is the capacity for extending control over the environment. Man has the capacity for achievement, that is, the potential for value based on doing.

Doing value differs from being value in some important ways. First, while each person has being value simply because he is created in the image of God, doing value must be acquired or earned. It is the extent to which an individual develops the potential he has. Secondly, while being value is absolute and universal, possessed to the same degree by everyone, doing value is relative. People differ in the amount and in the nature of their potential. Doing value is not based on potential itself; it is based on the extent to which one develops whatever potential he has.

If we had some way of measuring human value, we could say with certainty that in terms of being value each person's worth is the same. In terms of doing value each person could possibly be worth the same as any other person; that is, each person could measure up to one hundred percent of his potential. Individual differences in doing value are due not to differences in potential, but to differences in the extent to which each person achieves his potential.

The distinction between being value and doing value provides the foundation for the education of exceptional persons and for their Christian education in particular. If we understand and accept these two kinds of value, we can no longer ask, "Is he worth it?" Each person is worth it from two perspectives. He is worth it because he has being value, the same as any other person. But especially important for Christian educators, he is worth it because he has the same possibility for doing value as anyone else: one hundred percent of his potential, whatever that may be. With the same possibility for doing value as anyone else, the exceptional person is entitled to the same opportunity for developing that value as anyone else. The challenge that the exceptional person presents to Christian educators is not only to help them develop potential that is obvious, but to uncover potential that may be hidden behind handicaps.

Traditional Categories of Special Education: Aids in Defining Potential

Traditional categories of special education can be thought of as labels that identify limitations, or they can be thought of as information that gives insight into potential. The Christian educator should adopt the "potential" perspective, for it requires him to search actively for possibilities for *doing* value. The "limitations" perspective focuses on non-possibilities.

The categories that will be discussed in this section are disorders in hearing, vision, motor abilities, and behavior, as well as mental retardation. A description of each category will be given, along with a discussion of the major barriers to developing potential and the ways to overcome these barriers.

Hearing Disorders

A major concern in working with the hearing impaired is language development. Most individuals learn to understand concepts through hearing and learn how to express ideas through hearing others do so. The extent to which impaired hearing affects understanding and communicating is an important educational consideration. It is influenced by three factors: the degree of hearing loss, the age at which the loss occurred, and the type of defect. The degree of loss determines the extent to which sounds, especially speech sounds, are heard. The age at which the loss occurred is important because a loss suffered after age two has a much less severe effect on the development of speech and language. The type of defect is important because it determines the way in which the loss can be compensated for.

Degree of loss. The exact extent of a hearing loss is measured in decibels (dbs) on a device called an audiometer. Five levels of hearing loss have been defined, each having a more marked effect on understanding speech and, consequently, on language development. The person with a slight loss (26-40 db) may have difficulty hearing faint or distant speech. The person with a mild loss (41-55 db) can understand face-to-face conversation, but may miss as much as fifty percent of a class discussion. The person with a marked loss (56-70 db) can hear conversation only if it is very loud. He has difficulty in group discussions and probably will have difficulty in understanding some concepts. The person with a severe loss (71-90 db) may hear loud voices about one foot from the ear. He is likely to have marked defects in speech and language. The person with an extreme loss (91 db or more) may hear some loud sounds, but is more aware of vibrations than tonal patterns. He relies on vision more than hearing for communication.

The hearing impaired individual is classified as deaf or partially hearing, depending on the extent to which the sense of hearing is functional for learning language. If he can use hearing for learning language, he is partially hearing. If not, he is deaf.

Age at Onset of Loss. For the person classified as deaf, the age when the hearing loss occurs is an important factor in learning language. Losses occuring before about 18-24 months of age have a much more profound impact than losses that occur later in life. The deaf individual who suffers impaired hearing before the age of 18-24 months is referred to as "congenitally deaf." The individual who loses his hearing after that age is called "adventitiously deafened."

Type of Defect Resulting in Loss. The type of defect resulting in impaired hearing affects the extent to which the loss can be compensated for. There are three types of defects: conductive, sensory-neural, and central or perceptual. A conductive loss is one resulting from a defect of the outer or middle ear that interferes with the transmission of sound vibrations to the inner ear. A sensory-neural loss is one resulting from a defect of the inner ear that interferes with the reception of sound impulses at the nerve endings located there. A central or perceptual loss is one resulting from a defect of the auditory nerve pathways from the inner ear to the brain.

Conductive losses affect the intensity or loudness of the sound heard. They can, to a certain extent, be compensated for by amplifying sound and using an alternate route for transmitting the vibrations. This is the function of a hearing aid.

Sensory-neural or central losses affect the frequency or tone of the sound heard. A person with a sensory-neural or perceptual loss cannot hear certain sounds or ranges of sound. These cannot be restored, although hearing aids are often used to magnify those sounds that can be heard.

The Communication Barrier. For the hearing-impaired person, the main barrier preventing the development of potential is a communication barrier. Not only is there a problem with speech as a mode of understanding and communicating, but often the development of language is delayed, so that even when alternate modes of communication (such as signing or finger spelling) are used, some concepts may not be adequately understood.

Developing the ability to understand and communicate is the key to developing the potential of the hearing-impaired person. The three basic types of communication training for the deaf are oral, manual, and total communication. The goal of oral communication is that the individual be able to communicate with the broad community, not just with other hearing-impaired people. The emphasis is on speech reading and voice training. The learning process is a slow one.

The goal of the manual method is that the individual be able to understand and communicate as early as possible. Finger spelling and signing provide the mode of communicating and understanding. This method is learned much more rapidly than the oral method, but it restricts communication to those who know finger spelling and signing. This excludes most of the hearing community and creates another kind of isolation.

Total communication is an attempt to combine the benefits of the oral and manual methods. Its goal is that the individual use all of his resources to be able to understand and communicate as early as possible to as broad a community as possible. The child is encouraged from a very early age (parent-child programs may begin at birth) to use his voice and any residual hearing. He is also taught to understand and express himself through finger spelling, signing, and even natural gestures. The child trained in total communication should be able to use speech reading and vocalization to communicate with the hearing community, and still have the advantage of early language development. He will then be able to interact with both the hearing and with the deaf world.

Because in any given community he may find individuals

with manual, oral, or total communication training, the Christian educator must be prepared to adapt to any of these methods in order to overcome the communication barrier.

Vision Disorders

There are two classification systems for visual disorders: legal and educational. An individual is declared legally blind if central visual acuity is 20/200 or less in the better eye with best correction. The term 20/200 indicates that the individual can distinguish at 20 feet what the normal eye sees at 200 feet. An individual is declared to be legally partially sighted if his acuity in the better eye with best correction is better than 20/200 but less than 20/70.

The educational classification system is based on the individual's ability to use his vision for educational purposes. An individual is educationally blind if he must rely on braille rather than print for reading. He is partially sighted if he can read print given sufficient magnification or other special conditions. The distinction between the legal and educational classifications is important. Individuals with the same acuity (that is, the same legal status) may use their vision with differing degrees of effectiveness. An individual may be legally blind while educationally he is partially sighted, because he has learned to make good use of the vision he has.

Types of Visual Disorders. Visual disorders may be grouped into four types: disorders of the receptive structures, refractive disorders, defects in muscle functioning, and disorders due to some other interference in the visual system.

Disorders in receptive structures affect the retina or the optic nerve. The retina is the nerve structure that receives the visual image. Retrolental fibroplasia, a condition once common among premature infants, and detached retina are among the disorders affecting it. The optic nerve connects the retina to the brain. Deterioration of the optic nerve and severed optic nerve are among the conditions that can affect it.

Refractive disorders are probably the best known. These disorders interfere with the focusing of light on the retina that is essential to proper vision. They include myopia (nearsightedness), hyperopia (farsightedness), and astigmatism, an irregularity in the curvature of the lens or of the eyeball itself.

Muscle disorders interfere with the coordinated movement of the eyes. Among these disorders are "lazy eye," crossed eyes, the quick, jerky movement of the eyes, and double or multiple vision.

Disorders due to interference in the visual system include glaucoma, the build up of interocular fluids, and cataracts, the development of an opaque film on the lens.

The Experience Barrier. The major barrier to the development of potential in the visually impaired person is one of limited kinds of experience. Things that are learned visually by most of us must be learned through some other mode by the visually impaired person.

Lowenfeld suggests five basic principles by which the best use of other means for gaining experience can be made.

1. Individualization. Educational programs should be geared to the needs of each child.

2. Concreteness. As much as possible, the child should have direct experience with the things he is to learn. Knowledge should be gained through using real objects and events where possible and scale models or simulated events when necessary.

3. Unified instruction. Instruction should be integrated into a total life experience.

4. Additional stimulation. Incorporate as much stimulation of the sense of hearing, smell, taste, touch, and movement as possible.

5. Self-activity. The student should be encouraged to do most activities himself.

These principles are also appropriate for the partially sighted, although use of concreteness should be extended to include visual media adapted for their use. Additional stimulation should strongly encourage the child to use his vision as much as possible.

Disorders in Motor Abilities

The common features relating the disorders in this category is that they all in some way impair movement. A set of terms—the "plegias"—are used to describe the number and location of limbs affected by a motor disorder. These terms are defined as follows:

Monoplegia: one limb is affected
Hemiplegia: one side of the body is affected
Triplegia: three limbs are affected
Quadriplegia: all four limbs are affected

Diplegia: four limbs are affected, more involvement in the legs

Bilateral hemiplegia: four limbs are affected; more involvement in the arms

Although these terms are often used in connection with paralysis, they do not describe the nature of the disorder itself. They merely refer to the location of the affected area.

Two categories of motor disorders will be dealt with: cerebral palsy will be discussed, along with a brief description of some other disorders.

Cerebral Palsy. Cerebral palsy is a general term that includes five major types of motor disorders caused by brain damage:

1. Spasticity, the most common type, is characterized by a lack of coordination between muscle pairs that control voluntary movement. Purposeful movements are jerky and uncoordinated. Affected limbs may be drawn inward toward the body when the individual is at rest.

2. Athetosis, the second most common type, is characterized by involuntary movement, especially when the individual attempts deliberate, purposeful action. Throat and diaphragm muscles are often affected, so speech problems frequently accompany this condition.

3. Ataxia is the result of damage to the portion of the brain that controls balance. It is characterized by staggering, off-balance movement.

4. Tremor is characterized by small rhythmic involuntary movement of the affected limb or limbs.

5. Rigidity, as the name suggests, is characterized by a resistance to movement.

The brain injury that results in cerebral palsy can occur anytime before, during, or after birth. Prenatal infections or absence of oxygen may have been factors for those born with cerebral palsy. Injury, poisoning, high fever, or other factors can cause cerebral palsy at any time during the life span.

Since cerebral palsy is the result of brain damage, other conditions attributable to brain damage may accompany it. These include disorders of speech, hearing, and vision, and mental retardation.

Other Motor Disorders. Two other motor disorders are common enough to warrant a brief discussion. *Spina bifida* is a congenital condition characterized by a failure of the spine to close, leaving the spinal cord exposed at some point. It is often accompanied by hydrocephaly (increased cerebrospinal fluid in the skull) and in severe cases can lead to paralysis and loss of bladder and bowel control. *Muscular dystrophy* is a progressive disease affecting children and young adults in which muscle tissue is replaced by fatty tissue. The result is the gradual loss of voluntary muscle control. At present there is no known treatment that will reverse the progress of the disease.

Physical Barriers. The most obvious barriers to the development of potential for those with motor disorders are physical barriers. Stairs, narrow aisles, narrow halls and doorways, sanctuaries and rooms that cannot easily accommodate a wheelchair, and even certain procedures for passing communion or receiving an offering can inhibit the participation of individuals with motor disorders. Many physical barriers can be removed without costly structural changes. Consultation with an occupational or physical therapist (most hospitals have them on staff) might prove beneficial in learning some simple modifications that can help remove these barriers.

Behavior Disorders

Kirk defines a behavior disorder as a deviation from age appropriate behavior that significantly interferes with either the child's own growth and development or with the lives of others or both. Behavior disorders may be divided into two types: social maladjustment and emotional disturbance.

Social maladjustment is disruptive behavior that is unacceptable to society and violates cultural norms. It includes chronic disobedience, disruptiveness, defiance, and lack of cooperation.

Emotional disturbance refers to personal distress suffered by the individual. With some types of emotional disturbance, the individual does not withdraw from reality even though his distress may be intense. Among these types are chronic anxiety, a general uneasiness about the future not related to any specific cause and not focused on any specific object or event. Also included in this group are phobias (intense, irrational fears), obsessions (preoccupation with the same thought), and compulsions (repetitive, "driven" behavior).

Sometimes the emotional disturbance is such that the individual withdraws from reality. Such conditions include infantile autism (the individual fails to develop emotional relationships with others), regression (the individual reverts to a less mature level of behavior), and schizophrenia, characterized by severe withdrawal and the presence of conflicting impulses, thoughts, and ideas.

The "Self" Barrier. The main barrier inhibiting the behavior-disordered child's development of potential is, oddly enough, himself. Sometimes the individual unconsciously sets up barriers that inhibit his own development. (This fact does not contradict our "possibilities" orientation, nor does it suggest that society, family, or other individuals are not contributors to the problem.)

The first step in removing this barrier is to recognize that inappropriate behavior obscures but does not destroy potential. Such behavior should not be overlooked, but dealt with as a barrier behind which hides potential. The second step is to maintain consistent, realistic expectations. These can be determined by working closely with the individual's parents and the professionals involved. Procedures for holding the individual to these expectations should also be developed. Such expectations provide consistency for the child, and lend much-needed support to his parents.

The Mentally Retarded

The American Association on Mental Deficiency has defined mental retardation as follows: "Mental retardation refers to sub-average intellectual functioning which originates during the developmental period and is associated with impairment in adaptive behavior." In general, mentally retarded individuals are identified by their uniformly low performance on tests of ability and achievement. They seem subaverage in almost all areas of development—intellectual, social, emotional, and often physical.

Levels of Mental Retardation. The three levels of mental retardation are: the educable mentally retarded (EMR), the trainable mentally retarded (TMR), and the profoundly retarded.

The educable mentally retarded individual is one whose development is one-half to three-fourths the rate of the normal individual. He typically achieves a score between fifty and seventy-five on a mental ability test (a normal IQ score equals 100). Educational programs for the EMR include the basic academics, vocational training, and independent living skills.

The trainable mentally retarded individual is one whose rate of development is one-third to one-half that of the normal individual. He typically scores between 25 and 50 on general mental ability tests. Educational programs emphasize self-care and general safety skills, but happily there is a trend away from assuming that academic skills are totally beyond the TMR child's capabilities. Although TMR individuals are likely to require some kind of direct supervision over the entire lifespan, they may be expected to contribute both economically and socially to the well-being of the community.

The profoundly retarded individual is likely to score below 25 on tests of general mental ability. Educational programs emphasize sensory stimulation and the development of basic skills such as sitting, walking, self-feeding, and toileting. Usually the profoundly retarded individual requires direct care over his entire lifespan.

Causes of Mental Retardation. In most instances of mental retardation the cause is unknown. However, there are some known causes. These can be categorized as prenatal (before birth), perinatal (during the birth process), and postnatal (during the developmental years).

Prenatal causes of mental retardation include genetic ones such as Down's syndrome, drugs and toxic substances, incompatibility in the Rh blood factor, and maternal malnutrition. Some maternal illnesses can lead to retardation in the unborn infant. One such illness is rubella, or three-day measles. Rubella, if contracted by the mother during the first three months of pregnancy, can result not only in retardation in the infant but also in hearing and vision difficulties, absence or malformation of limbs, or severe heart disorders.

Perinatal causes of mental retardation include prolonged labor, other difficulty that interferes with the oxygen supply to the infant, or any physical trauma leading to brain injury.

Postnatal causes include physical trauma or interference with the oxygen supply to the brain. Toxic substances and malnutrition are other causes of postnatal mental retardation.

So far we have dealt with only organic causes of mental retardation. Environmental factors also have a strong influence on the extent to which an individual is able to use his inherent mental abilities. The extent to which environment affects intelligence is still being debated. However, it is fairly safe to say that many instances of mental retardation, especially at the EMR level, are directly related to a non-stimulating environment during the developmental years.

The Complexity Barrier. A primary barrier to developing potential for the mentally retarded might be called a complexity barrier. Many of the actions, events, concepts, and thought processes that we think of as single, simple entities are actually made up of several related entities. The normal individual is able to deal with this complexity. The greater the degree of retardation, the less a mentally retarded individual is able to handle it.

Task and concept analysis is an important tool in teaching the retarded. Here, to whatever extent is necessary, the teacher breaks down each task or concept into its components and their relationships. Tasks or concepts are then taught as a series of related events rather than a single event. Breaking down the complexity barrier is a key to uncovering and activating potential in the mentally retarded person.

Principles in Educating
the Exceptional Person

In addition to the barriers associated with each category of exceptionality, general factors also obscure potential for the exceptional person. These general factors give rise to a set of principles of Christian education that can help the teacher discover and help develop the potential of the exceptional person.

The first obscuring factor is that of limited or different experience. We have already discussed the problem of limited experience in visual disorders and mental retardation. Individuals in most other areas of exceptionality have also had limited or atypical experiences. Those with motor impairments as well as the visually impaired often lack the freedom to move and explore that others have. Those with sensory impairments miss out on experiences perceived through their impaired senses. Those with problems requiring hospitalization, institutionalization, or special schooling encounter a whole set of atypical experiences. Potential may be obscured in individuals with limited or different experiences.

A second obscuring factor is delayed development. Development is measured by certain milestones. Mobility milestones include sitting, crawling, and walking. Communication milestones include imitating sounds, speaking, and writing. Cognitive milestones include generalizing, categorizing, and dealing with abstractions. Delay in reaching these milestones can be an early indicator of mental or physical problems, but delay does not necessarily mean that the potential for their achievement is nonexistent. It may indicate that development must take a different course.

A third obscuring factor is unique expression. We often think of the hearing-impaired person when we think of unique modes of expression, but anyone's potential can be obscured when we fail to allow for unique modes of expression. We often associate the potential for kindness, for example, with the ability to "do something" for others. But we have come to define a certain range of possibilities for "doing something." We must redefine that range of possibilities when considering exceptional persons. A real-life example will illustrate this point.

The leaders of a Sunday morning class for exceptional persons were skeptical when Bob, a man with the use of only one arm, claimed he could play the guitar—until he presented several selections one Sunday morning. How did Bob do it? A friend of his, a man rather low in general mental ability, but with a good sense of rhythm, did the strumming while Bob fingered the chords. Bob's range of possibilities might have been restricted had not someone shown him this unique way of demonstrating them.

A fourth obscuring factor is unique abilities. The exceptional individual often has unique qualities or abilities or has developed certain qualities to a greater extent than others. Failure to recognize and use these abilities can limit the development of potential. The most obvious abilities are the great extent to which those with severely impaired vision are often able to use their senses of hearing, touch, and smell, or the way in which the severely hearing-impaired can detect very subtle changes in facial expression to distinguish speech sounds. But the exceptional person may possess other unique abilities that are just as significant: a highly developed quality of patience, a profound sense of gratitude, an uncommon willingness to accept others as they are. These qualities are unique in today's world and can serve as a foundation for developing potential in those exceptional persons in whom they are found.

From these four factors, we can derive a set of principles that can guide us in uncovering and developing potential in the exceptional person. These principles can help us contribute to the confirmation of being value and the development of doing value in exceptional persons:

1. Build on unique experiences and expand limited experiences in a direction that will encourage the discovery of new possibilities.

2. Act on the possibility that skills and concepts that have not naturally developed may be explicitly taught.

3. Search for unique ways for the individual to demonstrate his abilities or express his understanding.

4. Search for unique abilities and qualities and build on these for further growth and development.

Summary

Every person made by God is valued by Him regardless of that person's functional ability, or lack of it, in society. The thesis of this chapter has been that every person, even those severely handicapped and functionally dependent upon others, deserves opportunity to hear the message of God's love. To communicate that message requires an understanding of types of disorders and how to meet them. It requires a commitment to confirm "being" value and to develop "doing" value.

Projects

1. Visit a center for exceptional persons such as a special classroom, shelter care home, or sheltered workshop. If possible, arrange to participate in some social activity with the students or residents. Your goal: to discover possibilities and potential you have not been aware of.
2. On a sheet of paper list the four primary external barriers that hinder the development of potential in exceptional persons (communication, visual experience, physical barriers, and complexity). Under each heading list specific characteristics of your local church—the building itself and the services held in it on a typical Sunday—that contribute to these barriers. Suggest ways these barriers could be eliminated or modified.
3. Select one of the categories of exceptionality. Prepare a lesson (perhaps using one of the parables). Show how you have taken into account that category's primary barriers to developing potential, the general factors obscuring potential, and the general principles for educating the exceptional derived from these factors.

Selected Bibliography

Bogardus, LaDonna. *Christian Education of Retarded Persons.* Nashville: Abingdon, 1969.

Kirk, S.A. *Educating Exceptional Children.* Boston: Houghton-Mifflin, 1972.

Lowenfeld, B. *Psychological Considerations: The Visually Handicapped Child at School.* New York: John Day, 1973.

Smith, R. M. and J. Neisworth. *The Exceptional Child: A Functional Approach.* New York: McGraw-Hill, 1975.

CHAPTER

13

Audiovisual Methods

As you read, think about these questions:
—What were at least six ways in which visuals were used in the Bible?
—Name at least two examples of each type of visuals discussed in this chapter.
—What criteria guide selection of visuals for a given lesson?
—What equipment and materials should be included in an audiovisual center?

"A picture is worth a thousand words," states an old axiom. Visual aids communicate in a way not possible with words alone. A wise teacher uses everything at his disposal to communicate the truth of God's Word. Audiovisuals, used with the methods outlined in the previous chapters, are valuable communication tools.

A Biblical Basis for Using Visuals

Old Testament Visuals

God has always used visual media to communicate with His people. He spoke, and His message is recorded in the Bible. But He did more than speak. He also used a variety of visuals to reinforce His message, as can be seen in His dealings with the people of Israel during the exodus and wilderness wanderings.

God led Israel from the bondage of Egypt. Israel had been fully persuaded to leave Egypt, largely because of a visual demonstration of God's power through the plagues and by the work of the death angel,[1] but once the people had made their way out to the Red Sea, doubts arose. Egypt had always supplied their needs and had fed and sustained them. But now with the Egyptians in hot pursuit, angered at them, how were they to survive? Where was God now?

God chose to answer with a visual—a miracle of intervention. Exodus 14 records how God divided the Red Sea so that the Israelites crossed on dry land. When the Egyptians pursued them across the sea bed, the sea waters rushed over them, sending them to their deaths. To the Israelites it was a dramatic sign of God's power and presence with them.

Years later, when the Israelites were once again ready to cross a body of water (this time the Jordan River) to begin conquest of the promised land, God confirmed Joshua's leadership and reassured them of His presence when He parted the waters of the Jordan.[2] Again He reinforced His words with visual symbols to develop trust in Israelite hearts.

Not only did God use the visual media of miracles, but He also placed other more enduring visual aids in the midst of Israel. For example, He ordained the Nazarite vow as a visual reminder of Israel's unique purpose and function in the world. The Nazarite vow was taken voluntarily for a fixed period ranging from thirty days to life. During the time the vow was in effect, the Nazarite was to abstain from wine, grapes, and intoxicating beverages. He could not cut his hair or approach a dead body. The meaning of the vow, established by God, was to renounce the world and become set apart to God. The men and women who took the vow were visual reminders to the rest of Israel that national separation to God was a must if Israel was to fulfill her destiny in the world.[3]

Tassels were another type of visual. Numbers 15:37-40 records God's instructions for the Israelites to put tassels on the corners of their garments as a reminder of the commandments of God and the importance of obeying them. The visual made it difficult for them to forget their obligations.

Feasts were another aid to memory. Of the Passover Feast, God instructed, "This is a day you are to commemorate; . . . When your children ask you 'What does this ceremony mean to you?' then tell them, 'It is the Passover sacrifice to the Lord, who passed over the houses of the Israelites in Egypt and spared our homes when he struck down the Egyptians.' "[4] Feasts were vivid reminders to Israelite adults of God's power and care. Those same feasts stimulated children to ask questions, providing excellent opportunities for oral teaching about God's care.

The tabernacle served as a visual, a clear declaration to Israel that "God is in our midst." It stood as silent testimony that God walked with Israel.[5]

Old Testament examples abound: God presented His message to His people using visual media. He wanted them to know beyond any doubt who He was and how they could walk with Him.

Jesus' Use of Visuals

Careful analysis of the Gospels reveals Jesus' liberal use of visual media to illustrate and reinforce His God-given message. "Look at the birds of the air," He directed, surely pointing to birds flying overhead, when He wanted to emphasize the futility of anxiety. "See how the lilies of the field grow," He added to reinforce the same concept.[6]

Jesus' parables abound with everyday pictures, vividly painted to communicate abstract truth. "A farmer went out to sow his seed," He began as He illustrated possible responses to the proclamation of God's Word.[7] Sowers and seed were commonplace, something understood by all who were listening to Him. Another time He began, "The kingdom of heaven is like a man who sowed good seed in his field,"[8] and taught them the reality of good and evil existing side by side in the world until the judgment. In parable after parable He developed an understanding of the nature of the kingdom of God.

Jesus pictured the Father's love in another set of parables. "What do you think?" He asked. "If any man owns a hundred sheep, and one of them wanders away, will he not leave the ninety-nine on the hills and go to look for the one that wandered off?"[9] Acquainted as they were with shepherds and sheep, His listeners immediately pictured a wayward lamb being hunted by a good shepherd, and they caught a glimpse of God. He illustrated the same truth by telling a story of a woman searching relentlessly for a lost coin and of a father waiting patiently for a rebellious son.[10]

The Lord's Supper was begun by Jesus as a visual reminder

to man of every age of His suffering for sin. "Take and eat; this is my body," Jesus instructed as He gave the Passover bread to the disciples. "Drink from it, all of you. This is my blood of the covenant, which is poured out for many for the forgiveness of sins," He said as He took the Passover cup.[11] To this day the Communion pictures the suffering and death of Jesus to all who believe.

Anyone intent on spending time reading the Gospels can find many more examples of Jesus' use of visuals. The visuals mentioned are only a few examples of His abundant use of illustrations to communicate abstract ideas.

The Visual of Baptism

Besides the Lord's Supper, baptism is the most expressive visual presented in the New Testament. The immersion of a penitent believer in water pictures far more than a body dipped beneath water.

Paul explains the significance of baptism in Romans 6:4-7:

> We were therefore buried with him through baptism into death in order that, just as Christ was raised from the dead through the glory of the Father, we too may live a new life.
> If we have been united with him in his death, we will certainly also be united with him in his resurrection. For we know that our old self was crucified with him so that the body of sin might be rendered powerless, that we should no longer be slaves to sin—because anyone who has died has been freed from sin.[12]

A baptism pictures death and resurrection. The candidate enters the water. As he is plunged beneath the water, he stops breathing. At that moment, the observer pictures Jesus' death, and the one being baptized is identified with that death. But then the person being baptized reappears from beneath the water, a vivid reminder that Jesus emerged from the tomb triumphant over sin and death. The baptized person is clearly identified as a new person, having died to sin and put on Christ.

Baptism, like the Lord's Supper, is an expressive visual, reminding those who participate of Jesus' death, burial, and resurrection. The picture is worth a thousand words!

Values of Audiovisual Aids

Overcome Barriers to Learning

The language barrier is formidable at every age level, but

especially so for children who lack experiences and who cannot yet think abstractly. A teacher must be creative to be able to present abstract Biblical material in a visual medium understandable to the learner—this is no small task.

Children (and adults too, for that matter) can easily memorize words without learning their meaning, or with incorrect meanings. The results would be humorous if they were not so serious. Gene Getz lists several illustrations that demonstrate the misunderstandings that often occur:

"Gladly, the cross-eyed bear"
"Jesus wants me for a sun bean"
"Don't forget to play"
"When the sins go marching in"
"Sweet peas, the gift of God's love"
"There's not a friend like the lonely Jesus"[13]

Audiovisuals help to overcome the language barrier because they clarify words and meanings.

Make Learning Interesting

Audiovisuals make learning interesting because they provide an appeal to more than one sense. Speech appeals only to the auditory sense, but when visuals supplement the spoken words, an appeal is made to the sense of sight as well.

Audiovisuals also provide the basis for discussion, another way to stimulate interest. They stimulate questions, provide the foundation for problem solving, and present new information, all of which can be talked about in preparation for additional learning. Not all visuals need be commercially prepared. Pupils can make visuals themselves, as part of a learning activity. They participate in learning by visualizing the material to be learned—a process that helps hold their interest.

Make Learning Permanent

Helping pupils to remember is a supreme challenge to any teacher. It is a major problem for the Bible teacher, who usually experiences an interval of seven days between class meetings.

One reason that information is forgotten is that it is not related to life experience. Visuals help the student remember by tying the two together.

Visuals also provide meaningful associations that assist memory. People remember what is important to them and what they understand clearly.

Types of Audiovisuals

The following chart illustrates the process of learning and the importance of visual experiences in the absence of direct experience.[14]

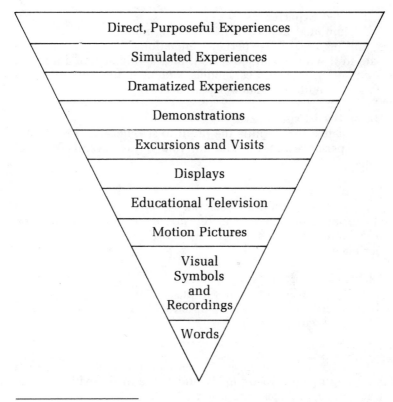

Figure 13-1. Comparative effectiveness of different kinds of learning experiences.

Figure 13-1 is a helpful reminder that direct, purposeful experiences are the most effective kind of learning experience. A full range of sensory experience contributes information and understanding to learning experiences.

Not all learning can be direct, however. In many cases direct experience is not an efficient, or even possible, way to learn something. One could resort to verbal symbols, but verbal symbols alone provide little linking between new information and previous experience. The cone of experience is helpful for the teacher to recall the audiovisual experiences available to link verbal symbols with direct experiences.

Simulated Experiences

A simulated experience is a representation of real life. It simplifies a real-life experience and allows the pupil to participate in it with the added benefit of the guidance of a teacher. Simulation, case studies, models, and mock-ups are useful visuals to provide simulated experience.

Dramatized Experiences

Dramatization permits the pupil to see, hear, and feel ideas and experiences. Plays, skits, and role plays are valuable visual tools.

Demonstrations

A demonstration is a visualized explanation. Visual symbols are usually incorporated in the presentation of a demonstration. Demonstrations are often used to prepare for direct experience.

Excursions and Visits

Study trips permit pupils to observe people and objects in their natural environment. Coupled with later discussion, field trips are a valuable tool.

Displays

Displays are to be observed, not manipulated or handled at any length. Both ready-made and home-made exhibits illustrate concepts, ideas, and information.

Television and Motion Pictures

Films compress both time and space and bring them to the classroom. They omit unnecessary material and concentrate on important points. They reconstruct experiences and involve the pupils imaginatively.

Visual Symbols and Recordings

Still pictures, recordings, and radio provide visual and auditory experiences far from direct experience, but considerably better than verbal symbols alone. Filmstrips, slides, overhead transparencies, flannelgraph figures, standup figures, dioramas, tapes, records, cartoons, stick figures, flat pictures, and photographs are types of still pictures and recordings useful for the classroom.

Words
Verbal symbols, or words, contain no visual clues to their meaning. Used with every other experience on the cone, they too are essential for learning.

Evaluating Audiovisual Material

From the plethora of material available, both ready-made and home-made, a teacher must choose visual materials for a given lesson or unit. The following criteria will help determine the suitability of any visual.[15]

1. Does the visual give a true picture of the idea it represents?
2. Does it contribute meaningful content to the topic?
3. Is it appropriate for the age, intelligence, and experience of the learners?
4. Is the physical condition of the visual satisfactory?
5. Will the visual stimulate thinking?
6. Is it worth the time, expense, and effort involved?

Organizing Audiovisual Materials

Audiovisual Center
A local church should accumulate, preserve, and organize a wide variety of visual tools. Visual aids and equipment should be available to everyone. A well-organized audiovisual center can make this possible.

The Christian education committee or other governing body may appoint a coordinator for the center. It is the coordinator's job to organize and distribute materials. All materials should be kept in a centralized place so that files may be maintained and distribution monitored.

Items to provide in the center include:

Books and Pamphlets	Objects
Charts	Photographs
Drawings	Posters
Films	Records
Filmstrips	Slides
Flannelboard Figures	Supplies for art,
Flat Pictures	bulletin boards, etc.
Graphs	Tapes
Maps	Teaching Kits
Models	Transparencies

These should be organized so that they can be easily located. Many of these items can be bought separately, but many could be added from used visual packets at the end of each Sunday-school quarter and after vacation Bible school.

A good audiovisual center will also include equipment as follows:

Bulletin boards (portable)	Overhead projector
Chalkboards (portable)	Projection screen
Film splicers	Record players
Filmstrip projector	16mm projector
Flannelboards	Slide projector
Individual filmstrip viewers	Tape recorders and players

Adequate storage space for all equipment and materials is also essential.

Personal Files

An individual should also organize his personal storehouse of audiovisual materials into files if he wishes to preserve them for use again and again. At the beginning a file folder for each type of item may be adequate. Eventually those will need to be subdivided.

The following outline might be helpful for subdividing pictures:[16]

Old Testament	New Testament	Modern Scenes
Creation	John the Baptist	Animals
Cain and Abel	Jesus	Going to Church
Abraham	Birth	Helping
Isaac	Childhood	Missions

Jacob   Temptation   Nature
Joseph   With Children   Praying
Moses   Teaching   Bible
Joshua   Miracles   Sharing
Samuel   Parables   Singing
Ruth   Passion Week   Worship
David   Resurrection   Flowers
Kings   Post-Resurrection   Trees
Daniel   Others   Buildings
Other Prophets   Apostles   Churches
                     Peter   People
                     John   Historical Events
                     Stephen   Sports
                     Paul   Travel
                     Others

Any subheading could be further divided as necessary.

Summary

Audiovisuals are valuable tools to make learning interesting and permanent. Not at all a modern invention, visuals were used effectively by God in the Old Testament. Jesus demonstrated and validated their use during His ministry. A wide variety of visual media is available for organization and use by Bible teachers who want to vitalize their teaching.

Project

Using the lesson plans you prepared for teaching preschoolers, elementary children, youth, and adults, plan at least three visuals you could use for each lesson. Tell why you chose the visuals you did.

Selected Bibliography

Brown, James B., Richard B. Lewis, and Fred F. Harderoad. *Instruction: Materials and Methods* (second edition). New York: McGraw-Hill, 1964.

Dale, Edgar. *Audio-Visual Methods in Teaching.* (third edition). New York: Dryden Press, 1969.

Getz, Gene. *Audio-Visual Media in Christian Education.* Chicago: Moody Press, 1972.

¹Exodus 7—12
²Joshua 3:8-10, 14-16
³See Numbers 6:1-15; Judges 13:5, 14; 1 Samuel 1:11, and Luke 1:15
⁴Exodus 12:14, 26, 27
⁵See Exodus 25:8; 33:7-11; 40:38; Numbers 9:15; 10:33-35; 1 Samuel 4:3-11; and 1 Kings 8:27
⁶Matthew 6:26, 28
⁷Matthew 13:3-9
⁸Matthew 13:24-30; see also Matthew 13:31-33
⁹Matthew 18:12-14; see also Luke 15:4-7
¹⁰Luke 15:8-32
¹¹See Matthew 26:26-29; Luke 22:15-20; and 1 Corinthians 10:16
¹²Romans 6:4-7
¹³AUDIO-VISUAL MEDIA IN CHRISTIAN EDUCATION, by Gene A. Getz, copyright 1972, Moody Bible Institute of Chicago. Moody Press. pp. 26, 27. Used by permission.
¹⁴Dale, pp. 107-135
¹⁵*Ibid.*, pp. 173-179
¹⁶Getz, pp. 123-125. (see reference 13)

14

Helping the Family Teach

As you read, think about these questions:
—What is the purpose of the family?
—What are the Biblical functions of parents?
—What problems face the contemporary family?
—How can the church help the family to fulfill its Biblical function?

God made the family. At the dawn of creation, before God expressed final satisfaction with the world He had fashioned, He created woman to go with man. "It is not good for man to be alone; I will provide a partner for him,"[1] God said, and He made woman from the side of man. "For this reason a man will leave his father and mother and be united to his wife, and they will become one flesh,"[2] God announced. Marriage and the home were a reality.

The Family in the Bible

God's intentions for the family were closely stated in the Bible. Eve was to be a partner with Adam, and both Adam and Eve were to provide companionship for the Lord God.[3] They were to rule over Eden, and they were set free to subdue creation to serve their needs.[4] They were also instructed to be fruitful and to populate the earth, sanctifying the sexual union that was theirs. The creation of the family unit was the crowning point of creation, and the remainder of God's creation was placed under their care and keeping.

Man's noble purpose was tainted, however, when he succumbed to sin. The purpose of the home remained the same, and man still retained his God-given responsibility for creation. But the appearance of sin severed man's perfect relationship with God, and introduced mistrust and tension between man and his partner. Sexual union was still a part of God's plan for the home, but children born to that union would be brought forth in pain. Marriage was still sanctified by God, but henceforth there would be a certain disharmony and tension between man and woman that could be resolved only when man reached full maturity in Jesus Christ.

Guidelines for the family are set forth in the Old Testament, but not until the era of the new covenant did the family rediscover its full potential. Gene Getz, in his book *The Measure of a Family*, asserts that the Christian home in the New Testament was almost synonymous with the church. This, he suggests, is why the New Testament says relatively little about the family unit. What was written to the church was also written to individual families. The family is the church in miniature, according to Getz. The truly Christian family will demonstrate the marks of a mature church.

Biblical Guidelines for the Family

Both the Old Testament and the New Testament seem to assume that under normal circumstances a home will be blessed with children. Therefore, other than the creation passage in Genesis, the laws for personal sexual conduct in Leviticus, and the treatise on marriage as a picture of the church in Ephesians, specific instructions for the family center in the business of childrearing. What are these guidelines to parents?

Teach With Words
Parents were instructed to teach their children. God commanded that parents were to verbally instruct their children in the faith:

O my people, hear my teaching;
    listen to the words of my mouth.
I will open my mouth in parables,
    I will utter things hidden from of old—
things we have heard and known,
    things our fathers have told us.
We will not hide them from their children;
    we will tell the next generation
the praiseworthy deeds of the Lord,
    his power, and the wonders he has done.
He decreed statutes for Jacob
    and established the law in Israel,
which he commanded our forefathers
    to teach their children,
so the next generation would know them,
    even the children yet to be born,
    and they in turn would tell their children.
Then they would put their trust in God
    and would not forget his deeds
    but would keep his commands.
They would not be like their forefathers
    a stubborn and rebellious generation,
whose hearts were not loyal to God,
    whose spirits were not faithful to him.[5]

Paul restates this principle: "You fathers, again, must not goad your children to resentment, but give them the instruction, and the correction, which belongs to a Christian upbringing."[6]

Teach by Example

God knew that children would watch their parents prepare for worship. Deuteronomy 6:4-9 identifies parents' responsibility to communicate faith by example:

Hear, O Israel: The Lord our God, the Lord is one. Love the Lord your God with all your heart and with all your soul and with all your strength. These commandments that I give you today are to be upon your hearts. Impress them on your children. Talk about them when you sit at home and when you walk along the road, when you lie down and when you get up. Tie them as symbols on your hands and bind them on your foreheads. Write them on the doorframes of your houses and on your gates.[7]

Parents teach by the way they themselves observe the Word of God. Under normal conditions, children become much like what their parents are, largely by copying their parents' model. Children critically eye parents' behavior patterns and decide if their behavior is consistent with their words. They observe parents' responses to joy and disaster. Then they usually begin to respond to situations much as their parents do.

Teaching by example is as much informal as it is formal. Family devotions, holiday traditions, mealtime prayers, bedtime prayers, and family conversation provide the atmosphere in which faith is communicated—if words and actions agree.

Discipline

Parents are also instructed to discipline their children. Proverbs records the positive results of effective discipline and the negative results of poor discipline.

* Rod and reprimand impart wisdom, but a boy who runs wild brings shame on his mother.

* A father who spares the rod hates his son, but one who loves him keeps him in order.

* Correct your son, and he will be a comfort to you and bring you delights of every kind.

* Start a boy on the right road, and even in old age he will not leave it.[8]

Discipline is more than mere correction. It also requires parents to direct a child's behavior into appropriate channels in an effort to lead him to healthy self-discipline. Paul's advice to the Ephesian parents applies here, too: "You fathers, again, must not goad your children to resentment, but give them the instruction, and the correction, which belong to a Christian upbringing."[6] Discipline is to be administered directly, positively, and in a spirit of love. "Fathers, do not exasperate your children, for fear they grow disheartened"[9] Paul further instructed.

Effective discipline is administered with a child's age level, capabilities, and emotional response in mind. Rules should be appropriate for the child's age, not demanding more than the child can produce. Discipline preserves the dignity of the child by protecting him from nagging and ridicule, yet, at the same time, consistently insists upon clearly defined behavior standards.

Firm authoritative discipline (as opposed to a permissive or authoritarian style) results in well-socialized, emotionally secure children who grow up to be responsible adults with healthy self-esteem and the capacity to love and care for others. Children who are disciplined feel worthwhile and loved.

Contemporary Problems Facing the Family

The contemporary family is confronted with strains and stresses from all sides. Families have changed dramatically in the past three decades. Many of those changes have created grave threats to family solidarity.

One major change has been a shift from a partnership with fixed roles to a partnership with fluid roles. Before World War II, family patterns were clearly defined. Fathers were bread-winners, and sons usually followed in their vocational footsteps. Mothers were homemakers, and daughters were expected to follow their example. But such fixed roles no longer apply. In many cases, both parents work, and a wide range of vocational possibilities exist for both boys and girls.

A second change, resulting from a highly mobile society, is the shift from an extended family to a nuclear family unit. Prior to the past three decades, when most people married they settled near their parents. Families included grandparents, cousins, aunts, and uncles as well as parents. Holidays and Sundays brought together the whole clan. Children grew up with the security of knowing who they were in relation to their family heritage. Parents enjoyed the advantage of knowing that the values and lifestyle they taught to their children were rein-forced by the larger clan. But most families no longer enjoy that luxury. In this day of high mobilization, families see the extended clan no more than once a year, leaving parents very much alone with their childrearing responsibilities and leaving children without benefit of a sense of heritage.

A third change centers in increasing technology. Almost every family owns an abundance of labor-saving devices: dishwashers, microwave ovens, trash compactors, automatic washers and dryers, vacuum cleaners, and power lawnmowers, to mention a few. Whatonce was an all-day chore to cook and clean and keep a house now takes much less time. What once were chores for children are no longer practical demands for them. Changing technology permits more leisure time for parents and decreases the possibilities for teaching children work and responsibility. In our consumer-oriented society, technol-

ogy creates economic pressures as well. People are pressured to
buy whatever new product or gadget that is advertised.

A fourth change is what some term an era of child-
centeredness. In early American history, children were considered to be of prime importance for their contribution to the
family. At an early age, they were set to work to share in the
family economy. Children were seen as miniature adults who
existed to serve, not to be served. But now parents are contributors to their children's livelihood, not just in childhood,
but into adolescence and even young adulthood. Children exist
to be given to, not so much to be received from. Parents are
advised to protect a child's self-esteem and to beware of discipline that will damage the child's psyche. No one would find
fault with the more humane treatment of children, but when
children are made the center of the family, undue stress is
brought to bear on family life.

All of these changes have brought about greater personal
freedom, an advantage not enjoyed by previous generations.
Yet in the pursuit of personal freedom, family solidarity suffers
unless parents understand the pressures and deal with them.

Marriage was once an institution that survived for better or
for worse, because the institution superseded individual identity of the two people in it. But marriage is now a companionship arrangement based upon internal cohesion more than on
tradition. However, internal cohesion must be nurtured
carefully—it is a quality not easily achieved in contemporary
society. Some marriages—far too many of them—fail to survive.

The family is not doomed in contemporary society, but it is
besieged. The family that succeeds will be the family in which
the parents acknowledge the stresses, covenant together to
meet and overcome the challenges, and observe Biblical
guidelines for communicating values to their children.

The Church and the Family

The church must help families to realize their potential as
"the church in miniature." An effective teaching program, described in this book, will provide strength and nurture for each
member of the family. But by itself that is inadequate, for faith
is transmitted more by the family than it is through formal
instruction.

Larry Richards, writing in *Ventures in Family Living*, suggests three ways in which the church can help families to teach:[10]

1. Train parents for their educative role.
2. Relate individual church ministries to the parental ministry.
3. Administer the church program to help rather than to hinder family life.

Train Parents

Any congregation can train parents for their role as parents. Such training begins in the youth department when teens explore the essentials of a Christian marriage, perhaps long before they seriously contemplate marriage themselves. Training continues into the young adult and adult classes.

A minister who is concerned for the family can also help train parents for their teaching role. *Sermons* should reflect understanding of family life and application of Biblical principles to family living. *Premarital counseling* can uncover areas of needed growth before marriage takes place. Good *pastoral work* puts the minister in touch with the needs of families and provides opportunities for *marriage and family counseling.*

Teaching agencies such as Sunday school or evening discussion groups can feature periodic elective classes dealing with family topics. The possible topics are numerous: couple communication, conflict resolution, discipline, how to communicate faith, how to teach Scripture to children, understanding teenagers, how to be a single parent. Elective classes can provide an opportunity for exchange of ideas, and mutual support for those experiencing similar needs.

Many churches provide a wide variety of family resources in the *church library*. Books, tapes, and pamphlets should be available for loan or purchase.

Some churches sponsor a *family month*, featuring the family and its needs and functions. Sermons, classes, films, and special family activities are often included. For example, one Illinois church observed family month with relevant sermons every Sunday for a month, two elective Sunday-school classes, more elective Sunday evening classes, and a series of family fellowship activities.

Family camps and *retreats* are another way for families to be equipped for their teaching function. Materials and suggestions should be available not only for church-planned family camping activities, but also for families that go camping by themselves.

Resources for *family nights* may also be suggested and made available by the church. A series of family night activities could be suggested for special occasions.

Relate Home to Church

Individual church agencies should be tied together with the home. Too often the church teacher and the parent have no idea of what each other is doing.

Parent-teacher meetings help acquaint parents with what their children really do at church; they also serve to familiarize teachers with home situations. Such meetings may be regular and formal, or the same purpose may be accomplished with programs for parents in individual classes or agencies. For example, one church planned at least one parent program per year at every age level of every program. These should be planned for different days, so that parents with more than one child can attend each.

Another helpful way of tying church and home together is for each teaching program to provide *quarterly curriculum previews* with suggestions of how parents can expand and reinforce curriculum concepts at home. At least one publisher provides such helps for vacation Bible school through a family enrichment calendar.

Home visitation is another link between church and home. Teachers should be encouraged and equipped to do such pastoral work. The teacher who does his homework well will use curriculum far more effectively.

Careful Administration

The church intent on building families is a church that *evaluates existing programs* and plans for ways to improve. It is a church that administers carefully.

Careful administration calls for a *one-job-only policy*. Some churches fragment the family by overly involving parents in church activities, leaving little time for one another. A one-job-only policy recognizes the limitations of a volunteer's time and attempts to avoid using parents so much that their children are harmed.

A family-centered church will search for ways to *combine*

meetings into fewer nights of the week. One or two nights per week can become focal points for committee meetings, board meetings, choirs, and the other activities in the church calendar. This can be accomplished with careful scheduling.

Some church activities should be *activities for the whole family*. One Oklahoma church features three or four such programs per year. At Halloween, for example, each youth and adult class prepared and manned a booth for a type of Halloween carnival that the children of the congregation attended. Creative planning will generate similar ideas.

Summary

The family was instituted by God. Its purpose was, and still is, to bring glory to God. But the modern family is besieged by many problems. The church must recognize its responsibility to help the family become the church in miniature, as God intended.

Projects

1. Analyze your home church to determine how well it helps prepare parents to teach. In what ways does it do so? In what areas can improvement be made?
2. Write a short paper outlining the Biblical teaching about marriage and the family. How can the church help couples and parents to achieve this ideal?

Selected Bibliography

Marriage Enrichment
Christensen, Larry. *The Christian Family*. Minneapolis: Bethany Fellowship, 1970.
Otto, Herbert A. (ed.) *Marriage and Family Enrichment*. Nashville: Abingdon, 1976.
Wright, H. Norman. *The Christian Faces . . . Emotions, Marriage, and Family Relationships*. Denver: Christian Marriage Enrichment, 1975.
_____. *Premarital Counseling*. Chicago: Moody Press, 1977.

Family Enrichment
Getz, Gene. *The Measure of a Family*. Glendale: Gospel Light, 1976.
Haystead, Wesley. *You Can't Begin Too Soon*. Glendale: Gospel Light, 1974.

Rickerson, Wayne. *Getting Your Family Together*. Glendale: Gospel Light, 1977.

_____. *Good Times for Your Family*. Glendale: Gospel Light, 1976.

_____. *How to Help the Christian Home*. Glendale: Gospel Light, 1976.

Staton, Knofel. *Home Can Be a Happy Place*. Cincinnati: Standard, 1977.

Ward, Ted. *Values Begin at Home*. Wheaton: Scripture Press, 1979.

Zuck, Roy B. and Gene A., Getz (ed.) *Ventures in Family Living*. Chicago: Moody Press, 1971.

---

[1]Genesis 2:18, NEB
[2]Genesis 2:24
[3]Genesis 3:8
[4]Genesis 1:28
[5]Psalm 78:1-8
[6]Ephesians 6:4, NEB
[7]Deuteronomy 6:4-9
[8]Proverbs 29:15; 13:24; 29:17; 22:6, NEB
[9]Colossians 3:21, NEB
[10]From *Ventures in Family Living*, by Zuck/Getz, Copyright 1971. Moody Press, Moody Bible Institute of Chicago. p. 138. Used by permission.

15

Building and Equipping for Christian Education

As you read, think about these questions:
—What are three trends for new buildings?
—How should a congregation plan for adequate educational facilities?
—What space and equipment should be available for each age level?
—How can existing space be adapted to meet educational needs?

Good Christian education can occur in any kind of facility (or none at all), if teachers are committed models of faith who center their instruction in the Word of God. But to a great degree, the church building and facilities determine the kind of program that will take place within its walls. The congregation that is genuinely concerned with the teaching mission of the church will periodically analyze their use of space and equipment in an effort to enhance the efforts of faithful teachers. As Lois LeBar says, "Our building tells the community what we think of our God. It either aids or hinders the attainment of our goals."[1]

Current Trends in Building

Larger Classrooms
If a modern church building is to be planned for effective Christian education, it will feature larger classrooms than have

been traditionally available. Traditional teaching philosophy calls for learners to enter the classroom, find a chair, and sit for the remainder of the class session, which requires minimal space. Larger rooms are made necessary by a changing teaching philosophy. The use of an activity-oriented style of teaching requires more space than a traditional teaching approach requires.

Chapter 8 presented a plan of organization for preschoolers in which departments were deliberately kept to twenty or less in number in order to permit interest centers, large groups, and small permanent groups. This organization is best achieved in a space large enough to provide for all activities to be completed in one room. Small separate rooms for each permanent group are unnecessary. The teaching plan for other age levels also calls for larger class areas to allow for the use of a wide variety of Bible learning activities.

Multiple Use of Space

A second trend in modern church buildings is the multiple use of space. Church buildings are expensive structures, often used only three to five hours a week. It is not economical to provide separate space for every kind of church program. Therefore, gymnasiums may become multi-purpose rooms that are used for recreational, fellowship, and educational purposes. Fellowship areas double for fellowship and educational space, and several programs a week may meet in classroom facilities.

Some congregations plan new programs to make full use of facilities. For example, a congregation in Illinois uses preschool facilities not only for the usual Sunday school, graded worship, youth meetings, and Wednesday evening program, but also conducts two sessions of preschool each weekday. Another Illinois congregation conducts a Christian school during the week in facilities used by elementary children on Sunday. That kind of use calls for flexible room arrangements, but it makes efficient use of otherwise expensive space and equipment.

Effective multiple use of space rests upon four conditions:

1. Thorough analysis of the needs of all current programs and all anticipated needs.

2. Careful coordination of scheduling for the use of facilities.

3. Training of leadership for the coordination of use.
4. Provision for adequate custodial service.

Emphasis on Environment

Classroom environment is created primarily by a loving teacher who provides warmth and acceptance, but it is also affected by physical surroundings. Buildings today take into account the need for adequate lighting, cheerful colors, attractive floor covering, equipment appropriate to the age level, and picturesque landscaping. All of these environmental considerations affect attitudes toward learning. Older buildings can also be made to conform to this trend.

Planning for Building and Equipment

Develop a Statement of Teaching Philosophy

Harry Atkinson insisted on the necessity of a well-thought-out teaching philosophy: "The backbone of a good educational building is a clearly conceived program of procedures to be carried out within its walls."[2] A building should be planned according to the kinds of functions that will occur within it. Classroom requirements, for example, are directly related to teaching philosophy. The traditional style of teaching can be used well in small rooms, while an activity orientation to teaching demands more space per pupil and larger rooms that lend themselves to both large-group and small-group activities.

Teachers and educational leaders should formulate a workable teaching philosophy before facilities are planned and provided. Failure of a congregation to clarify its teaching philosophy leaves it vulnerable for an architect's philosophy to be imposed upon it. If the unstated philosophies of both congregation and architect are compatible, all is well. But should those philosophies turn out to be opposite, the congregation will experience undue disappointment and difficulty.

A Master Plan for Space and Equipment

The next step for effective space planning and utilization is to develop a master plan for space and equipment. A list should be made of the number of persons for which space is to be provided (both current and projected figures). This list will allow a projection to be made of rooms needed, required floor space, and equipment needs.

Sunday-school Size

	1-99	100-299	300-499	500-899	900 & Up
Infants and Toddlers	1	1	2	3	4
2's and 3's	1	1	2	3	4
4's and 5's	1	1	2	3	4
Grades 1-2	1	1 large or 2 small	2 large or 4 small	2 large or 6 small	4 large or 12 small
Grades 3-4	Same as Grades 1-2				
Grades 5-6	Same as Grades 1-2				
Grades 7-9	1	1	1 lg. rm. Classrooms for groups of 12-15	2 lg. rms. Classrooms for groups of 12-15	3 lg. rms. Classrooms for groups of 12-15
Grades 10-12		Same as Grades 7-9			
Adults	2	3	4	8	12

Figure 15-1. Classroom requirements based on Sunday-school size

In *Building and Equipping for Christian Education*, Atkinson outlines probable needs for congregations of various sizes. Figure 15-1 adapts his suggestions to fit the organizational philosophy presented in earlier chapters of this book.

List Activities for Each Space

The next step toward efficient use of building and equipment is to list all activities, both Sunday and weekday, for each group. This list should include the times and frequency of use by community groups, like Scouts, that use facilities on a regular basis. This simple procedure allows for planned multiple use of facilities and omission of unnecessary space.

General Considerations for Usable Space

Every congregation should take the following considerations[3] into account when planning for educational space. Observance of these guidelines will create comfortable, satisfying space.

1. Circulation. Access to the building should be easy. If at all possible, entrance to a room should be from outside or from a hallway so that a working group need not be disturbed. Avoid winding hallways and limited foyer areas.

2. Roomy classrooms. A generally recommended room proportion is three feet of width to four of length. Window space is desirable.

3. Floors. Floor covering should be selected for durability, attractiveness, and ease of maintenance. Carpeting helps to control sound.

4. Toilets. Make separate provision for young children so that facilities may be geared to their size. If such provision cannot be made, provide step stools to help the children.

5. Heating and ventilation. These should provide for comfort.

6. Lighting and electrical outlets. Provide adequate lighting. Place light switches conveniently. Have at least one electrical outlet on each wall, more in large spaces such as fellowship areas.

7. Coat hangers. These should be convenient to classrooms and at an appropriate height for the age level using them.

8. Storage. Free-standing closets are commended because of their flexibility. Open storage shelves are also valuable for children's areas.

9. Drinking fountains. These should be easily accessible and, if possible, at a height appropriate to the age level using them (a step stool could be provided for children).

10. Acoustics. Carpeting, draperies, and acoustical ceiling tile help to control sound.

The Needs of Each Age Group

Early Childhood

The basic space requirement for preschoolers is thirty to thirty-five square feet of space per child, or rooms of 600-700 square feet, if the guidelines of Chapter 8 are observed.

Babies and toddlers should be housed in bright, cheery rooms located on the ground floor near the worship center to provide easy access for parents. Cribs, play pens, and washable toys are essential; so are extra diapers, facial tissues, sheets, changing tables, shelves for diaper bags, and rocking chairs. A sink should be located in the room. A Bible, pictures, and mobiles create a warm environment. Rooms designed for toddlers only will add a few puzzles and books, cardboard blocks, trucks and cars, and a rocking horse or riding toy.

Rooms for children of ages two through five need the following items:

Art supplies	Housekeeping equipment
Autoharp	and furnishings
Bible	Nature materials
Blocks	Pictures
Book rack	Play dough
Books	Puzzle rack
Chairs (seats 10-12"	Puzzles
from floor)	Record player
Child's rocker	Records
Coatracks	Tables (20-22" high)
Crayons	Tackboard (27" from floor)
Doll bed	Trucks and cars
Dolls	Wastebasket

Much preschool equipment can be built by men in the church.[4]

Elementary Children

Elementary children need twenty to twenty-five square feet per child if a church plans to follow the organizational guidelines outlined in Chapter 9. A room of 750-900 square feet is required if all activity for a specific department occurs within a single room (which is the recommended procedure). These rooms should be on ground level or above to provide adequate lighting and the most appealing environment.

A checklist of equipment and supplies provide guidance for planning:

Art supplies	Hymnals	Record player
Bibles	Maps	Records
Book rack	Open shelves	Scissors
Books	Paper	Tables (22-26" high)
Cabinet	Pencils	Tackboard
Chairs (seats 12-16"	Piano or autoharp	Wastebasket
above floor)		

Much of this equipment can also be built by members of the congregation.[4]

Youth

Youth areas need to provide eighteen to twenty square feet of space per pupil; that calls for classrooms of 225-300 square feet. Although most teaching in youth departments is done in small permanent groups, a department assembly room would be helpful. A permanent group could meet in this room, too.

Use the following list as a guide for planning equipment needs:

Art supplies	Chalkboards	Record players
Bibles	Hymnals	Small tables
Bible study aids	Pencils	Tackboards
Cabinets	Piano	
Chairs	Posters	

Adults

Adult learners require ten to fifteen square feet per pupil, or 300-450 square feet for a class of thirty. Rooms for young adults should be easily accessible to early childhood rooms. Older adult rooms must be accessible without the use of many stairs.

A checklist for equipment and supplies for adults is similar to that for youth:

Art supplies	Chairs	Pictures
Bibles	Chalkboards	Tables
Bible study aids	Hymnals	Tackboards
Books	Maps	
Cabinets	Pencils	

Administrative Space

Administrative space is essential for an education program. Offices should be provided for paid educational staff. A church library should be available (it may double as a classroom) as well as an audiovisual center. Central storage space is also essential. A small office is helpful for volunteer Sunday-school administrators' use and for records and materials.

Adaptation of Existing Space

Not every congregation has ideal space and equipment. In addition, enrollment at various age levels fluctuates, requiring periodic analysis of space usage. How can less-than-ideal facilities be renovated?

Every congregation needs to analyze space requirements and assignments every year or two. With shifting enrollments, space can be reassigned to relieve crowded areas or for more efficient use by a different age group.

Be alert for ways to use adjoining rooms. Perhaps some walls could be removed to create larger areas. Separating a large class or department into adjoining rooms allows some large group activity without excessive moving even if walls must remain in place.

Look for added space near the church building. Houses can be bought and converted into class and assembly rooms. Schools or club rooms can be rented. Small adult classes could meet in nearby homes. Mobile homes can be placed on the parking lot and used for class areas. Where there is a need and a will to meet it, there is a way, however unorthodox it may be.

A good coat of paint will improve many a room, even if it does not provide added space. A regular cleanup/paint-up day would be an asset for every congregation. Removal of unused equipment and supplies can help to utilize space to its fullest.

Most schools will be unable to acquire all needed equipment immediately. A priority checklist should be developed to guide future acquisitions.

Have some items built by men of the congregation. Cribs, home living equipment, chalkboards, bulletin boards, book racks, tables, shelves, and cabinets can be provided at great savings.[4]

Appeals to the congregation will often provide donations of toys, homemaking equipment, books, and other items. Whatever is donated will have to be evaluated for usability. Usable items can be placed into service and unusable ones destroyed.

Summary

Adequate space and equipment contribute to good teaching, but they seldom happen except by careful design. This chapter has presented a plan for determining what a congregation needs for each age level and suggestions for improving existing space. The best rule is this: *do the best with what you have.* Nothing substitutes for cleanliness, cheerfulness, and orderliness. Then using the guidelines developed for space and equipment, make whatever changes are possible. Improvement will be evident before you know it!

Project

Take a tour of a church building and analyze the space and equipment you find in it. Determine the square footage in each classroom and how many pupils meet in each. Take along the checklist of suggested equipment and supplies to find out what is available for each age level. Comment on your general impressions of each room when you first saw it. From what you observed, how could the building and facilities be improved?

Selected Bibliography

Atkinson, C. Harry. *Building and Equipping for Christian Education* (revised editon). New York: National Council of Churches of Christ in the USA, 1963.

Boone, Eldon M., Jr. *Working with Preschoolers in Sunday School.* Nashville: Convention Press, 1974.

Fulbright, Robert and Eugene Chamberlain. *Working with Children in Sunday School.* Nashville: Convention Press, 1974.

LeBar, Lois. *Focus on People in Christian Education.* Old Tappan, New Jersey: Revell, 1968.

---

[1]LeBar, p. 91

[2]Atkinson, p. 12. Used by permission, Division of Education and Ministry, National Council of the Churches of Christ in the U.S.A.

[3]*Ibid.,* pp. 17-21

[4]For suggested designs of much of the children's equipment, see the books by Boone and by Fulbright and Chamberlain listed above.

Part Three

ADMINISTRATION OF CHRISTIAN EDUCATION

Section Outline

The first section of this book dealt with the history, philosophy, and objectives of Christian education. The second section dealt with age-group characteristics, special education, teaching methods, and facilities. These sections have laid valuable groundwork for the following chapters, which apply these theories and principles in real-life situations.

The testing point of theory is in the local congregation, as it is put into practice in the lives of leaders and members. Yet if one were to ask a typical congregation what its greatest weakness was, more likely than not its answer would be "lack of leadership." We can see the importance of good leadership, competent administration, and effective use of the educational agencies available to the local church.

If Christian education remains nothing more than an academic activity, a course to be taken to fulfill a requirement, then we have failed. Our times are too desperate to allow Christian education to be no more than a scholarly inquiry. In the words of Dr. James DeForest Murch, we must "teach or perish!"

16

Christian Education in the Local Church

As you read, think about these questions:
—Why is a philosophy of education important for the church's educational program?
—Why does a church's educational program need objectives?
—What are the more important agencies a church may use in its educational program?
—How can various educational agencies be correlated for a more effective educational program?

The educational mandate for the local church is a major element in the Great Commission.[1] Although the command to teach as a part of the church's mission is clear and precise, how the church is to carry out this mission is not at all clear. This omission of specific instructions for carrying out the command to teach seems deliberate. Christ wanted His church to be able to adopt whatever methods were most appropriate to the cultural situation it found itself in. We would hardly expect the church of the first three centuries, when it was an illegal religion and its meetings often had to be held in secret, to employ the same educational agencies that the medieval church used. In the Middle Ages the church in western Europe enjoyed a place of prominence and privilege, but its educational efforts were hampered by the fact that a majority of the citizens could not read or write. And the educational agencies the church finds most effective in our modern, thoroughly secularized society are quite different from those used in either the third or the thirteenth centuries.

Good stewardship requires that every congregation make the best possible use of the educational resources and opportunities at its disposal. The local congregation must be organized for its task. Various educational agencies have developed over the years that are used in modified form by the modern church to carry out its educational responsibilities. Few congregations will use all of these agencies, but an awareness of the most important of them is needed in order to understand how they can be used in the local church.

Organizing the Local Church for Christian Education

Philosophy and Objectives

Those who talk about a philosophy of education for the local church run the risk of being thought too scholarly and impractical. But actually preparing a philosophy is no more than an attempt to state in some orderly fashion what one believes about education in the local church: what authority determines its goals and methods, who is responsible for it, what is its content, and by what processes it is to be accomplished.

Once a congregation has settled these matters (the Scriptures provide the basic guidelines for the church's educational philosophy), then it is ready to turn its attention to its educational objectives. Objectives are statements of specific outcomes that a congregation intends to reach as a result of its philosophy. Programs and agencies are ways of implementing philosophy and achieving objectives. Every objective ought to be a positive element in the church's effort to fulfill its total mission.

The Sunday school, vacation Bible school, youth meetings, and similar agencies are not just separate organizations that happen to involve many of the same people and use the same facilities. Each of these agencies has an important function to perform within the total framework of the church. These functions must be coordinated to avoid duplication and conflict.

Who's in Charge?

Ordinarily each congregation will be under the oversight of

some kind of a governing body. In some churches the governing body may be the board of elders or the board of trustees. In others, it may be called simply the church board. The educational activities of the church are one of the areas in which the governing body exercises its oversight. Often this responsibility is delegated to a board of Christian education or a Christian education cabinet. Under the direction of this Christian education board, the minister or the minister of Christian education (often called the director of Christian education), the youth minister, the minister of music, and the Sunday-school superintendent work to administer and help carry out the educational program of the church.

The board of Christian education should be responsible for coordinating all of the educational activities: scheduling (a master calendar of activities should be kept in the church office), recruiting and training leaders, selecting curriculum materials, purchasing supplies, and supervising facilities and equipment. Careful supervision of the program will eliminate unnecessary and wasteful duplication and insure that important areas of Christian education are not overlooked. The board of Christian education should also make sure that the doctrines proclaimed from the pulpit are not contradicted or obscured by the teaching in the classrooms.

Educational Agencies in the Local Church

In a typical congregation, a variety of agencies will be employed, each fitting into the church's total educational mission.

The Sunday School

When one thinks of the educational activities of the local church, one immediately thinks of the Sunday school (also called the Sabbath school, the church school, or the Bible school). The Sunday school dates back to 1780 when in Gloucester, England, Robert Raikes hired teachers to work with children on Sunday. The teachers imparted to them the rudiments of education along with some knowledge of the Bible. Raikes' efforts were soon copied by others. Before long the Sunday school began to receive wide acceptance, although not without considerable opposition from some quarters. The Sunday school made its appearance in the United States only a few

years after Raikes' initial efforts and since then has become a
firmly established agency on the American scene.

At least three characteristics have marked the Sunday school
during its 200-year history. Although clergymen have been involved in the movement during its whole history, the Sunday
school has been largely a lay movement. The majority of its
leaders and its teachers have not been professional religious
leaders but have been unpaid volunteers drawn from the membership of the church. The second characteristic of the Sunday
school movement is that it has been ecumenical, that is, its
organizations have reached across many denominations, and
the International Lesson Series outlines used in many Sunday
schools have been and are still prepared by scholars from many
denominations. The third characteristic of the Sunday school
movement has been the strong emphasis it has put on Bible
teaching. On this point, the Sunday school stands in contrast to
other teaching agencies that have often stressed creeds, catechisms, or denominational doctrines.

In the typical church, the Sunday school meets during the
hour before the Sunday morning worship, although a few
churches hold the worship service first with the Sunday school
following. Rapidly growing churches holding multiple worship services may sandwich the Sunday school between the
early and later worship services or hold it simultaneously with
the worship service. In rare circumstances, Sunday school may
be held Sunday afternoon or evening.

Even in the smallest schools some organization is required:
this will include a superintendent, a secretary-treasurer, and a
teacher for each class. Somewhat larger schools may have three
departments—children, youth, and adult—each with its own
departmental superintendent and other officers. Still larger
schools may have even more departments—crib, toddler, nursery, beginner, primary, middler, junior, young teen, youth,
young adult, and adult.

Schools are conducted in a variety of ways. Often they begin
with an opening assembly, which includes a brief devotional
period of congregational singing, prayer, and Scripture reading, along with announcements and activities promoting the
school. This is followed by a class period that runs from thirty
to forty-five minutes (some schools hold the assembly after the
class period). In larger schools each department might have its
own assembly, preceded or followed by a class period.

For their printed curriculum materials a Sunday school may choose from a bewildering array of attractive quarterlies, leaflets, workbooks, and take-home papers. These are produced both by denominational publishing houses and independent religious publishers. Never has such a variety of materials been available to teachers. The biggest problem for a Sunday school is to select those materials that best support its educational philosophy and its theological stance.

Facilities for the Sunday school may vary from one open room that serves both for classes and a worship sanctuary to an elaborate and well-equipped educational plant that will accommodate hundreds of students. Teachers may vary from one person who is drafted on the spot though unprepared and reluctant, to teachers and helpers who are dedicated and often as skillful and highly trained as public school teachers. With such a range of facilities, curriculum materials, equipment, and teachers, there is little wonder that the results are so spotty and often so disappointing.

For this reason, the modern Sunday school is not without its critics. "The most wasted hour in the week!" charged one critic. Or take, for example, the question, "When is a school not a school?" The answers is "When it's a Sunday school!" But in spite of its weakness, which its critics point out and its friends lament, the Sunday school still has a lot going for it. How else can we explain its remarkable 200-year endurance?

Let us pause and examine some of its strengths. First of all, the Sunday school has done more to teach the Bible and instill morals to more people than any other agency of the church during the past two centuries. A major thrust of the Sunday school is evangelism. Some estimates state that from eighty to ninety percent of the persons who are won to Christ are first reached through the Sunday school. Sunday schools are valuable because they afford an opportunity for fellowship. The relaxed and informal setting of the classroom, along with other class activities, allows for fellowship among members that cannot be enjoyed in the more formal atmosphere of a worship service. The Sunday school also provides excellent leadership training both through classroom learning and through in-service experience. In spite of its shortcomings, the Sunday school performs a function in the church's educational ministry that cannot be filled by any other agency. For this reason it is likely to be with us for many years to come.

Sunday Evening Programs

When we think of Sunday evening programs, we usually think of youth programs. Actually the educational opportunities on Sunday evening may include little children and adults as well as young people.

Today the Sunday evening youth programs have taken on a wide variety of forms and activities. Many denominations maintain their own youth organizations for which they provide printed curriculum materials. Independent publishing houses and youth organizations also have made available a wide selection of programs and materials. Programs are available for small children, teenagers, and adults. Next to the Sunday school, Sunday evening programs provide more Christian education opportunities than any other agency.

Most of the Sunday evening programs are designed for children and youth. When there are enough persons involved to make this feasible, the Sunday evening program usually follows the same age divisions used in the Sunday school. A growing number of churches add a youth minister (who may serve on a full- or part-time basis) to their paid staff. Most of his effort is often spent on planning and supervising the Sunday evening program. Among his responsibilities will be the recruiting and training of youth sponsors, the selection of curriculum materials, the planning of services and other programs including socials and recreation, coordinating the youth program with other activities, developing leaders among the youth, and involving youth in the total church program.

Sunday evening youth programs are important for several reasons. They reinforce and supplement the learning gained in Sunday school. Since Sunday evening programs allow for more flexibility than the Sunday school does, it is possible to meet the needs of the students almost as soon as they become apparent. Sunday evening programs usually involve more student activity than the Sunday school does. Children and young people have more opportunities to develop leadership skills and other talents. The Sunday evening program also allows opportunities for fellowship that are more limited in the Sunday school.

The Sunday evening program is not without its problems. It is sometimes a struggle to recruit enough dedicated sponsors. Printed materials, often lacking in real substance, must be carefully evaluated before they are used. Since the program attempts to meet a great variety of needs, probably no single set of curriculum materials can be used exclusively. Leaders and sponsors must maintain a high level of enthusiasm to hold the interest of young people. This makes severe physical and emotional demands on them, resulting in a rapid turnover in personnel. Young people often come under criticism for their dress and speech by adults. This leads to misunderstanding and tensions. Yet in spite of all these problems, the Sunday evening program is well worth what it costs in time, effort, and money.

Vacation Bible School

The first vacation Bible schools (also called daily vacation Bible school or vacation church school) were held in the 1890's. Since that time, the movement has grown to the point that thousands of schools involving millions of students are held every year. While the movement began among Protestant churches, today it also includes Roman Catholic and Orthodox churches, making it one of the most significant Christian education efforts of this century.

Vacation Bible school, as the name suggests, is ordinarily held during the summer vacation, although schools have been held during the Christmas and Easter vacations and on weekends. At one time schools sometimes ran for five or more weeks, but more recently this has been reduced to two weeks or even one week. Schools are usually held in the morning (though some are held evenings). Other time arrangements are sometimes made such as holding the school one day a week for several weeks, holding two sessions during the day (one in the morning and one in the afternoon), holding it over a weekend, or splitting the school with sessions for small children in the morning and young people and adults in the evening.

Vacation Bible school offers several advantages over other church educational agencies:

1. It is a valuable supplement to the Sunday school, increasing by up to fifty percent the amount of time available for teaching.

2. It affords an opportunity for concentrated learning where lessons may be reinforced daily rather than having a week lapse between lessons.

3. It offers a variety of learning, worship, and fellowship opportunities. Students learn through Bible storytelling, pup-

pets, crafts, workbooks, and visuals.

4. It gives an opportunity to involve many church members who are not otherwise taking an active part in church activities.

5. Vacation Bible school can be used to train new teachers and workers.

6. Vacation Bible school offers many opportunities for evangelism and outreach for the local church. Many children will attend vacation Bible school who do not attend the Sunday school, and as a result they can be reached for Sunday school and the church.

Vacation Bible school curriculum materials are produced by a number of denominational and independent publishers. These reflect a wide variety of theologies and educational philosophies. Many publishers have courses designed for either a five-day or a ten-day program. Along with the basic lesson materials, many courses offer visuals, worship program materials, prepared crafts, and promotional materials. These colorful and innovative materials make it possible for any church, regardless of size, to have an effective vacation Bible school, even with inexperienced teachers.

Midweek Programs

Church members of earlier generations usually met on a weekday evening for prayer. The prayer meeting was usually followed by Bible study. This practice is still followed in some congregations, for it meets the needs of many for worship and fellowship. But increasingly in urban churches a different approach is being followed. Opportunities for prayer and Bible study may still be featured, but often other church functions will also be carried on the same evening. There are likely to be graded classes for children and young people. The night may also be used for choir practice, teacher training programs, or teachers' meetings, officers' meetings, and other meetings. The practice of holding all these meetings on one night solves some of the transportation problems that result from a multiplicity of meetings scattered through the week. It also allows family to attend together, a significant consideration in view of all the forces that seem intent upon shattering the family.

One of the chief weaknesses of the midweek program is that it is not well organized to meet specific needs in the church's total educational program. Since attendance is usually only a fraction of the attendance at Sunday school or church, it does not, in the thinking of many, warrant a great deal of time being spent on it. How unfortunate is this attitude! Properly planned and conducted, the midweek program can reinforce Bible learning gained through other agencies. It can supplement this learning by teaching in greater detail, or by exploring subjects that do not seem appropriate to the Sunday school. While few publishers have provided materials specifically designed for the midweek program, a great variety of elective courses are available, which can be profitably used.

Weekday Programs

Many churches are so located that they can reach many children through a program after school, or in some communities where released time arrangements have been made, during school hours. These programs take several forms, but usually meet for about an hour and involve not only Bible study but crafts and recreation. While some programs include students from elementary school through high school, most serve only elementary school and junior high students. A variety of materials are used in these studies. Some chruches prepare their own materials. Others use vacation Bible school materials or Sunday school materials from a publisher other than those used in Sunday school. Some interdenominational organizations such as the Awana Youth Association, the Christian Service Brigade for boys, and the Pioneer Girls for girls provide programs that are widely used. Some churches have been able to use other organizations such as the Boy Scouts, Girl Scouts, and Campfire Girls to reach young people for the church.

Weekday programs allow a church to supplement Bible learning gained through other agencies. They also provide an avenue to help meet the legitimate social needs of children and young people. Since the learning situations are often less structured than those found in Sunday school, learning can be more spontaneous and enthusiastic. These programs also offer excellent opportunities for evangelism because they often attract many youngsters not reached by any other church program.

Children's Worship

Many churches now provide separate worship services for children. These may be further divided into junior, primary, beginner, and nursery worship services. Although the main emphasis in these programs is on the worship experience, they still afford many excellent opportunities for Christian teaching.

Children's church has several distinct advantages:

1. It provides a worship service that is geared to the children's needs and to their level of understanding.

2. Children are sometimes a distractive influence in the adult worship. Since they are in their own service, this distraction is removed.

3. Children's worship often relieves an overcrowded situation in the sanctuary. This allows better utilization of the facilities.

4. Adults working in the program develop their talents and are able to use them for the Lord.

5. Children, by participating in a service at their own level, are able to develop their talents.

It is difficult to hold a child's interest for an hour or longer in a worship service. Bible games, crafts, workbook activities, and other learning activities help to keep variety in the program. These may be interspersed with songs, Bible reading, prayers, storytelling, and object lessons. All of these helps and activities should be used in such a sequence that each child is led into an attitude of reverence toward God.

A variety of materials that will be helpful in children's worship programs is available from religious publishers. These include program books, Bible quiz and game books, children's songbooks, crafts, object lesson books, and both projected and non-projected visuals.

Camping

While many phases of Christian camping take place outside the local church and beyond its immediate control, some types of camping can be conducted by the local congregation. In addition, the church's educational program is greatly enriched by those who are involved in camping activities outside the local church.

Camping offers some unique eduational advantages (these are discussed in Chapter 24). Camping, perhaps more than any other educational agency of the church, involves the total person: spiritual, mental, social, and physical. It is a 24-hour-a-day learning experience and its setting is more spontaneous and unstructured. In addition, camping can take advantage of an outdoor environment, a matter of growing importance as our population becomes more urbanized.

Among the types of camping that may be effectively employed by the local church is day camping. In this type of camping students spend all or part of a day in a camping situation, but are not at camp overnight. This type of camping may be carried on at a regular campground or in public parks or other such facilities. The local church provides the leadership and planned activities, often the transportation to and from the campsite, and sometimes a lunch if the program lasts all day. The program includes crafts, recreation, and Bible study. Since day camping does involve some expense, a small fee is often charged the students.

The local church may also employ other types of camping such as weekend campouts, trip camping such as backpacking and canoeing, and adventure camping such as whitewatering and rappelling. All of these can provide learning experiences for students and deserve a place in the church's educational program if it is to meet the needs of all of its members.

Summary

In the chapter we have discussed briefly some of the agencies that the church may use in its total program of Christian education. Some of these are dealt with at greater length in other chapters. Others, such as the church kindergarten and the Christian day school, have not been discussed because they require resources usually beyond the reach of the local church. Other agencies certainly can and ought to be used by the church as the need and opportunity arises. The church is not limited to only a few traditional educational agencies. Indeed, as the future seems ever more uncertain, the church must not only modify traditional agencies but seek new agencies if it is to meet future challenges.

Project

Interview the minister or other person responsible for the educational program of a local church. From this person learn what educational agencies are being used by the congregation and approximately how many students are involved in each. Indicate what agencies the church might be able to use, but is not currently using in its program.

Selected Bibliography

Bower, Robert E. *Administering Christian Education*. Grand Rapids, Michigan: Eerdmans, 1964.

Evangelical Teacher Training Association. *Church Educational Agencies*. Wheaton, Illinois: Evangelical Teacher Training Association, 1968.

Hakes, J. Edward. *An Introduction to Evangelical Christian Education*. Chicago: Moody Press, 1964.

LeBar, Lois E. *Focus on People in Christian Education*. Old Tappan, New Jersey: Revell, 1968.

Lynn, Robert W., and Elliott Wright. *The Big Little School*. New York: Harper and Row, 1971.

Matthews, Charles. *Vacation Bible School*. Cincinnati: Standard Publishing, 1966.

Murch, James DeForest. *Christian Education and the Local Church* (revised edition). Cincinnati: Standard Publishing, 1958.

Speck, Henry E., Jr. *The Church's Educational Program*. Austin, Texas: R. B. Sweet Company, 1963.

Vieth, Paul. *The Church School*. Philadelphia: Christian Education Press, 1957.

---

[1]Matthew 28:18-20

Administering Christian Education

by Gerald Denny

As you read, think about these questions:
—What is a comprehensive definition for the phrase "administering Christian education"?
—What is the purpose of Christian education administration?
—What are the four major areas included in achieving the purpose of administration?
—What are the key principles of Christian education administration?
—What kind of leadership should characterize Christian education administration?

Administering Christian education in a local church is a wide-ranging, complex, and challenging job. Every interest and ability a person brings to this task can be utilized. No two workdays are alike. The variety, the involvement with people, and the interaction with the Word all combine to make administration an exciting and fulfilling type of work. Administration is an essential and holy responsibility. The goals of the church cannot be achieved without it.

The Scope of Administration

Administering Christian education involves four different processes:

1. Overseeing—knowing what is going on in one's area of responsibility and authority.

2. Directing—pointing out the goals and philosophy of one's educational ministry and exerting positive influence to reach those goals.

3. Coordinating—increasing efficiency and effectiveness by tying together all activities within one's area of responsibility.

4. Contributing—helping others to overcome the obstacles they face in their teaching ministry.

This fourfold process should be Biblical, systematic, and positive. Successful administration involves a thorough knowledge of human development: (1) how people learn; (2) when different concepts can best be learned; (3) what atmosphere and methodology best fits the subject matter to be learned; and, (4) how to coordinate and reinforce learning experiences so that maximum spiritual growth occurs. The results are worth the effort.

Plans that are Biblically-oriented, systematic, and positive result in programming. This programming also maximizes the effectiveness of the methods that are followed, whether the programs relate to enlistment of workers or to planning a Bible lesson.

The Purpose of Administration

The starting point for effective administration is a clear understanding of the purpose of the church. The purpose of the church is to help people become what God wants them to be. This involves reaching out to prospective members and building up present church members in Christ.

The process of administering Christian education (overseeing, directing, coordinating, and contributing), so that people are helped to become what God wants them to be, is summed up by the word *discipling*. Every Christian education administrator should strive to help people become discipled for Christ. Each person touched by Christian education should be growing in likeness to Christ and in effective ministry for Christ's church. To be discipled for Jesus Christ is a continual process for every Christian until death ends the process and Christ grants perfection.

The Christian should grow as a disciple of Christ in four major areas:

1. Love (of God and people)
2. Ministry (fellowship and service)
3. Purity (of doctrine and life)
4. Spiritual Reproduction (evangelism and nurture)

All four of these areas are included in the term *discipleship.* The local church is to be a body of love, ministry, purity, and spiritual reproduction. Each church member is to have a deep love for God and people, a relationship of Christian fellowship with other church members, a thorough knowledge of God's Word and obedience to it, and increasing effectiveness in leading others to Christ.

These goals are common to all Christians. But the local church is also made up of individuals with different abilities, interests, and personalities. A major aspect of the purpose of Christian education administration is to help each member find his unique place of life and ministry within the local church.

Planning in Administration

The administrator should devote plenty of time to thoughtful and prayerful planning. Good planning takes time, but it is essential if confusion and inefficiency are to be minimized. The curriculum planner, for example, should ask some key questions before attempting to develop a curriculum for his Sunday school or for a particular age group: What kind of learning experiences are needed? In what order should they occur? What resources are available to help achieve the specific objectives of these learning experiences? How can the teacher tell whether the desired learning has occurred? In order to relate these questions to the goal of achieving mature Christian discipleship, plans must be broken down into more specific categories.

As an example, one might take the category of love, particularly as it relates to increasing one's love for God. First, clearly specify the long-range goal (for example, to grow in love for God with all one's being—heart, soul, mind, and strength[1]). Second, set some short-range goals with dates attached to them. Third, determine to what extent the individuals have already achieved the short-term goals (written statements on "How I Feel About God" might help to assess the character and level of a person's love for God). Fourth, find prepared material that will assist you in achieving the short-range objective. If you cannot locate adequate prepared resources, adapt what you can from prepared resources and then prepare additional resources to fill in the gaps (or do it all from scratch). Fifth, after the first three months, evaluate what progress has occurred in reaching the goals (for example, a second statement on "How I Feel About God" might be compared with the thoughts expressed in the first statement).

Planning should be broken down into small manageable steps that occur over specific time intervals (plans should also be written down). The plans should evidence faith and vision tempered by realism. Discouragement comes quickly when one expects to accomplish too much in too short a time.

The planner should maintain proper balance between time given to planning and time given to implementing the plan. There is much truth in the statement, "If you are given three hours to chop down a tree, spend the first two sharpening the ax." Planning is the "ax sharpening." It is better not to go at all than to go with obviously poor plans. Chopping with a dull ax is both frustrating and harmful. But one can plan too much, and continue to sharpen up plans for so long that they never get implemented. It is better to go with less than perfect plans than not to go at all.

Effective planning begins with prayer and is sustained by prayer. Often some parts of the plan are not clear to you at first. Instead of letting this stymie all progress, do as much as you are aware has to be done and trust God to help you through the parts that aren't clear. When plans are blocked by unforeseen obstacles, be flexible, but make your adaptations with your goals in mind.

Principles of Administration

Ten basic principles undergird the work of the administrator at whatever level he is working. The administrator should:

1. Regularly pray and study the Bible.

2. Build credibility, trust, and love with those with whom he works.

3. Assess the needs of the people.

4. Make realistic, yet visionary plans based on Biblical principles and the needs of the people.

5. Translate plans into clearly written statements of goals and time schedules.

6. Periodically evaluate the progress made toward achieving his goals and make any adjustments necessary.

7. Model the kind of person, procedures, and practices he wants the Christian education workers to exhibit.

8. Learn from other educational administrators.

9. Mobilize members for ministry.

10. Build a broad base of leadership.

The Organizational Chart

Two organizational charts exist for every local church: (1) the way it is supposed to be, and (2) the way it really is. The administrator should try to merge these two ways into one.

The larger the church, the more levels of Christian education administration needed. Ideally, no administrator should have more than six people directly responsible to him.

The *superintendent of education* in Figure 17-1 is a member of the local church serving as a volunteer. The ministers mentioned in Figures 17-2 and 17-3 are paid staff members who have been trained in their particular responsibilities.

The *minister of education* in both Figures 2 and 3 serves as the administrator for the six leaders directly responsible to him. These additional staff members in Figure 3 are responsible for the detailed planning and day-by-day operation in their areas. The minister of education evaluates the plans and policies proposed by the leaders in these areas and provides the coordination of these individual ministries into the church's total educational ministry. The minister of education is also able to focus attention on other needs in the congregation (for example, missionary education, special education for the handicapped and gifted, ministry to internationals, maintenance of Christian unity with other congregations, reactivation of inactive members).

In both Figures 2 and 3 the *coordinator* is responsible for administering the church's total educational ministry for a particular age group (or in the case of adults, interest group). In the preschool area, for example, there may be an age group coordinator for birth to two-year-olds, another for two- and three-year-olds, and a third for four- and five-year-olds. The age group coordinator is responsible for overseeing the Sunday morning, Sunday night, Wednesday night, and other special educational activities for that age group.

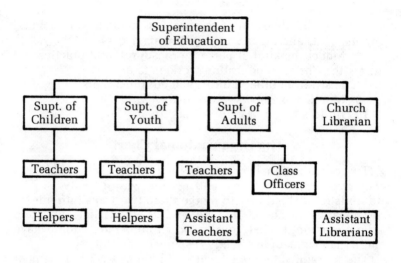

Figure 17-1. Organizational chart for a small church (under 300 in average attendance)

Department superintendents are responsible for overseeing the educational activities of a specific group at one specific time. An age group coordinator for two- and three-year-olds might have as many as six department superintendents under him: a Sunday morning department superintendent, a Sunday evening department superintendent, and a Wednesday evening department superintendent for two-year-olds; and the same arrangement for three-year-olds.

The teachers could be structured in many different ways (lead teachers and assistant teachers, co-teachers, or team teachers). The structure of the teaching responsibilities should be determined by the number of class members, their similarities and differences in spiritual, emotional, intellectual, and physical development, and the abilities and temperaments of the teachers involved.

The class officers of each adult Bible school class are responsible for overseeing, directing, coordinating, and contributing to the work of that class. In children's Sunday-school classes, the teacher usually fulfills this essential administrative role. The same type of role must be fulfilled by department superin-

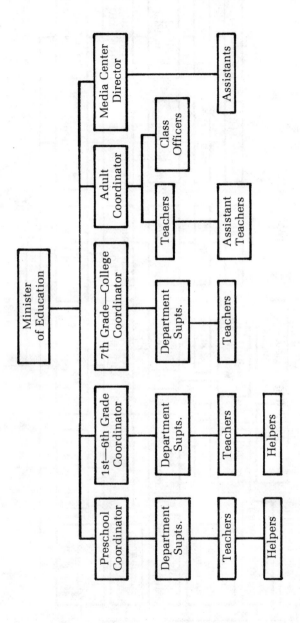

Figure 17-2. Organizational chart for a medium-sized church (between 300 and 800 average attendance)

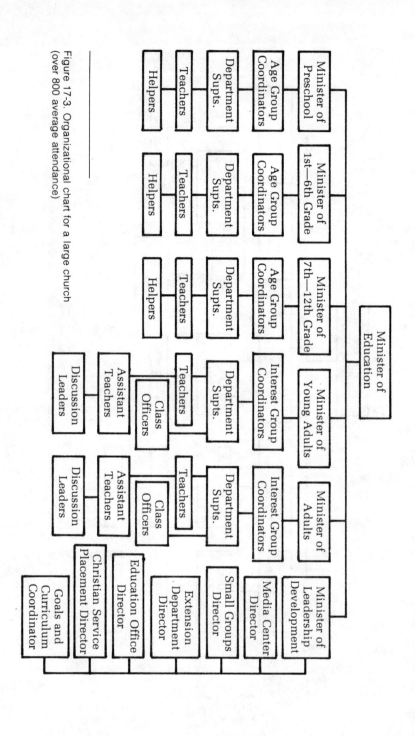

Figure 17-3. Organizational chart for a large church (over 800 average attendance)

tendents, only their administrative responsibility involves every class in that department.

The helpers include such people as greeters, record keepers, class shepherds, classroom decorators, song leaders, interest center leaders, supply chairpersons, research assistants, and social directors. Helpers should be recruited and trained to fulfill every need of the class.

Personnel Recruitment and Development

Recruitment

Personnel recruitment is essential for a functioning, growing educational ministry. The following principles for the administrator give direction:

1. Recognize that all things are possible with God.[2] God can provide the leaders needed for an effective, growing educational ministry.

2. Pray for specific personnel needs to be met. Enlist other individuals to pray. Pray that God will bring to your mind the right person for each place of service, and prepare that person to respond positively when asked to serve.

3. Have one person coordinate the asking of personnel to serve. This person needs to keep accurate records of who is serving where. Competition between leaders for a particular worker can be eliminated by clearing his name with the coordinator before asking him to serve. Discuss ahead of time the place where a particular person can best serve.

4. Be aware of other personnel needs and the agreed-upon order of priority in which the person should be asked. If the person refuses to serve in the originally requested area, the next possibility should be mentioned. If necessary, additional areas should be mentioned.

Normally, the one doing the recruiting should be the person with whom the one being recruited will most closely work (for example, a department superintendent should be recruited by his age group coordinator).

5. Give a written job description to the person being recruited. Make it as brief as possible, yet have it cover the essential points. It is also helpful to have a written organizational chart and a statement of educational objectives so the person can visualize where he would fit into the total educational ministry of the church.

6. Find prospective workers by utilizing talent and interest surveys, obtaining suggestions from those already serving, and checking through the church membership roll. One church follows the principle of asking all new members to serve in a small but important ministry (women as nursery workers, men as ushers). How they serve in those capacities will determine whether they will be asked to serve in more demanding areas of responsibility.

7. Visit in the home of the prospective worker when asking him to serve. This takes more effort than a phone call or a talk at the church building, but the dividends are worth the effort. You learn much about the person by a visit in the home and you deepen the ties that bind you together through such a visit.

8. Place your appeal on a spiritual level. Talk about the task as a ministry for Christ. Show how the task helps fulfill the commands of our Lord.

9. Provide pre-service training.

10. Shepherd those who become workers in the educational ministry of the church. If they fail to show up and you don't know why, for their sakes and the church's, find out. If they become frustrated or discouraged, give them the extra help they need plus an encouraging word.

11. Periodically recognize and honor those who are serving in the educational ministry of the church. This can be done through installation services, services of commitment and recognition, articles in the church paper, special sermons and Sunday-school lessons, personal notes of thanks, special seminars and retreats, and social get-togethers.

12. Set a goal of a certain number of prospective workers to be recruited each month. Make worker recruitment a continuous endeavor. Keep this ideal before you—every member of the local "family of God" should be fulfilling at least one specific Christian service responsibility for the growth and development of the "family."

Training Programs

Both a pre-service and an in-service training program must be developed for the ongoing ministry of education in the local church. A good pre-service training program involves some or all of the following items: observation of others doing the job, interviews with those experienced in the job (both in your church and in other churches), reading, listening to tapes, viewing films and filmstrips about the job, taking a class or classes relating to the job, and attending area seminars or workshops related to the job. These same items are also included in good continuing education programs.

A systematic plan for both pre-service and in-service training should be developed. This plan should be evaluated at least once a year and improvements made based upon past experience and the changing needs in your particular situation.

Delegating Responsibility

There is too much work in even the smallest congregation for one person to do all that needs to be done. When one person even attempts to do it all, he violates God's plan for the functioning of His church.[3] When a church has grown to the point that it has called a person there as the minister of education, an important part of that person's work is this matter of delegation.

Olan Hendricks quotes L.A. Allen's definition of delegation as follows: "Delegation is entrusting responsibility and authority and establishing lines of accountability."[4] For the sake of the spiritual growth of both individual members and the church as a whole, members must be entrusted with responsibility. But responsibility cannot be given without also giving the authority needed to fulfill the responsibility. For example, a person should not be held responsible for poor teaching in an adult class when he has no publicly recognized authority to correct the situation.

The effectiveness of delegation can be increased by establishing clear lines of accountability and procedures to follow in certain situations. For example, the policy should be determined ahead of time that if poor teaching or any other unresolved problem arises in an adult class, the class president is responsible to inform the adult department superintendent. If the class president is negligent at this point, the problem should still be detected by the adult superintendent when he periodically visits the class to observe how it is functioning. The adult superintendent and the class president should confer. The results of their discussion should be reported to the adult coordinator. If a plan of action is agreed upon, or if additional help is needed, the adult coordinator should report to the minister of education. Interaction should continue up and down this ladder of responsible authority until the problem is

successfully resolved. Sometimes the problem is so difficult
that the education committee must be consulted. At other
times, they may need to refer it to the church board. On rare
occasions, the problem might even go to a business meeting of
the entire congregation.

Usually, however, the problem can be properly resolved at a
level of authority nearer its source. Often those higher up the
ladder of delegated authority do not even need to hear about it.
That is why they have broken down the responsibility and
granted authority to those who can work closer to the week-
by-week functioning of an individual class. This arrangement
allows them to focus attention on the broad policies and issues
that affect whole groups of classes and even the whole church.

Leadership

Leadership Styles

Sociologists frequently categorize leadership style into three
major divisions: authoritarian, *laissez-faire*, and democratic
leadership.

The authoritarian leader is a dictator. He may be a benign
dictator who loves his people and works for their best interests,
but nevertheless, he controls the decision-making process and
the purse strings. He decides what is allowed and what is not
allowed. The group is shaped and controlled by him.

The *laissez-faire* leader really is no leader at all. He is a
leader in name only. People pretty much go their own way.
Either inefficiency, confusion, and anarchy reign or some
power "behind the throne" is actually functioning as the
leader. Often the *laissez-faire* leader is the kind of leader people want—a "good old boy" who won't bother them, lets things
go pretty much as they always have, and maintains the status
quo (which, as one speaker put it, is a Latin phrase meaning
"the mess we are in").

The democratic leader "does not necessarily differ from the
authoritarian leader in amount of power but he does differ in
the way he exercises his power." As Krech, Crutchfield, and
Ballachey further explain: "The democratic leader seeks to
evoke maximum involvement and participation of every
member in the group activities and in the determination of
group objectives. He seeks to encourage and reinforce interpersonal relations throughout the group so as to strengthen it. He

seeks to reduce intragroup tension and conflict. He seeks to prevent the development of a hierarchical group structure in which special privilege and status differentials predominate."[5]

The Scriptural model of leadership in the church begins with Jesus Christ, the all-wise, loving, just, and perfect head of the church. He is an authoritarian monarch, a benevolent dictator. He has imparted gifts of leadership to men. Paul had a benevolent authoritarian leadership style in which he communicated the previously written revelation of God to a church eager for divine direction.

The goal of the apostles' leadership, along with the early evangelists, prophets, and pastor-teachers, was to equip Christians for the various ministries needed to upbuild and extend the church.[6] The example and teaching of Paul are instructive at this point. His goal was to work himself out of the central leadership position in a local church. He wanted elders to be appointed in every church he started as soon as enough men were qualified for the position. He wanted them to assume the leadership of that church, so that he could leave and start another one.

Bible scholars disagree as to how the elders were selected in each church. But there can be little doubt that in the first Christian congregation (Jerusalem) deacons were selected by a democratic process involving the members of the church.[7] It is plausible to assume that this same process was used in selecting elders as well. When Paul instructed Titus to appoint elders in Crete,[8] perhaps he followed the Jerusalem church example in selecting deacons, and his "appointment" was merely a confirmation of the congregation's selections (similar to the setting aside ceremony the apostles performed for the Jerusalem deacons in Acts 6:6).

From this brief Scriptural overview, it appears that different leadership styles are appropriate at different phases in the life of the church. When a church was just starting, it needed some leader to function in a beneficial authoritarian style. When a church was established to the degree that men were qualified to become elders, the leadership style shifted to a democratic style of leadership. That is, the elders attempted to carry out Paul's directive in Ephesians 4; as pastor-teachers, they equipped church members to fulfill particular ministries in the church. By so doing, they encouraged a broadening of the leadership base and a sharing of the responsibility and authority.

Authority still rested on the shoulders of the elders as the ones responsible before God for the spiritual welfare of the flock,[9] but the exercise of their authority was through their example, not their commands.

The Servant-Leader

When Jesus' disciples heard that the mother of James and John had asked Him to give her boys chief seats of authority in His coming kingdom, they were upset. Jesus called them together and told them about true leadership in God's kingdom here on earth: "You know that the rulers of the Gentiles lord it over them, and their high officials exercise authority over them. Not so with you. Instead, whoever wants to become great among you must first be your servant, and whoever wants to be first must be your slave—just as the Son of Man did not come to be served but to serve, and to give His life a ransom for many."[10]

Leaders who "exercise authority over others" may have a place in society at large, but not in Christ's church. No matter what degree of rightful authority one has in the church (the total authority of Jesus, or the delegated authority of the elders or deacons), the style of leadership is to be that of a servant. Even if authoritarian leadership is needed at a particular point in time, it should be carried out as a service to others. There is no place for self-seeking or personal advancement in any Christian leader.

Like Christ, leaders in the church are to view their role as servants of others. They have not been placed in positions of leadership to be served by others. Their position of leadership provides opportunity to model the likeness of Christ for the sake of the church. They are to let Christ's ministering spirit pervade and transform the whole body of believers through them and through others they infect with the spirit of service. This unique exercise of Christian leadership will have an impact in the world outside the church. Unbelievers who are tired of the impersonal, dog-eat-dog existence in the workaday world will be drawn to this community of caring and service. The church, when properly led, stands in bold and refreshing contrast to the world around it.

Richards, in his book *A Theology of Christian Education,* suggests three central characteristics of the servant-leader.[11]

1. "The servant is a person who is *among,* not *over* those

whom he leads." As such, he is on the same level as the others; they perceive him as like them. Knowing that they stand equal with the servant-leader and have his respect makes it easier for them to share ideas, feelings, thoughts, and attitudes. Communication channels are open to two-way flow—either party can initiate communication, respond, or share. Within the church, either can minister and either respond.

2. The servant expends his life on behalf of others. "The servant task is to serve others *in that which is important* to God. . . . His primary concern and ministry is the building up of the body and its members."

3. The servant leads by example. He leads more by what he is and does than by what he says. Words are important only as they are undergirded by the servant's quality of life and spirit. The servant-leader is not a weak individual with little or no authority. He is an inwardly strong person who, by virtue of his Christlike example, bears a powerful authority.

Summary

Administration in Christian education must be constantly growing. Administering Christian education in a local church takes all the wisdom, skill, and Christlikeness one can bring to the task. Because he is working with growing Christians, he must model a growing Christian. People will learn from him as they observe how he handles mistakes and failures, how he responds to obstacles, how he deals with changing situations, and how he solves personal and interpersonal problems.

The growing Christian education administrator is one who recognizes his weaknesses and takes specific steps to correct them. He chooses seminars to attend and keeps current on available resources (tapes, books) that might better equip him for service. He gets on the mailing list of churches across the country that have a growing program of Christian education. He takes the initiative to seek out and interview leaders in the field of Christian education. He gets to know fellow administrators and discusses their mutual ministry of Christian education. He continues learning, growing, and serving as long as the Lord gives him the opportunity to do so. His is a high and holy task with tremendous eternal rewards (both for him and for those he has influenced). It demands the very best that he can give.

Project

Draw an organizational chart for the administration of Christian education in your local church. Be as complete as possible. How closely does your chart resemble the chart in this chapter that corresponds to your church's size? In what areas can the administration function more efficiently?

Selected Bibliography

Books

Douglas, Stephen B., and Bruce E. Cook, *The Ministry of Management* (second edition). Arrowhead Springs, California: Campus Crusade for Christ, 1973.

Gangel, Kenneth O. *Competent To Lead.* Chicago: Moody Press, 1974.

Hendricks, Olan. *Management for the Christian Worker.* Santa Barbara, California: Quill Publications, 1976.

LeBar, Lois E. *Focus On People In Christian Education.* Old Tappan, New Jersey: Revell, 1968.

Krech, David, Richard S. Crutchfield, and Egerton L. Ballachey. *Individual In Society: A Textbook of Social Psychology.* New York: McGraw-Hill, 1962.

Richards, Lawrence O. *A Theology of Christian Education.* Grand Rapids, Michigan: Zondervan, 1975.

Sanders, J. Oswald. *Spiritual Leadership.* Chicago: Moody Press, 1967.

Schaller, Lyle E. *The Decision Makers.* Nashville: Abingdon, 1974.

Cassette Tapes

Brandt, Henry. *Leadership in Management* (3 tapes). San Bernardino, California: Campus Cusade for Christ.

Hendricks, Howard. *Motivation and How to Lead* (3 tapes). Costa Mesa, California: One Way Library.

Organizations

Christian Leadership Dynamics, Inc.
    Suite 620 (100 Northcreek)
    Atlanta, Georgia 30327
International Center for Learning
    110 West Broadway
    Glendale, California 91204
World Vision (Christian Leadership Letter)
    Box "O"
    Monrovia, California 91016
Worldwide Discipleship Association, Inc.
    Airport International Center/Suite 315
    1001 Virginia Avenue
    Atlanta, Georgia 30354

Yokefellow Institute
  920 Earlham Drive
  Richmond, Indiana 47374

---

[1]Mark 12:30
[2]Matthew 19:26
[3]See Acts 6:1-4; Ephesians 4:11-16; Romans 12:4-8
[4]Hendricks, p. 83
[5]From *Individual in Society* by Krech, Crutchfield, and Ballachey. Copyright 1962, McGraw-Hill. Used with the permission of McGraw-Hill Book Company.
[6]Ephesians 4:11-16
[7]Acts 6:1-6
[8]Titus 1:5
[9]1 Peter 5:1,2
[10]Matthew 20:25-28
[11]A THEOLOGY OF CHRISTIAN EDUCATION by Lawrence O. Richards. Copyright © 1975 by The Zondervan Corporation, pp. 133, 134. Used by permission.

18

Leadership for Christian Education

As you read, think about these questions:
—What is leadership?
—What kinds of leaders are needed in the church?
—How can the church develop leaders?
—What methods do churches use to train leaders? At what times can these methods best be used?
—How can the church maintain high standards for its leaders?

Ask any congregation about its greatest need. Almost invariably the reply will be, "Competent, dedicated leaders." The problem is universally recognized, but why has no one solved it?

Perhaps one reason is that *leadership* has not been clearly defined. Without a clear definition of leadership, we have not recruited or trained leaders, nor have we adequately identified those who are leaders even when they were available.

Defining Leadership

As He has dealt with His people across the centuries, God has chosen to do so through men and women, not through angels nor other celestial beings at His command. Those whom He selected were qualified to lead and certified through training and dedication. We think immediately of people like Moses and David. Moses was schooled in all of the wisdom of ancient Egypt. Then God allowed him to mature for forty years in the wilderness of Midian. David learned to walk close to God as he kept his lonely vigil over his father's sheep. When God finally needed him to lead the nation of Israel, David was ready.

Problems in Defining Leadership

The meaning of leadership seems obvious. A leader is the person in charge, the dominant person, the man or woman standing up in the front. He is the one who wears the uniform, or who possesses certain traits we have come to associate with leadership. But these traditional and widely accepted definitions really explain little about leadership.

After only a few minutes of observing an elementary schoolroom, for example, it is often possible to discern the intellectual leaders within the group. They have not been appointed to any special position, nor do they wear a uniform to distinguish them as leaders. Yet other students and the teacher clearly recognize that they are leaders.

Then the same class goes out to the playground for recess and decides to play a game of baseball. Quickly the athletic leaders, who may or may not be the same as the intellectual leaders, become apparent. They, like the intellectual leaders, are not officially chosen, nor do they wear any special uniform. Yet everyone on the playground recognizes them as leaders.

One reason that we have difficulty in defining leadership is that we often confuse two aspects of leadership. On one hand we think of a leader as one who has been elected or appointed, formally or informally, to a certain role in a particular social setting. That setting can be a playground, a factory, an office, or a church board meeting. On the other hand, we sometimes define leadership in terms of his ability to function in a given role whether or not that role is an authoritative one. We further confuse the issue when we attempt to describe leadership in terms of certain innate qualities or attributes.

This leads us to another important question: Are leaders born or made? We sometimes comment that a person is a "born leader;" at first glance we may decide that leaders are born. Heredity (nature) is decisive in some leadership situations. One is not likely to become the leading center in the National Basketball Association unless nature has endowed him with a seven-foot-tall body, quick reflexes, and a strong heart. Nor is one likely to become a nuclear physicist unless he has an I.Q. considerably above average.

Yet nurture (training) is also important in developing leaders. Not every seven-footer becomes a basketball star, nor does everyone with an I.Q. of 140 become a nuclear physicist. Nature may limit the areas in which one may exercise leadership, but nurture determines whether or not one becomes a leader in those areas (or what kind of leader he becomes).

Some Contemporary Concepts of Leadership

In recent years a great deal of research has been done in the area of leadership. Because of the highly competitve nature of our secular society, business, industry, government, and education must have capable leadership if they are to survive and grow. This research can also help Christians develop insights into the recruiting and training of leaders for the Lord's work.

Much of this research centers on group behavior or group dynamics. Persons behave differently when they are involved in different group situations. A calm, sedate member of a Sunday school class may have been a screaming, arm-waving fanatic at a football game the prior afternoon. Leadership grows out of a group situation. The person who best meets the needs of the group in that situation is likely to emerge as the leader.

Modern concepts of leadership put great emphasis upon creativity. In a more stable, tradition-bound society, leadership could spend its energies defending and maintaining the status quo. But in our modern, rapidly changing world, such a stance is difficult to maintain and, if maintained very long, can be disastrous both to the organization and the leader himself. Most of us are familiar with dying churches whose motto is "We've always done it this way" or "We've never done that before."

Another important aspect of modern leadership is communication. Rare indeed is the leader today who can isolate himself from his fellow workers, appearing only occasionally to dictate orders. Research clearly indicates that a group performs better when it is knowledgeable about the organization and is involved in setting goals and making decisions. Christian leaders should apply this insight to the work of the church.

Numerous studies have also been made of the personality traits displayed by leaders. These intangible qualities are often difficult to identify and evaluate. How can one person be a dynamic leader while another, just as talented, intelligent, and well-educated, lacks this personal dynamism? We have come to call these intangible qualities "charisma." Perhaps in this area we are getting close to the "gifts" Paul was talking about in 1 Corinthians 12.

Biblical Concepts of Leadership

Since God chose to carry out His mission to the world through human beings, the Scriptures have a great deal to say about leadership. What God reveals to us about leadership comes both from positive teaching and from many examples of God-led men.

God's leaders were people who had been cleansed and transformed. We immediately think of Isaiah and his confrontation with God, or Saul of Tarsus on the road to Damascus.[1]

God's leaders were dedicated persons, not willing to allow inconvenience or suffering to turn them aside from their calling. Jeremiah could endure all kinds of ridicule and mistreatment because he had a fire that burned in his bones.[2] The apostles could face the threats of religious officials, counting it joy to suffer for their Lord.

God called men who were prepared to carry out the tasks He assigned them. Moses had an excellent education when God called him; Paul was an outstanding scholar. Some dismissed the apostles as poor, unlearned peasants, even though they had spent three years at the feet of the greatest Teacher who ever lived. God may be able to use a person who has little education or preparation for leadership, but God can make greater use of people who are prepared.

The Scriptures suggest several other qualities that God looks for when He chooses leaders. Among these are humility, enthusiasm, perseverance, compassion, creativity, vision, and the ability to work with others. God also seeks persons whose lives are open to the leading of the Holy Spirit.

Kinds of Leaders Needed

Paul appropriately compared the church to the human body, in which each member fills an important role that cannot be properly filled by any other member. Eyes can see but they cannot hear; feet can walk but they cannot talk. If this was true of the first century church, it is even more true of the church today. Advanced technology is forcing us to become specialists, and even the church in its educational work cannot escape those pressures for greater specialization. As a result, persons involved in the educational program of the local church must give increased attention to preparing persons to meet these needs, some of which we will discuss in greater detail.

Church Officers

There might have been a time when a church, especially a small congregation, could have gotten along with a hit-or-miss approach to carrying out its mission, using whatever volunteers might have been handy. But that day is past, and even a small congregation needs officers who understand their tasks and have had some preparation for fulfilling them. Every congregation should develop elders, deacons, financial officers, and persons serving in the areas of evangelism, missions, fellowship, education, and benevolence. Sometimes this preparation will involve classes for these areas. In other cases it will require directed reading and personal study or internships and on-the-job training.

Workers in the Church's Educational Programs

The education programs of the typical church will involve more people in more different activities than any other church programs. For this reason, those who lead in this area need special preparation. Since the Sunday school is the largest and most visible educational activity of the church, capable leadership in all its activities is important. A Sunday school ordinarily will have a superintendent, assistant superintendent, secretary, and treasurer. Most classes within the school will have their own officers.

As important as these officers are, the teachers are more important. The effectiveness of the teachers in communicating God's Word to their students will largely determine the effectiveness of the church's educational program. Yet teachers are often selected in the most haphazard fashion, thrust into the classroom with little or no training, and left largely to their own initiative and resources. Is it any wonder that so little learning takes place in a typical Sunday school? (Yet, amazingly, much learning can occur under these circumstances.) Persons who would serve as teachers need courses in Bible content, teaching methods, and educational psychology. While teachers can, and often do, acquire this information on their own, it can be more readily and quickly acquired in regular classes or directed studies.

Youth Workers

A church that neglects its youth is a church that is failing in an important part of its mission. Trained leaders are vital if a youth program is to succeed. Even with a youth minister on the staff, there is a need for volunteers to work in various youth programs. Youth coaches or sponsors will need special training to prepare them for their work. They will also need on-the-job training to learn how to help meet the needs of young people.

Worship Leaders

The public worship services of the church afford many people meaningful religious experiences. Yet if these services are disorganized or clumsily carried out, they have other, less desirable results. For this reason, we need to be concerned about those who lead or participate in public worship. The educational program of every church should provide training in such areas as music and song leading, public prayer, ushering, taking the collection, and serving communion.

Miscellaneous Activities

Numerous other activities of the church require trained leaders. A congregation should feel responsible for training these leaders and requiring that trained leaders fill these positions. Among these are activities such as children's worship services, vacation Bible school, nurseries, recreation programs, retreats, camps, and calling.

Developing Leaders

While certain skills or abilities that the church needs (organists or pianists, for example) can be gained from outside the church, most of a church's skilled leadership must be trained by the church. Several steps are necessary to ensure an effective leadership training program within a local church.

Discovering Potential Leaders

The first step in any program is to find those who have skills or who have the potential to gain these skills needed by the church. The minister, church officers, and especially Sunday-school teachers should be alert to those who have such potential. The Sunday-school teacher is usually the key person for recruiting leaders. Because the class is often a small group and because class meetings and socials often provide opportunities for informal discussions, the teacher can come to know his students better. This gives him a chance to evaluate a student's talents or sometimes to discover hidden talent.

Many congregations use a talent survey questionnaire to discover potential leaders. Such a survey should be taken at least once a year; people sometimes acquire new skills or develop new interests that can be used by the Lord. New members can be encouraged to fill out the questionnaire at the time they join the congregation.

A church must not overlook children and young people in its search for capable volunteers. Every congregation should try to involve as many of them as possible both in service activities and in various training programs. These experiences prepare them for the day when they can accept larger responsibilities.

Leadership Training Programs

The content of any training program will depend upon the length of the course. But probably a more serious problem for most churches will be determining the time to hold such a study. Below are suggested some possible times and methods along with their advantages and disadvantages for holding such classes:

1. During the regular Sunday school hour. More students are likely to be available at this time than at any other time during the week. But, on the other hand, the regular teachers could not attend these sessions unless some provision can be made for substitute teachers. Some churches have held these once a month, allowing the substitute teacher to take over the class while the regular teacher attends the training session.

2. Sunday evening. Sunday evening training sessions have been quite popular with many churches. These may be held at the same time as the youth meetings.

3. Midweek evening. Some churches have found this is a good time for training sessions. Probably the most serious

drawback to the midweek evening session is that it usually attracts fewer attendants.

4. Weekday sessions. Some churches have successful weekday Bible studies. Since these are usually held in the morning, they are likely to attract more housewives than anyone else. Training sessions can be held at these meetings.

5. Vacation Bible school. Many churches now hold vacation Bible school at night. It is often possible to have classes for youth and adults at a night vacation Bible school. This affords an excellent opportunity for leadership training classes.

6. Weekend leadership training clinics. One or two sessions can be held on Friday night; sessions are held Saturday morning and occasionally Sunday afternoon. Thus on a weekend it is possible to attend as many as a half-dozen hour-long sessions. Often two or more churches hold the clinic cooperatively. When several churches work together, several different courses can be offered at once; thus a variety of leadership training needs can be met at the same time. A combined school may be able to enlist Christian college personnel or other experts as teachers.

7. Cooperative training programs. In some areas several churches pool their resources and hold training sessions that may meet one night a week for six or eight weeks. Outside experts may be used as teachers or resource persons.

8. Christian college sponsored programs. Many Christian colleges offer classes designed to train leaders for the local church. These may be available on the college campus or through extension programs.

9. Camp leadership training programs. Many Christian camps offer these in their summer camping schedule. These may be for a week or perhaps for a weekend.

10. Religious publishers. Some religious publishers offer a variety of programs and published materials designed to strengthen leadership in the local church.

11. Conventions. Denominational conventions and conventions sponsored by Sunday-school associations often provide clinics for leaders and teachers.

12. Correspondence courses. Some publishers and other organizations offer correspondence courses for teachers and leaders. Even if one is not able to participate in any of the other training programs, he can (in his own home for a nominal expense) prepare himself for more effective Christian service.

On-the-Job Training

Leadership involves acquiring knowledge, but it also necessitates acquiring skills. Knowledge may be gained by reading and classroom studies, but skills can be gained only through practice. One may read a book on swimming and "know how" to swim, but one doesn't really learn to swim until he gets into the water. Thus it is vital that a church provide on-the-job training for its teachers and leaders.

In preparing one for personal calling, classroom instruction is certainly helpful, but it alone will not make one an experienced caller. Besides his formal instruction, the novice should accompany an experienced caller. In real life situations, the novice can observe the experienced caller and can quickly learn to participate in the conversation.

In the same way, an inexperienced teacher can work with a veteran teacher, observing and sharing in the classroom activities. As the novice gains more experience, he gains confidence as well.

On-the-job training or an internship is just as important for any other type of leadership. For this reason, then, every congregation should include on-the-job training as a regular part of its leadership training program. It should not be looked upon as a frill or as an extra that is optional. Jesus himself set an example in preparing the twelve through on-the-job training.

Maintaining Leadership Standards

One of the most dangerous pitfalls of leadership in any organization is that it often becomes complacent. It is normal for a leader to attempt to reduce his repeated activities to routines. This allows one to go through his normal activities without spending a great deal of time and energy thinking about them. But routines often become ruts, and, as someone has observed, a grave is nothing but a rut with both ends filled in. To avoid getting into ruts, we need to make ample provisions for regular renewal in our Christian education programs.

Maintaining Spiritual Standards of Leaders

One might suppose that once a leader reached a high level of spiritual maturity he could rest secure in the knowledge that further spiritual struggle was unnecessary. But such is not the case. God requires absolute moral perfection of us. Since we don't even begin to come close to perfection in this life, we must constantly struggle to keep reaching higher. Our surroundings do not help us to do this. We do not live in Heaven, but in a world horribly stained by sin. Just as one cannot enter a coal mine without becoming contaminated by coal dust, so one cannot live long in this world without being contaminated by sin. Satan is constantly at our side, seeking to cause us to fall. When one is content to stand still spiritually, he is actually losing ground.

Teachers and leaders must be encouraged to look to their own devotional lives. Various helps (such as devotional guides or systematic Bible reading schedules) can be made available to help them in their Bible study and prayer. Many publishers have such materials available, or the church may prepare its own materials to meet special needs.

While one's private spiritual growth is essential, there is also a place for sharing together in achieving devotional growth. Many churches provide regular opportunities for spiritual growth through prayer and Bible study sessions. Teachers' meetings and church board meetings afford opportunities for inspiration and spiritual guidance. Some churches plan retreats for their teachers and leaders. These are most effective when conducted away from the busy routines of life. Such retreats can be used for instruction, for planning, and for spiritual renewal. Leaders return to their tasks with new enthusiasm and resources for the challenges before them.

Continuing Education for Leaders

In our rapidly changing technological society, one has to learn what amounts to a whole new profession about every ten years. Professionals such as physicians, lawyers, and public school teachers must regularly take refresher courses to bring them up-to-date. A physician who practiced medicine as he did twenty years ago would be charged with malpractice. Salesmen and other business leaders frequently attend seminars and clinics to keep them abreast of the changes in their fields.

Sunday-school teachers and other church leaders face the same problems. While the teacher's task is to share the timeless truths of the Bible with his students, yet the methods and opportunities for that sharing change constantly. Any teacher who does not take advantage of these changes is shortchanging his students.

To meet this problem, local congregations should provide

leadership training programs on a regular basis. Further, churches should make it clear that they expect their leaders to become involved in these programs. A church should maintain a library of books and other materials that will stimulate teachers and other leaders to develop their skills. Many churches encourage leaders to attend clinics, workshops, and conventions by paying all or part of the expenses involved.

Evaluating Leaders

Still another aspect of preparing and maintaining good leadership is evaluation. Unfortunately, evaluation has negative overtones for many people. It sounds like testing or inspecting. As a result, many seek to avoid evaluation. But the members of a congregation are continually evaluating their leaders, though not in a formal way. When attendance in the Sunday-school class declines, the students may be indicating by their actions that the teacher is not meeting their needs. Or when the members of the congregation fail to meet the budget, they may be telling the leaders that they are not satisfied with their leadership. Though some may seek to do so, leaders cannot avoid being evaluated.

While informal evaluation goes on all the time, there is also a place for regular formal evaluation of teachers and leaders. Leaders can be evaluated by others, but self-evaluation is also helpful. Many persons, especially those who feel insecure in their positions, fear evaluations as some kind of an inquisition. But a positive emphasis can help them to look upon evaluations as opportunities to improve their skills for the Lord.

Summary

The need for competent leaders in the local church has never been greater. Church leaders today must function in a variety of roles: organizer, planner, decision maker, promoter, inspirer, counselor, model. Christian stewardship demands that we give our best to the Lord—and then do better. For this reason, then, the Christian education program of every church must include a comprehensive plan for recruiting and training leaders. To do less is to invite disaster.

Projects

1. Determine the leadership needs of a local congregation.

2. Design a leadership program that would meet the needs of the congregation you analyzed, including the types of leadership needed, the number of potential trainees, instructors, curriculum materials, and time of meeting for training classes.

Selected Bibliography

Dobbins, Gaines. *Learning to Lead*. Nashville: Broadman Press, 1968.

Duckert, Mary. *Help! I Run a Sunday School*. Philadelphia: Westminster Press, 1971.

Engstrom, Ted. W. *The Making of a Christian Leader*. Grand Rapids, Michigan: Zondervan, 1976.

Gangel, Kenneth O. *Competent to Lead*. Chicago: Moody Press, 1974.

_____. *Leadership for Church Education*. Chicago: Moody Press, 1970.

Kilinski, Kenneth K. and Jerry Wofford. *Organization and Leadership in the Local Church*. Grand Rapids, Michigan: Zondervan, 1973.

Leavitt, Guy P. (revised by Eleanor Daniel). *Teach With Success*. Cincinnati: Standard Publishing, 1978.

_____. (revised by A. Leon Langston). *Superintend With Success*. Cincinnati: Standard Publishing, 1980.

McDonough, Reginald M. *Working With Volunteer Leaders in the Church*. Nashville: Broadman Press, 1976.

Robinson, Godfrey C., and Stephen F. Winward. *Church Worker's Handbook*. Valley Forge, Pennsylvania: Judson Press, 1972.

Towns, Elmer. *The Successful Sunday School and Teachers Guidebook*. Carol Stream, Illinois: Creation House, 1976.

Sources for Teacher Training Materials

Standard Publishing Company
    8121 Hamilton Ave.
    Cincinnati, Ohio 45231

Evangelical Teacher Training Association
    Box 327
    Wheaton, Illinois 60187

International Center for Learning
    Gospel Light Publications
    Box 1650
    Glendale, California 91209

---

[1] Isaiah 6:1-10, Acts 9
[2] Jeremiah 20:9

CHAPTER

19

Evaluating Christian Education

As you read, think about these questions:
—Why is evaluation of the church's Christian education program important?
—What are some ways to evaluate?
—What should be evaluated?
—When should evaluation be carried out?

A person carefully studies his cancelled checks and compares them with his check stubs. He is evaluating. A business firm closes down for two days to take inventory. It is evaluating. A teacher averages scores in her gradebook and finally puts down a grade. She is evaluating. A coach watches players in practice as he makes out his starting line-up. He is evaluating. The process of evaluation goes on almost constantly and takes numerous forms.

We not only evaluate physical things that can be counted, weighed, or measured, but we often evaluate mental activities. Every pop quiz or final examination is a form of evaluation for the student—and the teacher. As Christians we must also be involved in various types of spiritual evaluations. Paul wrote, "A man ought to examine himself before he eats of the bread and drinks of the cup."[1] John had in mind another kind of evaluation when he wrote, "Dear friends, do not believe every spirit, but test the spirits to see whether they are from God, because many false prophets have gone out into the world."[2]

Why Evaluate?

To Determine Whether Goals Have Been Reached

An effective Christian education program must have goals or objectives. These goals may be very general or quite detailed. They may be short-term or long-term. They may deal with such readily measurable items as attendance or offerings, or with the spiritual growth of students, something much more difficult to measure. But goals serve little real purpose if no provisions are made to see whether they are being met.

Unless definite goals have been established, we have no basis for evaluating whether progress has been made. For this reason, goals ought to be as specific as possible and in terms that can be readily measured wherever possible.

To Help Establish New Goals

Goals are like mileposts along a road. They are to be reached and then left behind as new goals are met. Suppose an attendance goal is set for the Sunday school. When that goal is met, a new goal must be set. But suppose the goal is not reached, and attendance falls substantially below the goal. This may indicate that the goal was unrealistically high, and should be revised downward. Whether the new goal is higher or lower, it has been changed because of a process of evaluation.

To Help Determine Personnel Efficiency

Neither the Sunday school nor any other educational program of the church is stronger than its leaders. The best leaders available should be involved in every program. To make sure that the best leaders are involved, we must evaluate them and the alternative leaders at hand.

The most capable people we have need to be busy and working in the Christian education program. Therefore, we evaluate a person's capabilities before we assign him a job. But the evaluation process continues as he continues in that job.

To Discover Weaknesses

The most obvious use of evaluation is to determine weaknesses. A failure to reach a goal is apparent to everyone, but it is important also to know why the failure occurred. Suppose that we had set an attendance goal for a certain Sunday, but fell short of reaching the goal. If there had been a ten-inch snowfall on the previous night, we could readily understand the poor attendance. But suppose the weather was excellent and there were no other conflicts that might interfere with attendance. Then we would need to probe deeper to find the reason for the failure to reach the goal. Once we were able to isolate the reason for the failure, we could take appropriate action to avoid similar failures in the future.

To Discover Strengths

Although we are inclined to think mainly of the negative aspects of evaluation, the positive aspects are just as important. When a program is successful, we need to be made aware of that fact. We need to know why the program succeeded so that we can use the ideas to help make future programs successful. The reasons why a program succeeded may not always be obvious, so we may have to spend some effort finding them.

To Stimulate Growth and Learning

Most of us work better when we know what we are working for. We also work better when we know how well we are doing in reaching our objectives. A lagging student, for instance, might be motivated to work harder by a failing grade on a test. The evaluation gave him a basis for understanding what the teacher expected of him and how well he measured up to those expectations. But in the same way a high grade can lead a student to work harder to maintain the high average. Similarly, when one evaluates his prayer life or his stewardship, he might be stimulated to work to improve them.

How to Evaluate

Once we have established reasons for evaluating our Christian education programs, we need to establish definite methods of carrying out the process. We must have definite methods of gaining the facts we need, and we must have ways of determining what these facts mean.

Two Kinds of Evaluation

Our approach can be confined to two different kinds of

evaluation: process and results. In the first of these, we are concerned about how the established goal is reached. For example, we may observe how a teacher teaches his lesson. How does he introduce the lesson? How does he get his students into the Scripture? How does he lead the students to apply the Scripture to their lives? How does he get student involvement in the teaching-learning process? How does he close the lesson?

All of these questions deal with process. We are concerned about the process or method in order to find ways of doing the job better. If the job is being done well, we want to be able to share good ideas with others.

We are interested in the process, but we are also interested in the end results of that process. No matter how effective a song leader seems to be, if he does not lead people into worshipful praise of God through his song leading, then his efforts leave something to be desired. A teacher may be an exciting storyteller or be adept at using audiovisuals, but if the lives of his students are not changed, then something is wrong.

We must also, then, measure for results in the lives of those we serve. Is attendance and participation in various church programs increasing? If so, this usually tells us that the people's interest and commitment is growing. Is there greater concern about the missions and benevolent activities of the church? If so, this may indicate that our teaching is taking root in the lives of the members. In this kind of evaluation, we are measuring results.

Use Measurable Goals

If evaluation is to be meaningful, we must begin with goals that establish a basis for comparison. Statistical goals (attendance figures, offerings, number of baptisms) can be easily measured as long as accurate records are kept. Each organization within the church should have someone designated to keep records. Records should be checked regularly for accuracy. Standard forms are helpful for maintaining these records in the same form from year to year even though different persons keep them. Copies of these records should be kept on file in the office of the director of Christian education or the person who is responsible for the church's educational program.

Not all the important goals in Christian education can be reduced to statistics. Cognitive learning, that is, learning that deals with the acquisition of factual information, can be measured by tests. But affective learning, the kind of learning that deals with the change of attitudes and emotions, cannot be as easily measured. About the best we can do is to measure the change in people's outward behavior or changes in the pupil's report of his attitudes. We can set up goals that will measure this change in behavior. Such goals will then let us evaluate certain phases of our education program.

Personnel Feedback

One helpful way of evaluating a Christian education program is to determine how the teachers and leaders involved in it feel about it. Can they see specific evidence that students are involved and learning? Are they satisfied with their own efforts? Can they find ways to improve their teaching? Are there adequate supplies and equipment to do the job?

The answers to such questions as these can be helpful, not only to the teachers or leaders involved, but also to those who plan and administer the programs. These evaluations, which ought to be conducted regularly, can be used in many ways to improve the total work of the church. (The evaluation questionnaire included at the close of this chapter will help in these evaluations.)

Student Feedback

The students themselves are in a better position than anyone to know whether their spiritual and educational needs are being met. Student feedback can be observed in several different ways. Attendance and attitudes in class are means commonly used. Interviews or questionnaires can also provide helpful information.

Suppose that the attendance in the junior girls' class has suffered a steady decline during the past several months. The matter is discussed with the teacher, who began teaching the class a year ago. She indicates that there seems to be a lack of interest on the part of the students and an increase in discipline problems (these two trends usually go together). Then we interview some of the students. They indicate a lack of interest in the lessons, confirming the teacher's report on the situation. Then one of the students indicates that the teacher always reads the lesson, there is little discussion, and little application of the lesson to life.

This kind of evaluation helps us to pinpoint the source of the problem. Once we know that the problem lies in the lesson presentation, we may now suggest tactfully some ways in which the teacher can make her lessons more interesting.

What to Evaluate

Since the purpose of evaluation is to find ways to improve the total education program of the church, we need to evaluate the entire program. But this is often an overwhelming undertaking, if we try to do it all at once. The various aspects of the program should be evaluated one by one over a period of time. Below are listed some of the areas that may be profitably evaluated. Since some of these areas are discussed in other chapters or covered by the survey form at the close of this chapter, this listing does not go into great detail.

Goals

An effective program for Christian education within the local church will have general, overall goals and more specific goals for each area. These goals ought to be reexamined at least once a year (more often in many situations). In almost every congregation, some changing or restatement of objectives will be necessary. Regular evaluation of goals will prevent their becoming out-of-date or impractical.

Programs

Separate programs within the total program need to be evaluated frequently. For example, vacation Bible school should be evaluated as soon as it has been concluded while information and attitudes are still fresh in the minds of the participants. A teacher training class should be evaluated not only when it is concluded, but also several weeks or months later to determine its long-range effectiveness.

Organizations

Organizations within the church should be subject to regular evaluation. Are they performing a useful function? Can they be made more effective? Are they duplicating activities that can be more efficiently carried out by other organizations? Even the most elaborate organizational charts and detailed job descriptions for all positions within the educational program can soon become useless without frequent evaluation and updating.

Personnel

Persons serving within the various programs are always being evaluated, at least informally, by their peers and their students. Because so much of this evaluation is informal, it is not useful for improvement. But formal evaluation of teachers and leaders is often feared and resented, and so it must be done tactfully.

Facilities

Since the available physical facilities play a great part in shaping and limiting the church's educational program, facilities and equipment should be evaluated at regular intervals. Equipment can be updated or kept in good repair and facilities can be remodeled and used more efficiently.

Records

All church records, especially those dealing with educational work, should be checked frequently to keep them up to date and accurate. For purposes of evaluation it is helpful to keep them available in one central location and on standard forms.

Curriculum

In its broadest sense, curriculum concerns all the activities within the church that help the church reach its educational objectives. Certainly this is a subject for constant evaluation. Sometimes people restrict the use of curriculum to printed lesson material. Such materials should be kept under close scrutiny to ensure their doctrinal fidelity, their educational soundness, their usefulness to the teachers working with them, their attractiveness to the students, and their appropriateness to the church's educational objectives.

Students

In the final analysis, nothing is more important than what happens to the student in the educational program. Unless there is clear evidence of Christian growth, with each person becoming more Christlike in his attitudes and behavior, then the program has fallen short of its primary objective.

Testing for cognitive learning is relatively simple and should be done more frequently than it is. Admittedly, tests have a negative connotation for many people, but with the proper approach testing can be done regularly in the Sunday school and similar formal learning situations. Testing for spiritual growth is far more difficult, but it should be done if we are to help people meet their needs.

When to Evaluate

Many churches do not take evaluation seriously until they are faced with a serious problem. Then hastily and often with less than happy results, leaders try to find out what went wrong. Assuredly, evaluation is necessary in a crisis situation, but frequent and regular evaluations can often head off problems before they become real crises.

Methods of systematic evaluation should be set up within the congregation. Carried out in this way, evaluations do not seem nearly so threatening to the persons involved. In many aspects of the program, annual evaluations are adequate. Others may require quarterly or monthly attention. Teachers should be encouraged to evaluate their lessons each week, at least for their own benefit.

Summary

When we talk about evaluation, it may seem idealistic, impractical, or unimportant in the typical congregation. But nothing could be further from the truth. As we have already noted, some types of evaluation—at least informally—are always taking place. Our main concern, then, becomes one of going about the process in a more systematic and efficient manner. The forms that have been included with this chapter may help teachers and leaders do that.

Project

Evaluate the Christian education program of a local congregation, using the evaluation form beginning on the next page (or any appropriate parts of it).

Evaluation Questionnaire

A. Objectives

1. Does the church have objectives for its total program?
   □ Yes □ No
2. Are these written down and readily available? □ Yes □ No
3. By whom were these objectives designed? (Check more than one if appropriate.)
   - □ Minister
   - □ Church board or other governing body
   - □ Committee chairmen
   - □ Members of the congregation
4. Does the church have objectives for its educational program?
   □ Yes □ No
5. Are these written down and readily available? □ Yes □ No
6. By whom were these objectives designed? (Check more than one if appropriate.)
   - □ Minister
   - □ Church board or other governing body
   - □ Committee chairmen
   - □ Sunday-school superintendent
   - □ Teachers
   - □ Students
7. Have objectives been established for each department?
   □ Yes □ No
   For each class? □ Yes □ No
8. When were these objectives last evaluated and revised?
   □ Within the last year □ The last five years □ Never

B. Organization and Administration

1. Does the Sunday school have a superintendent? □ Yes □ No
2. Does each department have a superintendent? □ Yes □ No
3. How many departments are there in the Sunday school? _____
4. How many classes? _____
5. How many teachers? _____
   Assistant teachers or helpers? _____
6. Do you have regular meetings of the teachers? □ Yes □ No
   How frequently do they meet?
   □ Annually □ Quarterly □ Monthly
7. Does the church have a regular leadership training program?
   □ Yes □ No
8. In addition to the Sunday school, what other regular agencies does the church use in its educational program?
   - □ Sunday evening classes
   - □ Youth meetings
   - □ Children's church or extended Sunday school sessions
   - □ Mid-week classes
   - □ Vacation Bible school
   - □ Camp
   - □ Retreats
   - □ Kindergarten
   - □ Week-day classes
   - □ Other

C. Records
1. Are attendance records kept for various church activities?
   □ Worship   □ Mid-week service
   □ Sunday school   □ Other
   □ Sunday evening service
2. Are these records kept in such a way that comparisons can easily be
   made with last year's figures?   □ Yes □ No
   Figures from five years ago?   □ Yes □ No
3. Are these records kept in a convenient location?   □ Yes □ No
4. Are these records regularly used to evaluate the progress of the
   church's educational program?   □ Yes □ No
5. Are more or less detailed records kept on individual students?
                                                           □ Yes □ No

D. Facilities and Equipment
1. Do the educational facilities allow for easy departmentaliza-
   tion of the Sunday school?   □ Yes □ No
2. Are classrooms assigned in such a way as to allow for easy movement of students?   □ Yes □ No
3. How many square feet of floor space per student are provided in
   each department?
   Nursery_____   Middler_____   Senior High_____
   Beginner_____   Junior_____   Adult_____
   Primary_____   Junior High_____
4. Indicate which of the following are located in classrooms:
   □ Chalkboards   □ Pictures
   □ Bulletin boards   □ Maps and charts
5. Indicate which of the following are available to teachers:
   □ Flannelboards   □ Filmstrip projectors
   □ Flannelboard materials   □ Overhead projectors
   □ Pictures   □ Overhead transparencies
   □ Slide projectors

E. Curriculum
1. Has the church attempted to correlate all of its learning activities in
   relation to one another and to its educational objectives?
                                                           □ Yes □ No
2. Does the curriculum provide for both student needs and student
   learning readiness?   □ Yes □ No
3. Who selects the printed curriculum materials?
   □ Minister   □ Individual teachers
   □ Superintendent   □ Other persons
   □ Committee
4. Do the curriculum materials present the Scriptures as the infallible,
   divinely inspired Word of God?   □ Yes □ No
5. Are the materials true to the Bible in terms of emphasis?
                                                           □ Yes □ No

6. Are the materials attractive and up-to-date in appearance?
☐ Yes ☐ No

7. Do the materials encourage students to apply the Bible to life situations? ☐ Yes ☐ No

8. Do the materials provide sufficient helps for the teachers?
☐ Yes ☐ No

9. Do the materials give a strong emphasis to evangelism?
☐ Yes ☐ No

10. Are the materials accurately graded to meet the needs of students at each age level? ☐ Yes ☐ No

Selected Bibliography

Byrne, H.W. *Christian Education for the Local Church.* Grand Rapids, Michigan: Zondervan, 1963.

Bower, Robert K. *Administering Christian Education.* Grand Rapids, Michigan: Eerdmans, 1964.

Edge, Findley B. *Teaching for Results.* Nashville: Broadman Press, 1956.

Leavitt, Guy P. (revised by Eleanor Daniel). *Teach With Success.* Cincinnati: Standard Publishing, 1978.

LeBar, Lois E. *Education That Is Christian.* Westwood, New Jersey: Revell, 1958.

Towns, Elmer. *The Successful Sunday School and Teachers Guidebook.* Carol Stream, Illinois: Creation House, 1976.

---

[1] 1 Corinthians 11:28
[2] 1 John 4:1

20

The Minister and Christian Education

As you read, think about these questions:
—What qualities and commitments should the minister have?
—What qualities should the minister have as an educator?
—What qualities should the minister have as an administrator?

The modern minister must be many things. He is expected to be a preacher, pastor, evangelist, counselor, administrator, teacher, and family man. The minister is also expected to have time to work at, if not excel in, all these pursuits.

Faced with impossible demands on his time and talents, the wise minister seeks to assign priorities to the tasks he is expected to do. This gives him a logical basis for allotting differing amounts of time for his duties. When he establishes job priorities, a minister must look to the needs of the situation rather than his own preferences. He must resist the temptation to allot a disproportionate amount of time to the activities that he enjoys the most, or at which he is most skilled.

The minister's academic preparation for his job rightfully emphasizes exegetical and language preparation. But practical skills—especially administrative and teaching skills—are not always developed, even though he will be expected to provide significant leadership in both areas.

A study conducted by the Accrediting Association of Bible Colleges indicated that ninety-six percent of the ministers responding would include more Christian education courses in their academic programs if they were preparing for the ministry again.

In most congregations the minister is the key to the educational program. Persons preparing for the ministry will have many opportunities in the area of Christian education. As part of their preparation for the preaching ministry, they should consider taking other courses in Christian education or to do further studying on their own.

The Minister as a Person

Any discussion of the minister and Christian education must begin with his own person. Usually a person can separate his personal life from his professional life, but the minister cannot. Every aspect of his work is influenced by the kind of person he is.

He must be a committed Christian. Because the temptations to pride and to routine professionalism are constant, every person preparing himself for the ministry needs to be reminded that his every activity stems from this commitment. He will encounter subtle pressures to sacrifice integrity to expediency, to compromise convictions, to settle for the good rather than insisting upon the best. The best antidote for these temptations is a frequent reminder of whose we are and whom we serve.

He must be a student of the Bible. Church members expect their minister to be an expert in the Scriptures. A Bible college or even a graduate seminary education can do little more than introduce a person to the Scriptures and give him a few tools that will help him do independent study. The Holy Word will yield its sweetest fruits only to those who engage in regular study over many years. If a primary task of the minister is to share these sweets with his people, he must be prepared to study diligently.

Very early in his ministry, a wise minister will establish study routines that bring him into an in-depth relationship with God's Word. He will set aside a special time each day or each week for Bible study, according to some systematic plan. One will want to occasionally follow a book-by-book study plan. At other times, topical studies may prove helpful. But almost any planned study is better than a hit-or-miss approach.

A minister will study the Scriptures for the purpose of sermon preparation. He will also study the Word to prepare to teach classes to the Sunday school, Sunday evening or mid-week studies, or various special classes. But while the minister must study the Word in order to share it with others, he must also allow it to speak to him and to his personal needs. To neglect this devotional study of Scripture is to come to look upon it as little more than a professional tool.

He should be committed to sound doctrine. One who is a student of God's Word will be concerned about sound doctrine, because in our day so many forces are at work to erode our doctrinal foundation. Basic Christian doctrines are under attack both from within and without the church. An even more serious danger may be posed by the subtle forces that would have us not repudiate, but compromise these crucial doctrines. The minister must resist the temptation to allow his feelings, rather than the Scriptures, to become the final authority in matters of doctrine. If the minister is to play his proper role in the educational program of the church, he must be a guardian and teacher of sound doctrine.

He should be a man of prayer. Like the Apostle Paul, he must learn to "pray without ceasing." And learn he must, for one does not build an effective prayer life just by wishing for it or talking about it. He must pray about his own personal needs, the needs of the congregation, and the needs of the community and the world.

Every program of the church ought to be planned in prayer, developed in prayer, and consummated in prayer. There is no way to measure the power that prayer can impart to a church program. Yet as important as prayer is, it must not become a convenient way to avoid the careful planning and hard work that successful church programming requires.

He should be a growing learner. The minister must be a student of the Scriptures, but he must also be a student of history, literature, sociology, psychology, science, politics, and current events. Guided by the Scriptures, he must build a Christian philosophy of life that allows him to give proper evaluation to all these areas of knowledge and to use them in his ministry to his people. Although his own interests and aptitudes will lead him to emphasize some areas more than others, yet no area of knowledge is beyond his proper concern. Since all truth is

God's truth, every particle of truth in the universe is important to him and may be useful as he attempts to meet the needs of his people. In no profession is a well-rounded education more important than in the ministry. It is a part of becoming "all things to all men." And to achieve this well-rounded education, a minister must be a lifelong student, not only of books, but of life.

He must love people. No man can effectively serve his people if he does not love them. He may perform many of the duties associated with his office, yet this service alone will never exude the warmth and enthusiasm that comes from a service of love. Such an attitude of love is nowhere more necessary than in the minister's relationship to his educational program and the people involved in it. It takes patience and understanding for one to lead others to grow in faith and knowledge. Love allows one to develop this patience and understanding.

He must understand and appreciate his role in Christian education. The minister must understand that he is the key to the success of the congregation's educational program. His attitude toward that program will go a long way toward determining whether it will fail or succeed. He needs to realize that his enthusiastic support for Christian education can become contagious, infecting the whole congregation.

The minister also needs to understand that a great deal of the support for his ministry will be generated by the educational program. A congregation that has been nurtured on God's Word will respond favorably when the Word is proclaimed from the pulpit. It will rise to meet the challenge of evangelism, stewardship, and service.

The Minister as an Educator

In many congregations the minister will be more knowledgeable about Christian education than any other member. In such situations he must exercise considerable leadership in Christian education. In other congregations, many competent educational leaders are available. In these congregations, the minister's leadership need not be so prominent. But regardless of the specific role he is required to fulfill, in every congregation the minister needs to be an educator.

He must have a sound philosophy of Christian education. To be effective, a Christian education program must be built upon a sound philosophy of education. Every person involved in Christian education has a philosophy of education that provides the basis for the decisions that he makes. Such a philosophy may be sophisticated and detailed, or rather simplistic and disorganized, or perhaps not even articulated.

The minister should take the lead in establishing a philosophy of Christian education that is grounded in Scriptures and meets the needs of the congregation. He would be wise to organize and write out his philosophy of education. In this way he can more readily share it with others, refine it, or improve it.

He should understand the importance of educational objectives. The minister needs to be involved with the leaders of the congregation as they develop the overall objectives for the congregation. Specific educational objectives should also be established by every agency, department, and Sunday-school class in the church.

He should have some understanding of educational psychology. It is hardly fair to expect the minister to be an expert, but he must understand some of the basic elements of psychology if he is to provide leadership for his congregation. He should know something about age level characteristics. He should understand how learners are motivated and the processes by which they learn.

An alert minister will soon find that the knowledge of educational psychology needed for the church's educational program will also be useful in other phases of his ministry. The same principles are as applicable to preaching as to teaching, for example.

He should have some understanding of teaching methods. Probably more Christian education programs fail in local churches because of poor and monotonous teaching methods than for any other reason. One reason teachers fail to use better teaching methods is the age-old problem of lethargy. Teachers have fallen into the habit of teaching in a certain manner, and they stubbornly resist all suggestions for change. Most teachers tend to teach the way that they were taught, thus perpetuating poor teaching methods. Further, teachers often feel a sense of security in using certain teaching methods. The lecture method often provides such a feeling of security. The teacher can present his position without being challenged by class members as he might be were he to use a discussion method that encourages feedback from students.

The minister may be qualified to conduct training courses for his teachers. If not, he should be concerned enough to see that teacher training courses are provided for them. But more important than teacher training classes is the example the minister sets. Some ministers prefer not to be tied down to teaching a Sunday-school class regularly. Others may consider this a very important way to become close to some of their members. This is a matter for each minister to decide on the basis of his own interests and the needs of the congregation. He will, however, almost certainly teach some classes, such as a class for new members or one for church officers. If he knows and uses a variety of good teaching methods, he can create a persuasive model for others to follow. In the long run, a good model is likely to be a far more effective method in improving teaching than is any number of training classes.

He must be a counselor. Teachers and leaders in the church's educational program are certain to have problems even under the best of circumstances. They need someone to whom they can go for help and encouragement. If a minister is knowledgeable about Christian education, he is the logical person to provide such counseling.

The minister is often in a position to serve as a resource person for teachers. Most members of a church will look to the minister as the best Bible student and theologian in the congregation. But they will also turn to him for information about curriculum materials, supplies, equipment, and the newest trends in Christian education.

The Minister as an Administrator

In a congregation that has a minister of education, the minister may not be involved directly in the administration of the education program. But most congregations do not have a minister of education, and the minister must carry out many of the administrative duties that would ordinarily fall to the minister of education.

He must be an organizer and planner. Even the smallest congregation must be organized if its educational program is to be effective. The minister is usually best qualified to provide the leadership necessary for good organization. He is also in the best position to see the church program as a whole and to understand how education fits into it.

A good organizer first evaluates the resources of the congregation in terms of its objectives. He evaluates the persons available to work, and employs the agencies best suited to help the church achieve its objectives.

The minister also needs to be a good planner. He must work with the congregation to formulate long-range plans for achieving the church's educational objectives. He must also develop short-term plans to meet needs that arise each week and each month. Plans and coming events should be recorded on a master calendar. The church office is usually the best place to maintain a master calendar for all church activities.

He must work with others. One mistake that many ministers make is to take too many responsibilities upon themselves. They feel that because they are better qualified than most of the members, they must do the work. But the whole membership needs to be involved, not just to relieve the minister of many jobs, but that they too may learn and grow through experience.

An important task of the minister is to recruit and train leaders. Once leaders have been trained, the minister must be willing to delegate responsibilities to them.

The minister must learn to work effectively with others in the church. He must not see himself as a boss whose chief job is to give orders to others. The leaders with whom he works are volunteers, with whom coercion does not work. He should consider himself a member of a team on which each member has different, yet significant, responsibilities. He will frequently have to work with or through a board or committee of Christian education. While ordinarily he should not serve as chairman of this committee, he should be an *ex-officio* member of it and all other committees involved in education. If the minister does not learn to work harmoniously with others in the church's educational program, then other phases of his work will be hampered.

He must coordinate the educational program. Unless all educational agencies within the church are coordinated, serious overlapping or omissions may result. Since the minister is in the best position to see the church's total program, he is the best qualified member of the congregation to coordinate all aspects of it.

Some coordination is done in the organizing and planning activities previously mentioned. The choice of curriculum materials is another way that the program may be coordinated.

Unfortunately, in some churches each teacher is free to select his or her own materials. Since different publishers may have different philosophies of education and different theological stances, such a cafeteria approach to the selection of curriculum materials can lead to confusion and even disaster. The minister should provide wise leadership in helping select and use curriculum materials.

Coordination is also important in the utilization of facilities. By careful planning a church can learn to make the best possible use of the facilities it has. Occasionally a church may have to alter its programs to fit its facilities. When new facilities are planned or older facilities remodeled, the minister should be involved in developing and coordinating the plans and carrying them out.

He must promote the educational program. A minister who understands the importance of Christian education to his ministry will be an enthusiastic promoter of all the church's educational activities. He must regularly explain these activities to the congregation, since many members will not understand them nor appreciate their value.

This support for education must be made from the pulpit, in the church bulletin and church paper, in committee meetings, and in private conversations. The minister should use every opportunity to praise those who work in educational programs. He should also seek for ways to show how Christian education has influenced the lives of the church members.

Summary

The specific ways that a minister is involved in the educational work of his church will vary depending upon his own talents and the needs of the congregation. But he must be involved, for every phase of his ministry will be vitally affected by what happens in the educational program. Evangelism, stewardship, pulpit work, counseling, and pastoral work are all influenced by how effectively the Word is learned by the members of the congregation.

Project

Interview a minister and find out how he is involved in Christian education in the congregation where he ministers.

Selected Bibliography

Bower, Robert K. *Administering Christian Education*. Grand Rapids, Michigan: Eerdmans, 1964.

Gangel, Kenneth O. *Leadership for Church Education*. Chicago: Moody Press, 1970.

LeBar, Lois E. *Focus on People in Church Education*. Old Tappan, New Jersey: Revell, 1968.

Lentz, Richard, Paul H. Vieth, and Ray L. Henthorne. *Our Teaching Ministry*. St. Louis: Christian Board of Publication, 1967.

Miller, Randolph Crump. *Christian Nurture and the Church*. New York: Charles Scribner's Sons, 1961.

Person, Peter P. *The Minister in Christian Education*. Grand Rapids, Michigan: Baker, 1960.

Towns, Elmer. *The Successful Sunday School and Teachers Guidebook*. Carol Stream, Illinois: Creation House, 1976.

CHAPTER

21

The Minister of Christian Education

by W. Edward Fine

As you read, think about these questions:
—What qualifications should the minister of Christian education have?
—What are the responsibilities of the minister of Christian education?
—What are the relationships of the minister of Christian education with the paid staff, church officers, and volunteer workers?
—What are some of the possible sources of stress in the life of the minister of Christian education?

Realizing the importance of Christian education, churches in increasing numbers are calling persons especially trained to provide leadership for the educational program of the local church.

The title "Minister of Education" is often reserved for those who have been ordained and work in the field of Christian education. The title "Director of Christian Education" is frequently given to those men and women who are not ordained for the ministry. Though not ordained, such a person should still be qualified for the position by education and, if possible, by practical experience. The following information may be used as guidelines for both ministers and directors of Christian education.

His Qualifications

The apostle Paul's sense of a call from God gave him great commitment, perseverance, and determination. He wrote to the Corinthians that he was "called to be an apostle of Christ Jesus by the will of God."[1] Today's educational leader should also be aware of his call to ministry.

Commitment

The primary qualification of a minister of Christian education must be a mature and growing commitment to God and Jesus Christ. God calls a minister of education to know God, so that he "may be filled to the measure of all the fullness of God,"[2] to become "mature, attaining to the whole measure of the fullness of Christ."[3] The minister of education must grow more like Christ and help others to do so by his example.

Professional Training

The professional training of the minister of education should include work in education and church administration. A good background in Bible and theology is basic, since this is what he will teach others. A thorough knowledge of educational philosophy, psychology, and principles of teaching is also essential.

The minister of education must continue to grow and develop through refresher courses, seminars, conferences, reading, observation, and other similar experiences. The educational leader who continues to grow professionally not only equips himself for more effective service, but also sets an example for those who work with him.

Personal Qualifications

A college degree does not mean that a minister of education is automatically capable of leading a local church. Evaluation of his qualifications should also be made on the basis of his Christian education, professional training and experience, personal qualities, and past performance as a leader. Desirable qualities (not necessarily in order of importance) include:

Spirituality	Love for people
Unselfishness	Neat and clean appearance
Humility	Studiousness

Self-control   Foresight
Emotional maturity   Leadership ability
Patience   Special talents
Obedience   Sincerity
Cooperativeness   Attractive personality
Growth in grace   Sense of honor
Good health   Diligence
                                Common sense

The minister of education should be able to lead others. He should not only know where he is going and how to get there, but he must also be able to influence others to cooperate with him. Flexibility on the part of a leader is absolutely essential in meeting the changing demands of a congregation. A leader who can adjust his leadership approach when the situation changes is more effective than one who functions the same way in every situation.

His Responsibilities

The church is not an organization that has an educational program; it *is* an educational program. Of all the religions of the world, Christianity is unique in placing its hope on teaching and nurture of believers.

Developing an Educational Program

The minister of education is primarily responsible for the development and success of the church's educational program—which is primarily concerned with developing people. The minister of education is expected to lead the church to:

1. Develop a philosophy of Christian education.
2. Build and implement a curriculum to meet the needs of the church.
3. Evaluate the educational program.
4. Recruit and train leaders.

An effective minister of education will lead the church to determine appropriate educational objectives, and then plan to meet them. Two types of planning are necessary. The first is short-term planning, which takes place on a week-to-week basis. Second is long-term planning, which may cover a period from one to five years. The long-range plans provide the framework for short-term planning.

Once the church has determined its educational objectives, the minister of education will lead church members to develop abilities that will assure the achievement of these objectives. Ordinarily he should not teach a Sunday-school class or direct a youth group himself. His primary responsibility is to be a teacher of teachers and a leader of leaders. If the entire church program is to profit, he must be free to observe and evaluate the program in action in order to correct weaknesses.

His success at achieving the church's educational objectives depends largely on his ability to build a cohesive team of workers. He must recognize that he is not primarily attempting to motivate individuals, but to build work teams that are committed to the attainment of the church's objectives. He must involve people in problem solving and decision making.

Rather than attacking the apparent weaknesses of the church program, the minister of education should build on the already existing strengths of the church. People will change, but slowly. It is best not to rush people into accepting a new concept, unless the change is an emergency measure. Under these circumstances, he should get as much support as possible for his proposed change, and monitor the change closely to be sure of its effectiveness.

The minister of education serves as an education resource expert and as advisor for the entire church program. Part of his duties involve not only the workers in the program, but also all the other resources available to the church. He will also help to lead the church to become closer in fellowship with one another. In addition, he will help the church determine what ministries can be developed to meet the unique needs of the community served by the church.

The minister of education needs to be cautious in his allocation of time and duties. Because of his background, experience, and abilities, he might most enjoy the part of his ministry that relates to administration. Some ministers of education spend so much time in administration that they neglect those areas of ministry concerned with outreach, teaching, and counseling. It is easy to become sheltered behind the desk!

Evaluating Educational Programs

The minister of Christian education must be constantly alert to changing trends in his field. New forms of Christian education continue to emerge in our day, as they have from the past.

For example, there is an increasing focus upon relationships. In a society that is becoming more and more impersonal, people have a desperate hunger to relate to one another. The purpose of relational Bible study is to deal with the Scriptures on a highly personal level rather than on an abstract verbal level. Another current interest stresses educating the affective domain (attitudes and emotions). Christian educators have had a tendency to treat learning as an exclusively cognitive process. A third new emphasis in education is active pupil involvement in learning. Much significant learning can be acquired through participation. Christian educators view involvement learning as preparation for daily engagement with the traumas, struggles, and sufferings experienced in this world. This is accomplished through discovering how the Bible can be applied to the learner's lifestyle. Yet another trend is the growing use of modern technology to develop various types of programmed instruction. This idea has given rise to the concept of specification of educational objectives and increased emphasis on the evaluation of learning.

As they become available, the minister of Christian education must study and evaluate new techniques and materials in the light of Scripture. He must be able to distinguish fads from effective new methods, adapt these methods to his own programs, and persuade and train workers to use these new ideas and equipment.

Knowledge of Available Materials

The minister of education must lead the church in an awareness of the available educational and curriculum materials. The minister of education needs to be able to lead church program leaders in evaluating, selecting, adapting, and producing curriculum materials appropriate for use in all aspects of the church's total educational program.

The minister of education should constantly be aware of the needs of his teachers and learners. Abraham Maslow identified a hierarchy of needs ranging from physiological needs, safety and security, belonging and acceptance, and self-esteem, to the highest need, self-actualization or fulfillment of one's potential. The behavior of an individual at any particular moment is usually determined by his strongest need at that moment. A study and application of these principles by leaders can help increase the effectiveness of one's leadership.

Selecting, Enlisting, and Training Workers

The church's educational program will succeed only to the extent that it has dedicated, trained workers led by a dedicated, trained leader.

One of the greatest challenges to the minister of education is the selection, enlistment, and training of workers. He should keep a list of potential leaders and teachers who could, if trained and/or challenged, fill vacancies. With the help and direction of God, all such positions can be filled. The minister of education must also provide pre-service and in-service education for his volunteer teachers and workers. Likewise, he must promote and direct regular teachers' planning sessions.

Encouraging Use of Facilities and Equipment

The environment in which teachers instruct can be either an asset or a liability. The minister of education is responsible to see that teachers use the facilities and equipment most advantageously. He will seek ways to improve the educational facilities while making the best use of those that he has.

The size of the classroom and the equipment needed depends on the age level and number of learners. A children's classroom should simulate their various everyday surroundings, while the adult classroom should provide study aids and additional resource materials for Bible study and life application.

Keeping Records

The Sunday school that knows its past has a future. Trends in attendance reveal a great deal about the educational program of a church, but such evaluations can be made only when accurate records are kept. Records can indicate the spiritual temperature of the Sunday school or class. Through records he knows who was present and who was absent, who were visitors, out-of-towners, or prospects.

Planning for Visitation

Records must be reinforced with a good visitation program of personal visits, phone calls, and post cards. People come when callers go. Like the servants in Jesus' parable, the minister should "Go out to the roads and country lanes and make them come in, so that my house will be full."[4]

His Interpersonal Relationships

Emphasis has been placed on the importance of the minister of education's professonal competence and his spiritual commitment. Yet it is possible for him to be competent and committed and still fail because he cannot relate to other people. For this reason, building interpersonal relationships must rank high in the concern and prayers of the minister of education.

With the Paid Staff

Much of the minister of education's work will be done behind the scenes; few will notice or give him the credit for what he does. He must be able to remain in the background while others enjoy the limelight, and so he must be constantly alert to the temptation of jealousy. He will respect the authority of his superiors, but at the same time he will not compromise his convictions just to maintain the appearance of harmony that does not really exist. In an aggressive program, disagreements among staff members may develop, yet even these tensions that occur can become creative opportunities for Christian growth. Loyalty to co-workers is the key.

With Church Officers

The minister of education must maintain open and effective lines of communication with the elected representatives of the congregation: the church board, the board of Christian education, and the Sunday-school council. He must work with the finance committee of the church to provide adequate resources for curriculum materials, equipment, supplies, and leadership development.

The minister of education should also involve department leaders and appropriate staff members in the resolution of philosophical, procedural, and scheduling problems. It is his task to see that there is coordination and balance among the various educational programs of the church.

With the Volunteer Staff

Working with the volunteer staff from the congregation is a must for the success of the minister of education. The average volunteer has a greater desire to be put to use than church leaders often realize. These volunteers require a greater amount of help and training than most church leaders believe. It is in the role of equipping others for service that many ministers of education find their greatest satisfaction. Continuing emphasis must be given to this training process.

Coping With Stressful Situations

Even under the best of circumstances, stresses are likely to develop in the life of the minister of education. Four general areas of stress confront the minister of education: career, job responsibility, family, and personal.

The minister of education's career seems particularly susceptible to stress during the first five years in his work. Much stress occurs because he has an inadequate self-image. Research shows that ministers of education want a professional self-image that reflects a strong "people-developing" ministry. Characteristics deemed most important are as follows: ability to get along with others, spiritual maturity, love for people, and a sense of divine call.

Conflicts with the senior minister are the source of considerable stress. A detailed job description accepted by both the minister of education and the congregation can eliminate many later misunderstandings. Job responsibilities should be clearly presented to the minister of education before he accepts a call to a church.

In the area of family, physical illness of a family member causes the highest degrees of stress. However, this type of stress is much less severe than job stress. In the area of personal stress, financial difficulties were the cause of stress most frequently cited by the research.

Vagueness and confusion still exist concerning who the minister of education *is* and *what is expected* of him. This lack of clarity hinders ministers of education from achieving their maximum effectiveness, it prevents churches from making full use of the potential services of the minister of education, and it hinders colleges and seminaries in adequately preparing persons to serve in the profession. These conditions tend to result in stress on the minister of education.

The most frequent particular coping response, in the survey, was to change churches. This response may free an individual from a stressful situation temporarily, but eventually he must deal with the source of stress and/or himself. His actions probably indicate that the minister of education either does not have the skills to manage stress constructively or that he lacks the motivation to attain such skills.

Most ministers of education surveyed met the stress with individual efforts to master the situation. The minister of education's spouse was listed in the survey as the one person most likely to be a source of support during stressful times.

Summary

The "Minister of Education" or "Director of Christian Education" is a man or woman called by a local congregation to lead and supervise its educational program. He is an individual called to a specific form of ministry, requiring adequate preparation for him to do the job. His responsibilities are to plan programs, recruit and equip workers, and coordinate the work of teaching in the local church. He is indeed a key figure in his congregation.

Project

Interview a director of Christian education. How does his work compare to what is described in this chapter?

Selected Bibliography

Byrne, Herbert W. *Christian Education for the Local Church*. Grand Rapids, Michigan: Zondervan, 1963.

Drucker, Peter. *The Effective Executive*. New York: Harper & Row, 1966.

Ezell, Mancel and Suzanne. *Being Creative*. Nashville: Broadman, 1974.

Gangel, Kenneth O. *Competent to Lead*. Chicago: Moody Press, 1974.

_____. *Leadership for Church Education*. Chicago: Moody Press, 1970.

_____. *The Effective Sunday School Superintendent*. Victor, 1975.

Getz, Gene A. *Sharpening the Focus of the Church*. Chicago: Moody Press, 1974.

Leavitt, Guy P. (revised by A. Leon Langston) *Superintend With Success*. Cincinnati: Standard, 1980.

MacKenzie, Alec. *The Time Trap*. American Management Association, 1972.

Richards, Lawrence O. *A Theology of Christian Education*. Grand Rapids, Michigan: Zondervan, 1975.

Schaller, Lyle A. *Parish Planning*. Nashville: Abingdon, 1971.

_____. *The Pastor and the People*. Nashville: Abingdon, 1973.

Wofford, Jerry, and Kenneth Kilinski. *Organization and Leadership in the Local Church.* Grand Rapids, Michigan: Zondervan, 1973.

---

[1] 1 Corinthians 1:1
[2] Ephesians 3:19
[3] Ephesians 4:13
[4] Luke 14:23

Part Four

BEYOND THE
LOCAL CHURCH

Section Outline

22. Interchurch and Parachurch Organizations
    A. The Development of These Organizations
    B. The Religious Education Association
    C. An Evaluation of Interchurch and Parachurch Organizations

23. The Christian School
    A. History of the Christian School Movement
    B. Philosophy of the Christian School
    C. The Christian School Teacher
    D. The Organizational Structure
    E. Has the Christian School a Right to Exist?
    F. The Future of the Christian School
    G. Sources of Additional Information

24. Christian Camping
    A. Definition and Purpose
    B. Objectives of Christian Camping
    C. A Brief History of Christian Camping
    D. Forms and Varieties of Camping
    E. Administering Camp
    F. The Camp Program

25. The Campus Ministry
    A. History of Campus Ministry
    B. Philosophy of Campus Ministry
    C. Types and Programs of Campus Ministry
    D. The Campus Minister

26. Christian Higher Education
    A. The Beginning of Colleges in America
    B. The Teaching of Religion in American Colleges
    C. Professional Training in Christian Education
    D. The Rise of Bible Colleges and Institutes

The local church is the focus of Christ's mission to the world. We stress that mission in terms of evangelism and education, the two basic thrusts according to the Great Commission. This volume has been concerned mainly with the program of Christian education that local churches need to develop to accomplish Christ's will for His people.

Some areas of Christian education lie beyond the local church. They may be cooperative ventures of several churches or groups of churches, such as Christian camping, campus ministries, colleges, and seminaries. Other parachurch agencies attempt to provide service to local church programs of Christian education.

Many have doubts about the continuing value of the public school. Christian schools are involved with the education of children and youth, and should be seen and evaluated in terms of the mandate of Christ to teach. The chapter by Dr. Chris Templar presents this option from the perspective of one who has studied the Christian school movement intensively as well as having personally participated in the program of a Christian school.

Christian education begins in the local church, but it must never end there. In this section, attention is given to those agencies and activities that are beyond the local congregation.

They contribute to the local church's program of nurture, and in some cases, the local church can develop cooperative programs. As such, these agencies must be considered and evaluated.

CHAPTER

22

Interchurch and Parachurch Organizations

As you read, think about these questions:
—What is meant by *parachurch organizations?*
—What are the contributions of these organizations?
—What is the Religious Education Association? What has been its accomplishments?
—How can we best evaluate these organizations?

Many regional, state, county, and city councils attempt to promote what some term "functional Christian unity" among churches. By encouraging cooperation among churches and/or denominations, they attempt to do for the total church population what one local church or single denomination can never do. Churches that participate receive certain benefits and a sense of ecumenical fellowship. One of the functional areas to which these councils address themselves is Christian education.

In addition to these interchurch and interdenominational councils (mostly related to the older, mainline denominations), numerous parachurch organizations have developed among evangelicals in the twentieth century. These organizations exist alongside the church and promote various aspects of church life.

The Development of These Organizations

Sunday-School Associations

The development of interchurch and parachurch organizations is largely an American phenomenon. In Europe with its state-church systems, such organizations have not been necessary until recently. But it was a European import—the Sunday school—that became the basis for many of these interchurch agencies.

In America, the Sunday school flourished outside official denominational control. Individuals and groups saw the value of the Sunday school for meeting the educational needs of the poorer classes. Soon Sunday-school societies, designed to promote Sunday school work, were also begun. The first of these societies was organized in 1790 in Philadelphia. Other early societies (or unions, as they were sometimes called) were begun in the larger cities of the East. In 1824, these Eastern unions were merged into a national organization, the American Sunday School Union, with the city organizations becoming arms of the national organization.

The American Sunday School Union, largely controlled by Christian lay people, set itself to the task of establishing a Sunday school in every center of population in America. It also began a series of national Sunday-school conventions and encouraged state and county conventions. These conventions were centers of information and inspiration for all who were interested in Sunday-school work.

When the conventions were extended to state, county, and local levels, the American Sunday School Union moved into the background. Permanent county and state Sunday-school organizations began in the 1850's, and some time later the International Sunday School Association (Canada had been included) was serving these state and county associations. The report of the Thirteenth International Sunday School Convention, meeting at San Francisco in 1911, revealed that every state and province in the United States and Canada had been organized and that 2,541 of their 3,254 counties had organizations as well. More than 53,000 conventions of all kinds had been held the previous year.

By the close of the nineteenth century, Sunday schools had become the teaching arm of American churches. Almost every denomination had welcomed the Sunday school by this time, and had developed some kind of denominational board or department to encourage and supervise Sunday-school work. Since the International Sunday School Association, with its state and county auxiliaries, was already on the scene giving leadership to the Sunday schools of America in a non-sectarian fashion, little opposition was expressed by the denominations. The International Association was promoting the Sunday school as a means of encouraging Bible study, and during the nineteenth century most denominations saw this as a beneficial thrust.

The International Council of Religious Education

By 1910 the scene had changed. Theological liberalism was already influencing denominational leadership. Many religious education leaders became dissatisfied with the Bible-teaching thrust and the lay leadership emphasis fostered by the International Sunday School Association. These leaders formed the Sunday School Council of Evangelical Denominations and determined to wrest the control of the Sunday-school movement from the International Association.

Conflict was resolved by the merger of the two organizations in 1922 into the International Council of Religious Education. Slowly but surely, denominational leaders assumed almost complete control, even though the merger guaranteed a continuation of joint control by denominational officials and laymen.[1] The International Council, led by Hugh Magill, provided educational leadership in several ways. Its journal, *International Journal of Religious Education*, soon became a leader in the field of Christian education. The Council in Christian Educational Research made achievements in the development of standards and in young people's work, under the leadership of Percy R. Hayward. Perhaps the most noted accomplishment was the work that led to the Revised Standard Version of the Bible. The International Council of Religious Education Bible Revision Committee, formed in 1929 under Luther Weigle's leadership, worked steadily through the next decade, producing the New Testament in 1946 and the Old Testament in 1952.

Voices of criticism were raised against the International Council of Religious Education. W. S. Athearn was critical of the highhandedness and the careful control of the organization by denominational leaders. Others were critical of liberal theological influence. Many conservative segments within denominations that officially cooperated made known their opposition to the theological liberalism within the Council through independent journals and other publications.

Other interchurch organizations existing at the time of the formation of the International Council of Religious Education related to other areas of church life. The Federal Council of Churches of Christ in America had been formed in 1908 as a cooperative tool of the major denominations. The National Council of Church Women was begun in 1929, the Christian Youth Council of North America was organized in 1934, and other smaller organizations were formed to relate to specific needs. In the 1940's the leadership of the International Council of Religious Education began to agitate for the amalgamation of all these organizations into a National Council.[2] The National Council of Churches of Christ of America was officially formed on November 29, 1959, in Cleveland, Ohio. The work of the International Council of Religious Education is now carried on by the Division of Christian Education of the National Council.

Many conservative critics saw in this the "growing superchurch," with its control reaching into thousands of local churches across the land. Such fear led many groups to look elsewhere for leadership and direction for their programs of Christian education. In 1939, a group of independent publishers met to discuss the Uniform Lesson system, now controlled by the International Council. All of these publishers were conscious of a growing dissatisfaction with curriculum trends. Dr. J. D. Murch, who represented Standard Publishing Company of Cincinnati, Ohio, was a leader at this meeting. He noted that the objections made to the system were mainly over its liberal and socialistic tendencies. This was one of the first meetings of conservative, evangelical churchmen to discuss common concerns in Christian education.

The National Association of Evangelicals

The National Association of Evangelicals was formed in 1942. Harold J. Ockenga, minister of the prestigious Park Street Church in Boston, became the Association's first president. J. Elwin Wright, George H. Ford, J. D. Murch, Paul S. Rees, and H. H. Savage were among the Association's members. The organization was established to promote evangelical cooperation without compromising the doctrinal integrity of the cooperating groups. Its membership was open to denominations, independent religious organizations, local churches, groups of churches, and individuals. Its purpose was clearly expressed:

> To provide a medium for voluntary united action among the several groups of Evangelical Christians of America, without, however, exercise of executive or legislative control over the constituent members. The fields of endeavor shall be Evangelism, Foreign Missions, Home Missions, Education, War Service, Public Relations, Moral Welfare, Radio, and such other fields of endeavor as the governing board may from time to time deem appropriate.[3]

Currently representing some thirty million evangelicals, the National Association of Evangelicals has constantly sought to promote Christian education. Its commissions on Christian Education and Youth have done much to promote Christian education and youth work on a wide level. *Christian Education in a Democracy,* edited by Frank Gaebelein, was published under N.A.E. auspices in 1951. This book has done much to provide a basis for Christian education among evangelicals. It includes chapters on church schools, Christian colleges and Bible colleges, youth, public schools, and Christian day schools.

Twenty-two years after the old International Sunday School Association was merged into the International Council, and the idea of a mass convention of lay and professional workers was lost, leadership in the National Association of Evangelicals proposed the organization of a National Sunday School Association upon strictly evangelical principles. One hundred evangelical leaders in Christian education called a convention to meet in Chicago, October 2-6, 1946. This was to be the constitutional convention of the new association. Over one thousand delegates were in the audience during this convention in which a constitution was adopted, the National Association of Evangelicals statement of beliefs were accepted, officers were elected, a uniform lesson project was approved, and a program of expansion was planned.

The National Sunday School Association provided much-needed leadership for a great Sunday school and Christian educational revival in America. During the late forties and fifties, the Association held yearly national Sunday-school conventions in various parts of the country and promoted the organization of state, regional, and metropolitan associations throughout the nation. A journal, *NSSA Link,* was established to promote and provide information for evangelical Sunday schools across the land. Through its various commissions—Research (now the National Association of Professors of Christian Education), Youth, Camp, and Denominational Sunday School Secretaries—it has been very influential in areas other than the Sunday school. A more recent affiliate, the National Association of Directors of Christian Education, has brought together those who are vocationally involved in the direction of Christian education in local churches. As Murch notes in his history of the National Association of Evangelicals, "three basic emphases characterize the work of the National Sunday School Association: (1) the Bible, (2) evangelism, and (3) spiritual power." *The Bible* had been restored to its rightful position as the textbook of the Sunday school; *evangelism* had been restored to its rightful place in the purpose of the Sunday school; and *spiritual power* had been restored to the whole Sunday school operation.

Other Parachurch Organizations

The American Bible Society, begun in the nineteenth century, continued to provide Bibles, Testaments, and Scripture portions for all groups. In more recent years this society, in cooperation with the United Bible Societies of Europe, has translated the Bible into many languages, printed these Bibles and Testaments, and distributed them through various missionary organizations. The American Tract Society served the churches through various tracts and other literature. In the twentieth century, the Wycliffe Bible Translators have been active in the translation and publication of Scriptures into some of the less spoken languages of the world.

The Christian Endeavor Society was the first organization promoting youth ministries. It began in the nineteenth century in the Williston Congregational Church in Portland, Maine, under the leadership of Francis Clark, and soon became an international movement, with societies in almost every Protestant church at home and abroad. When each denomination began its own youth program (Epworth League among Methodists, Westminster Fellowship among Presbyterians, and Baptist Young Peoples Union among Baptists), Christian Endeavor lost much of its constituency and today is a pale shadow of its former self. Many other youth organizations have developed within evangelicalism, such as Youth for Christ and Young Life, Bill Gothard's Basic Youth Conflicts seminars, and the Fellowship of Christian Athletes programs.

Among collegians such organizations as Inter-Varsity Fellowship and Campus Crusade have been effective in evangelism and Christian nurture. Other parachurch organizations have developed to meet the needs of children and young teens. Among these are the Christian Service Brigade program for boys, and the Pioneer Girls program for girls. These stress evangelism of children and families as well as Christian nurture and leadership development. They also encourage local churches to sponsor these through-the-week programs. Child Evangelism Fellowship works through children's clubs as well, and is evangelistic in nature.

Publishers

Various independent publishing concerns are also important parachurch organizations closely related to Christian education. With the rise and influence of liberalism in the major denominations, the publishing houses of these denominations began to produce curricular materials that were experience-centered and less committed to Biblical emphasis. As a result, many evangelicals within these denominations sought materials from publishers that continued to emphasize the Bible's supremacy. Few independent evangelical publishing houses produced Sunday-school and other educational literature at the time. Standard Publishing Company, an independent concern in Cincinnati, Ohio (closely related to conservative Christian Churches and Churches of Christ), Union Gospel Press of Cleveland, Ohio, and David C. Cook Publishing Company of Elgin, Illinois, were three such independent publishers committed to publishing literature that was Biblically sound.[4]

Other publishing ventures were launched. In 1925, C. H. Benson, a Presbyterian minister and head of the Christian Education Department of Moody Bible Institute, Chicago, began to direct his students in critical examination of all existing Sunday-school curriculum materials. His purpose was to develop a new series of graded materials that would provide complete, comprehensive, and consecutive Biblical instruction. In 1933, after eight years of investigation and experiment, they offered the public the "All Bible Graded Series." Since this date, Scripture Press has produced evangelical church school literature. Since then it has expanded operations to include publication of vacation Bible school materials, Christian books, and other printed and audiovisual aids.

About the time that Benson was developing the All Bible Graded Series in Chicago as an extension of Moody Bible Institute's work, another Presbyterian, Henrietta C. Mears, wa developing a similar program in a church on the west coast. Miss Mears was Christian education director of the First Presbyterian Church in Hollywood. Dissatisfied with her denomination's curriculum materials, she began to prepare closely-graded Bible teaching materials that attracted thousands to the local Sunday school. The enrollment jumped from 400 to 4,200 in two years' time. (Today this church leads its denomination in enrollment with over 5,000 members.) In 1933, Miss Mears founded the Gospel Light Publishing House to publish and market the materials she and others were preparing. Its growth, like that of Scripture Press, was rapid, and can be explained only in terms of the production of needed materials that exalt Christ and His Word. Other, smaller independent publishing houses have risen out of the same circumstances, but these two are prime examples of positive protest to liberalism's effect on Christian education.

The Religious Education Association

Perhaps the most significant organization to influence the modern religious education movement for good and ill was the Religious Education Association. It came into existence as a result of a conference of teachers, ministers, editors, superintendents of Sunday schools, and other religious education workers called in 1903 by William R. Harper, president of the University of Chicago. This call acme out of Harper's and others' deep concern about the inadequacies of Biblical instruction in the churches and the almost complete absence of religious instruction in the public schools. Among those who met in Chicago were outstanding leaders such as Edward Scribner Ames, James B. Angell, George A. Coe, Nicholas Murray Butler, John Dewey, Shailer Matthews, W. R. Harper, Frederick B. Eiselen, Francis G. Peabody, and Walter Dill Scott. They published a "decalogue of needs" to brief prospective members on the new organization's basic program:

1. To endeavor to define the true relation of religious and moral instruction with the instruction of history, science, literature, and other subjects in the public school;

2. to seek to show how to correlate religious and moral instruction with the instruction of history, science, and literature obtained in the public school;

3. to present and apply the established results of modern pedagogy and Bible study as related to religious and moral training;

4. to indicate the proper place of the Bible in religious and moral instruction and set forth the general and specific methods of using the Bible for this purpose;

5. to show the necessity and method of gradation of pupils according to age, capacity, and attainment, and of graded method for them;

6. to indicate how this new, higher ideal can be worked out in the churches and in other agencies;

7. to seek to create a graded curriculum enbodying the larger substance and better methods of moral and religious instruction commensurate with current biblical, theological, ethical, psychological, and other scientific knowledge;

8. to recommend for the study of the Bible, religion, and morality in ancient and modern times the best available sources as judged by the new ideal, and to promote further preparation of materials in the field;

9. to seek by all possible means to accomplish adequate training of moral and religious teachers, pointing out how to get and use needed knowledge, the necessary qualifications for teachers in training, and the best methods to serve them; and,

10. to seek to unite in common work all individuals and agencies laboring for this high ideal.[5]

The Association has largely followed this program throughout its history. As an association of individuals of various faiths, it has not been interested in religious politics or fostering ecclesiastical organizations. Laird T. Hites stated that three qualities have dominated its thinking and activity: *freedom,* the *pioneering spirit,* and *scientific control.*[6]

At first the Association was dubbed "the harmless hobby of academic theorists," but it soon won respect by means of practical achievement. Such ideals as those set forth by Walter S. Athearn in *The Church School,* which was the direct result of an R.E.A. commission, demonstrated the value of the Association to the educational program of local churches. It gave help in reviving and standardizing Bible departments in church-related colleges,[7] advocated teaching the Bible in accredited high schools, and made surveys that revealed needs and set forth methods of meeting these needs. Arlo Brown believed that in its early years, the R.E.A. "was perhaps the most potent single factor in crystallizing the sentiment in favor of better methods in religious education."[8]

Religious Education, the journalistic arm of the Association, has contributed richly to Christian education. It has served as a medium for exchange of new ideas, discussion and debate of issues, and critical appraisal of programs and procedures. Through the years it has supplied resource material (including statistical studies, bibliographies, critical book reviews, and other materials) by which one may keep abreast of the religious education movement in general.

The conservative evangelical will find inadequacies and deficiencies in the Association for its interfaith basis and its concern for scientific methodology, which has tended to set it over against a Biblical approach to Christian education. But it has had and still has a place in the vanguard of the religious education movement. One can recognize its limitations and still make use of its positive contributions to the glory of God.

An Evaluation of
Interchurch and Parachurch Organizations

Parachurch organizations are identified as institutional structures that have three things in common: "They are structured institutionally rather than organically or charismatically; they exist alongside or parallel to the church community; and they exist ostensibly to serve the Church."[9] Thus defined, any denominational structure, educational institution, or mission organization, as well as the organizations that have been mentioned in this chapter, is a parachurch organization. Board has estimated that there are 6,500 such parachurch organizations, counting both Protestant and Catholic.[10]

These organizations have proliferated and grown and gained influence and financial power. Some local church leaders are alarmed at their growth. Critics charge some of these organizations with "imbalance, doctrinal indifference, and exploitation of congregations for money and people," and that they "lack accountability to anyone but themselves." Parachurch groups are considered by some as "religion gone free enterprise."[11]

Leaders of these organizations respond that they are "arms of the church," specialists who help the churches to do their job. They may even add that they are doing what churches would be doing if they were not so traditional, reactionary, disorganized, or materialistically preoccupied with buildings, budgets and numbers.

The following principles can be applied to a proper evaluation of parachurch organizations:

1. Does the organization genuinely contribute to God's purpose? If it does not contribute in some way to building a Biblical church or helping such churches grow to maturity in Christ, then there is some question as to its validity.

2. Does it merit existence by its accountability? Parachurch organizations that take in millions of dollars without accounting financially and morally to their contributors are not helpers, but parasites.

3. Does it bring people into the church or lead people away from the church? If the organization does not promote the growth and health of local churches, there is doubt whether such agency should be supported by those committed to Biblical Christianity.

Parachurch organizations may well serve in ways that local churches cannot. For churches whose polity is not connectional or denominational, these organizations may prove helpful to them. Perhaps the parachurch organization can teach local churches somthing about human need and Biblical response. If a parachurch organization is doing what a local church could and should do, then local churches should learn this lesson and respond creatively to the need.

Summary

Independent extrachurch or parachurch organizations are not new. Some may consider missionary teams like Paul and Barnabas to be parachurch organizations. The monastic orders of the ancient church fit into this category, and the various mendicant, pastoral, and teaching orders of the Roman Catholic Church of the Middle Ages and Reformation Period were certainly parachurch organizations. The Moravian and Wesleyan revival and mission work was parachurch, until these movements constituted themselves into structured churches. The Sunday school itself began as a parachurch organization and was later embraced by churches to become an essential part of their teaching programs.

Such organizations have mushroomed since the 1930's, because of the growth and affluence of the American population, and because evangelicals have needed such organizations. The communications revolution in radio and television and the rise of new methods of direct mail fund raising have also aided in this proliferation. This is one of the prices paid for freedom of religion in this country.

Many of these organizations have benefitted the church and its educational program. They have been genuinely service-oriented and have been able to accomplish things that local churches could not accomplish themselves. Twentieth-century Christians must be knowledgeable and sensitive enough to evaluate these organizations in terms of God's purpose through the church and then to use those services definitely needed.

Project

Select a parachurch organization mentioned in this chapter. Go to the library and read the publications of that organization. Write a brief report indicating the nature and purpose of the organization and in what circumstances it would be helpful to you.

Selected Bibliography

Benson, C. H., History of Christian Education. Chicago: Moody Press.

Board, Stephen, "The Great Evangelical Power Shift," Eternity, June, 1979.

Bower, W. C. and P. R. Hayward, Protestantism Faces Its Educational Task Together. C. C. Nelson, 1909.

Brown, Arlo A. The History of Religious Education in Recent Times. New York: Abingdon Press, 1923.

Cully, K. B. (ed.) The Westminster Dictionary of Christian Education. Philadelphia: Westminster Press, 1963.

Ferguson, E. M. Historic Chapters in Christian Education in America. Revell, 1935.

Goddard, Burton L. (ed.) The Encyclopedia of Modern Christian Missions: The Agencies. Nelson, 1967.

Murch, J. D. Cooperation Without Compromise. Grand Rapids, Michigan: Eerdmans, 1956.

Snyder, Howard A. The Community of the King. Chicago: Inter-Varsity, 1977.

Taylor, Marvin J. (ed.) An Introduction to Christian Education. Nashville: Abingdon, 1966.

[1]See Chapter 3 for further details.

[2]Those that did merge included, in addition to those mentioned, the Council of Church Boards of Education, Foreign Mission Conference of North America, Home Missions Council of North America, Missionary Education Movement of the United States and Canada, and the United Stewardship Council.

[3]Murch, p. 66. Used by permission.

[4]A number of conservative, evangelical denominations such as the Southern Baptist Convention, the Lutheran Church, Missouri Synod, and many of the smaller Holiness and Pentecostal groups provide Biblically-oriented materials for their own people. These, however, were not independent and did not serve a wide and varied constituency.

[5]Bulletin No. 1, Religious Education Association, August, 1903.

[6]See "The Religious Education Association," in P. H. Lotz, L. W. Craford (eds.), *Studies in Religious Education* (Nashville: Cokesbury Press, 1931), p. 393.

[7]Both H. F. Cope and W. S. Athearn made surveys of the scope of religious teaching in church colleges and found the situation deplorable. These R.E.A. surveys stimulated the Council of the Church Boards of Education to study the situation and promote a vigorous campaign to "introduce Biblical courses into their church schools (colleges)." See W. S. Athearn, *An Adventure in Religious Education* (New York: The Century Co., 1930), p. 127.

[8]Brown, p. 178

[9]Taken from *The Community of the King* by Howard A. Snyder. © 1977 by Inter-Varsity Christian Fellowship of the USA and used by permission of InterVarsity Press.

[10]Board, p. 17

[11]*Ibid.* Reprinted by permission of ETERNITY Magazine, Copyright 1979, Evangelical Ministries, Inc., 1716 Spruce Street, Philadelphia, PA 19103.

CHAPTER

23

The Christian School

by Dr. Chris Templar

As you read, think about these questions:
—Who were the significant people in the development of the Christian school movement?
—How is the philosophy of integration applied within the Christian school?
—Identify the significant roles that the teacher must play in the Christian school.
—What stages must be implemented in order to develop a Christian curriculum?
—What are the arguments for and against the Christian school?

History of the Christian School Movement

Religion in the schools is not new in America. Its roots are to be found in early American history. The first American schools, at St. Augustine (1606), Boston (1635), and New Amsterdam (1638), educated individuals in Christian truths. This practice remained normal even after the emergence of public education and the establishment of independence. However, with the increasing secularization of society and education, Christian education was gradually eradicated from the schools.

Until recently, the development of the independent Christian school has been primarily influenced by the leadership and support of the National Union of Christian Schools located in Grand Rapids, Michigan, and the National Association of Christian Schools located in Wheaton, Illinois.

The National Union of Christian Schools grew out of the Christian school background in the Netherlands. Christian schools were developed in reaction to a ruling by King William II of the Netherlands, which decreed that public schools were to have a social and educational task only. Prior to this time they had been under the direction of the church. The first Christian school was in Nijmegen in 1840, followed by one in Greda in 1842. Several leaders in Christian school education, including Henry Beets, H. P. Scholte, and A. C. Van Raalten, later emigrated to America and brought with them this tradition of Christian schools.

The earliest Christian day school professional organization was founded in 1892 and known as the *Vereeniging Voor Christelijk Onderwijs Op Gereformerden Grandslag* (Society for Christian Board on the Reformed Faith). Ten or twelve schools were charter members of this organization, which later developed into the Chicago Alliance. This alliance appointed a committee consisting of Mark Fakkema, the first principal of Chicago Christian High School, Andrew Blystra, and Henry Kuiper to assess the standards of education in their schools. The committee reported that the standardization of the curriculum, the training of better teachers, and the issuing of textbooks were universal problems in the Christian schools, and it recommended that a national union be formed.

On September 1, 1920, representatives of thirty-seven school associations met in Chicago and formed the National Union of Christian Schools. The task of the National Union was clearly defined in articles Three and Four of the constitution of the Union. Article Three read: "The purpose of the Union is to further the interests of Christian Education which our schools have in common." Article Four read

This purpose of the Union shall be achieved by:
(a) Aiding the cause of Christian Normal Training
(b) Encouraging the publication of literature of a pedagogic nature
(c) Raising the standard of education
(d) Improving the economic position of the teacher

(e) Aiding one another as schools when necessary

(f) Supervision of the individual schools.[1]

From its inception the National Union was to be a service organization. In no way would it seek to dictate to individual schools.

Most of the independent non-parochial schools were to be found within the Reformed tradition until 1940 (an exception was the Portland School in Louisville, Kentucky). But by the early 1940's, the influence of the Christian school movement had extended well beyond the Reformed churches. In 1945, groups from non-Reformed church backgrounds bought a majority of the promotional literature that the National Union sold. Benson describes the situation:

> It became clear that with so many denominations seeking to develop Christian schools that a new type of organization was needed. The organization envisioned was to embrace all Christian schools which were parent-controlled or private, rather than parochial in polity. Membership in such an organization was to be based on a general doctrinal statement such as was identified with the National Association of Evangelicals.[2]

At the National Association of Evangelicals convention in Omaha, Nebraska in 1947, Frank Gaebelein of the Stony Brook School was appointed chairman of a committee that dealt with elementary and secondary education. This committee recommended that the National Association of Christian Schools be formed. This association became the guiding influence in the development of Christian day schools over the next twenty-five years. The National Association of Christian Schools was founded in 1947 with Mark Fakkema as its chief official.

At the height of its expansion in 1971, the National Association of Christian Schools had a membership of 364 schools, a growth of 120 schools in four years. In July, 1978, four months after its formation into a new organization, the Association of Christian Schools International had a membership of approximately 1,200 schools representing more than 150,000 students.

In 1950, the Christian school system was a rarity. Now citywide systems such as those to be found in Memphis, San Diego, and Los Angeles are increasing. Briarcrest Baptist School System in Memphis, Tennessee is an example of this trend. Established in 1973, the schools now meet in eleven locations and have a total enrollment of 3,850. The system has been described as "having just about everything: a lavish $6.5 million building and a well-educated corps of teachers (40 percent have masters degrees)."[3] Concerning this school, the *Wall Street Journal* commented:

> Briarcrest's concern for quality education is another difference. It offers all the standard academic subjects in addition to religious training, but above all, Briarcrest is financially sound.[4]

This development of the Christian school movement has been described as "an explosion" of unprecedented size. Just over a decade ago, Henry Buchanan and Bob Brown made the following observation about the growth of Christian schools:

> The most exciting development in education today is the rise of the Protestant church school. A rarity three decades ago, Protestant church schools are now being organized at the rate of 225 per year. If the enthusiasm does not wane, they will soon take a place of equal importance alongside the public and parochial schools.[5]

During the past decade, enrollment in Christian day schools affiliated with the national professional associations has soared by more than 700 percent. Christian day schools are now coming into existence at an estimated rate of three new schools a day.

Philosophy of the Christian School

What, then, are the specific features of these schools? W. J. Lanouette described them this way:

> These Christian schools aren't the familiar parochial schools of the main line religions: Roman Catholic, Episcopalian, Presbyterian, Lutheran, and the like. And, with few exceptions, they're not the all-white private academies begun to avoid public school desegregation. Rather, those in the movement apply the term "Christian Schools" to new and independent entities, most founded since World War II. All are evangelical, and most are conservative in outlook.[6]

Much criticism in the past has centered around the idea that parents who send their children to Christian schools shelter them from the real world. Both Kienel, executive director of the

Association of Christian Schools International, and Roy Low-rie, president of the Association of Christian Schools International and the principal of Delaware County Christian School, have vigorously protested against such criticism. An education that leaves out teachings about God, they said, gives the student an incomplete and erroneous picture of reality—it does not depict the "real world" at all. Especially teachings about man himself must be considered in the full light of Scripture. Further, any educational system that leaves God out of its teachings is itself making certain presuppositions that it takes on faith, and in this sense is also giving children a "religious" education, only this religion is one of secular humanism.[7]

The National Association of Christian Schools, under Mark Fakkema's leadership, developed an overall philosophy of education that is widely accepted among Christian schools today. This philosophy can be summarized as follows:

> The non-Christian philosophy has an integrating center in man, but the center of the Christian philosophy is God. . . . It is understood that the two resultant programs which are so separated in the beginning will never reach agreement, but rather, in the main, will stand in antithesis. It is because of this philosophic divergence that many Christian educators have concluded that the Christian day school is the only answer to the problem of providing a theocentric and thus Christocentric educational program for children.[8]

Certain examples substantiate his contention. Mathematics reveals a God who is unchangeable. Grammar speaks to us of His law and order of plan. The child also recognizes something of God as He reveals himself through nature. History is man in the laboratory of life demonstrating to himself and to his fellow men that he is a sinner in need of God's plan of redemption.

A true philosophy of education integrates all truth in God, and demonstrates the relationship of all subject matter to Him in a manner that honors God. Since all truth is God's truth, all curriculum material must be thought through from a Christian frame of reference.

The Christian School Teacher

The key person in the training of a child is the teacher. The teacher must reflect God's glory as he teaches Scripture. Mark Fakkema ascribed roles of privilege and responsibility to the teacher; the teacher must take seriously James' statement, "Not many of you should presume to be teachers, my brothers, because you know that we who teach will be judged more strictly."[9]

The concept of the Christian school makes special demands on the teacher. Not only must he be living the life of a growing, maturing Christian, but he must also be academically competent. Only the very best in all areas of the school life can truly bring glory to God.

When Paul talked about his role as a teacher to the church in Thessalonica, he said: "You know how we lived among you for your sake. You became imitators of us and of the Lord. . . . and so you became a model to all the believers in Macedonia and Achaia."[10] In Paul's life there was harmony among what he taught, how he taught it, and the life he lived. The same harmony is demanded of each Christian day school teacher. A truly Christian school is one staffed by Christian teachers where Christian values and a Christian world view permeate every part of its life.

Curriculum

The only satisfactory curriculum to the Christian teacher is one that has two components: a horizontal one (a relationship among facts) and a vertical one (a relationship with God). Scripture relates all things vertically to God in a threefold way. "All things" are said to be of God, through God, and for God. Every system of instruction that ignores or bypasses this vertical relationship (as secular instruction does) is inadequate, for not to know things in their vertical relationship is not to know their true origin and real purpose.

The importance of curriculum development and the role of curriculum in the Christian school were discussed in the 1920's by the National Union. At that time a need was expressed for the development of curriculum guides for teachers in order to help them to perform the necessary integration of the Bible and Biblical material with other subjects.

Current writers continue to emphasize the need for an integrated curriculum. John Burgess, chairman of the Division of Education at Gordon College, has sought to identify two types of integration—isolated and structured. Isolated integration is that which occurs when no comprehensive objectives guide the selection of Biblical elements to be introduced into the learning activity. This results in a curriculum containing a series of unrelated Biblical concepts. There is no conscious planning for one element to support another.

Burgess says that the structured integration approach involves long-range planning:

> This approach is characterized by the careful planning of Biblical integration over a significantly large portion of the curriculum. Objectives are identified and the Biblical elements are structured so as to support each other and to contribute to the accomplishment of common Biblical goals. . . . Structured integration should be accomplished at two major levels. It should take place as a corporate effort by the entire faculty of a school in the organization of the total curriculum and by an individual teacher over that portion of the curriculum which is his responsibility.[11]

Robert Miller, superintendent of Norfolk Christian Schools, presents the following scenario to illustrate what is implied by structured integration:

> A school is concerned with the subject of government. In the Christian school we cannot delete the normal material included in a government course but must first consider what Biblical principles apply to this area. As a result of a student's research and discussion with his peers, he will discover such truths as the following:
>
> 1. God is the supreme ruler, controlling nations and rulers.
> 2. When men refuse God's rule, He lets them rule themselves.
> 3. The powers that be are ordained of God. Since God has a hand in the placing of leaders, they should be respected and obeyed.
> 4. Believers must pray for their leaders.
> 5. Believers must support the government in taxes.
> 6. Civil authorities are a deterrent to evil, not to good.
> 7. When civil authorities conflict with God's Word we are to obey God.
> 8. God holds nations accountable for their actions.
> 9. God expects kings and government leaders to keep the promises they have made.
> 10. When a godly nation turns from God its sins are often worse than those of the heathen, and its judgment is greater.
> 11. The Bible encourages patriotism and love of country.
> 12. The Bible discourages rebellion and rioting.

For the Christian teacher these Biblical principles do not become an interesting supplement to the course but rather the basic propositions which will shape his planning and instruction. To be worthy of the name "Christian education" the course must not only analyze the interworking of our governmental structure but see it as it fits into God's plan and purpose. Only as these Biblical principles become an integrated part of the government course can it be said that the subject begins to reflect the unique philosophy of the Christian school. The heart of integration in Christian education is no less than "the living union of its subject matter, administration, and even its personnel, with the eternal and infinite pattern of God's truth."[12]

This underlying fact of God's authorship and purpose of government must be clearly presented to the student as a part of each subject he is taught. The student should see each subject from a God-centered instead of a man-centered perspective. This integration must finally be communicated to the student in such a manner that it becomes his frame of reference. He must be exposed not only to the results of the teacher's study, but to the whole process of integration. He himself must learn to put together the pieces of the puzzle. In this way he will develop his own Christian world view and be able to evaluate positively all materials to which he is exposed as his degree of maturity develops.

A factor that must be considered in any discussion of Christian school curriculum concerns regulations imposed by various states. At present this is a sensitive issue. Some states, such as North Carolina, apply only regulations concerning health and safety to the private schools within their area, while others require the use of approved textbooks and curricular materials. This issue is currently before the courts in several states. Many Christian schools regard these regulations as a contravention of the principle of the separation of church and state. They suggest that the philosophy of integration demands the freedom to use Christian textbooks in all subject areas.

Until recently this ideal has been hard to achieve. Few quality textbooks have been written from a Christian perspective for elementary and secondary education. With the growth of the Christian school movement the demand for this type of text has grown. Some Christian textbook publishers are beginning to offer fairly complete sets of materials, at least at the elementary level. The rate of production of quality high school texts is also accelerating. A partial list of Christian school textbook publishers is at the end of this chapter.

The Organizational Structure

Four types of organizational structures can be distinguished within the Christian school movement:

1. The private school is owned by an individual or family. Usually it is operated either by that individual or by a self-perpetuating group of trustees. The role of the board, if one exists, is advisory. Many of these schools are at the high school level, and some evangelical boarding schools fit into this category.

2. The church-organized school is organized by a church or denomination. A majority of the schools founded in the last decade are owned or operated either by one or a group of churches. This type of school is often run by a school board that is itself responsible to and appointed by the church board. It often uses the church's educational property. Church members frequently play an active role in various areas of the school's life and regard the enterprise as a part of their educational and mission outreach.

3. The parent society school is an independent Christian school started by a group of parents who form a legal corporation that owns the school property and appoints a board to manage the school. This corporation is often called a school society. An individual may have a child in the school and not be a member of the corporation, and some corporation members may not have immediate family members in the school.

4. The multigrade individualized education school is a recent development. Companies have prepared materials that allow for the development of a school that has very few pupils. Generally these companies train church leaders and administrators and sell them a complete curriculum package. These curriculum materials frequently use programmed textbooks through which the student moves at his own pace with needed help given by a supervisor. It is possible for several grades to meet in one room and for one supervisor to help all of them. This type of structure has made possible a Christian school with only a few pupils. In most cases churches sign a three-year contract with the production company that provides all that is needed to establish and run the school.

Has the Christian School a Right to Exist?

While Christian schools have existed in America throughout

this century, their right to exist has been constantly challenged. Some of the arguments that are raised on both sides of this debate are listed here.

Arguments for the Christian School

1. God's revelation is the basis for all truth (Luke 11:52; Proverbs 1:7).
2. God gave parents the responsibility to control the education of their children (Deuteronomy 6:7; Ephesians 6:4; Genesis 18:17-19).
3. God gave religious leaders a responsibility for teaching children (Deuteronomy 31:6-13).
4. Christian education must be education for the whole person (Proverbs 22:6).
5. God's education is always in contrast to man's education (Colossians 2:8).
6. Biblical education requires a submission of the intellect and will to the lordship of Christ (1 Corinthians 1:18-31; 2 Corinthians 10:5).
7. Every part of the educational process is related to God and, therefore, education cannot be divided into "secular" and "religious." It can take place only in an atmosphere where this relationship can be implemented.
8. The person to be educated is a unified personality. He is one as God is one. Therefore, his education cannot be departmentalized into "secular" and "religious."
9. The goal of all education, in church or school, is to help man more fully achieve the purpose of his life, that is, to know and serve God. Only the Christian school can eradicate the false dualism of "sacred" and "secular" and bring the two together, thus presenting a unified Christian world view.
10. Higher academic standards are possible because of devoted teachers, limited enrollment, and increased efficiency due to the wise stewardship of limited resources.
11. The small percentage of time children spend at home and church reinforces the need for the Christian school.
12. For the Christian, the highest incentive in learning and conduct is to glorify God. This incentive can be stressed in Christian schools in a way that is not possible for a Christian teacher in a public school. Thus the standards of the Christian home are reinforced and emphasized.

Arguments for the Public School

1. The public school is the only way the Christian voice may be heard in a tangible way in education. The Christian has a great responsibility towards his town's public schools. Withdrawal from them will abandon them to secular humanism.
2. Christian children should attend public schools in order to present a witness and to avoid being overly sheltered from the world. This promotes evangelism and a realistic viewpoint.
3. Public schools have better physical, financial, and transportation facilities and therefore provide for better education.
4. A strong parent-child relationship and a virile Christian home life coupled with public school offers the best combination.
5. Public school offers the traditional American way of education.
6. The public school offers full academic and athletic programs. In all, a much broader form of education is available in the public school.
7. Parents are already paying for public education through tax dollars. Rather than use its money to establish schools the church should devote this money to the cause of world missions and encourage parents to use the educational facilities that are already available to them.

The Future of the Christian School

Diversity is a feature of Christian schools, so it is impossible to generalize about them. Schools founded for inadequate reasons or on an unsound financial, Biblical, or administrative basis will experience problems and tend to bring criticism to the movement as a whole. On the positive side, there are signs that the movement is developing maturity. At the present time questions concerning the tax exempt status of these schools, racial integration, and curricula are among the issues being tested in lawsuits. The decisions that are finally reached in some of these areas will affect the future of the Christian school, but will not cause the end of this movement.

In the next decade there will be more teachers and administrators trained for ministry in the area of Christian schools. Better specialized curriculum materials will continue to be made available. More professional help will be offered to the schools through organizations such as the Association of Christian Schools International. The school has the potential of being a meaningful agent together with the home and the church, in providing for the total education of the child. Ministry within the Christian school, whether as a teacher, administrator, counselor, or one of the many auxiliary helpers will provide an increasing opportunity for meaningful Christian service.

Summary

The development of Christian schools in the last decade has been just short of phenomenal. The Christian school movement has roots back to the early settlement of this nation, even as far back as Europe for some religious groups. Public education nearly supplanted the evangelical Christian school movement for a hundred years, but the past decade has been the era of a return to private education. Even so, the quality of these schools depends upon a sound philosophy of education, effective teachers, and appropriate materials.

Sources of Additional Information

Christian Day School Professional Organizations

Association of Christian Schools International
P.O. Box 4097, Whittier, CA 90607

Christian Schools International
865 28th Street S.E., Grand Rapids, MI 49508

American Association of Christian Schools
6601 N.W. 167th Avenue, Miami, FL 33193

Southern Baptist Christian School Association
Nashville, TN

Christian Day School Curriculum Publishers

A Beka Book Publications
Pensacola Christian College
125 St. John Street, Pensacola, FL 32503

Association for Bible Curriculum Development
1515 N. Los Robles Avenue, Pasadena, CA 91104

Association of Christian Schools International
P.O. Box 4097, Whittier, CA 90607

Beacon Enterprises
P.O. Box 1296, Santa Cruz, CA 95061

Bob Jones University Press
Greenville, SC 29614

Christian Education Music Publishers
2285 W. 185th Pl., Lansing, IL 60538

Christian Light Publications
P.O. Box 1126, Harrisonburg, VA 22801

Christian Schools International (formerly N.U.C.S.)
865 28th Street, S.E., Grand Rapids, MI 49508

Creation-Life Publishers
P.O. Box 15666, San Diego, CA 92115

Rod and Staff Publishers
Crockett, KY 41413

Project

Visit a Christian school in your community. Find out its origins and
goals as well as teacher qualifications and textbooks. Observe a class
in action. How does this class differ from one in a public school?

Selected Bibliography

Allen, Wayne. "How We Began Our Christian Day School Ministry."
Church Administration, XX (June, 1978), p. 3.

Benson, Warren Sten. "A History of the National Association of Christian Schools During the Period of 1947-1972" (unpublished Ph.D.
dissertation, Loyola University, 1975), p.25.

Blanchard, John F. Jr. Education That Is Christian. Wheaton, Illinois:
National Association of Christian Schools.

Buchanan, Henry A., and Bob W. Brown. "Will Protestant Chruch
Schools Become a Third Force?" Christianity Today, XL (May 12,
1967), p. 3.

Burgess, John. "Considering the Individual in Structuring Biblical Integration." Christian Teacher, 12 (March-April, 1975), p. 17.

Clark, Gordon H. A Christian Philosophy of Education. Grand Rapids,
Michigan: Eerdmans, 1947.

Gaebelein, Frank. *The Pattern of God's Truth.* New York: Oxford University Press, 1954.

Haycock, Ruth. *Bible Truths for School Subjects.* Whittier, California: Association of Christian Schools International, 1979.

Hodge, Archibald Alexander. *The State and Religion.* Philadelphia: Christian Statesman Tracts, 1878, p. 6.

Kienel, Paul. "Should Parents Shelter Their Children From the Real World?" *Christian School Comment,* VIII (September, 1977), p. 1.

_____. *The Christian School: Why It Is Right For Your Child.* Wheaton, Illinois: Victor Books, 1974.

_____. *The Philosophy of Christian School Education.* Whittier, California: Association of Christian Schools International, 1977.

Kuiper, Henry, "The National Union Begins to Function." *Christian Home and School,* XXXII (June, 1954), p. 16.

Lanouette, William J. "Christian Schools Boom by Stressing That the Fourth R Is Religion." *The National Observer,* January 15, 1977, p. 1.

Lowrie, Roy. *Christian School Administration,* Wheaton, Illinois: National Association of Christian Schools, 1966.

_____. *Serving God on the Christian School Board.* Whittier, California: Western Association of Christian Schools, 1976.

Miller, Robert M., "Implementing the Christian Philosophy in Textbook Selection and General Curriculum Development," *The Philosophy of Christian School Education,* Paul A. Kienel, ed. Whittier, California: Association of Christian Schools International, 1977, pp. 132-133.

Van Dusen, Henry P. *God in Education.* New York: Charles Scribner's Sons, 1951.

---

[1]Kuiper, p. 16

[2]Benson, pp. 28, 29

[3]Allen, p. 3

[4]*Ibid.* From *Church Administration,* June 1978. © Copyright 1978 The Sunday School Board of the Southern Baptist Convention. All rights reserved. Used by permission.

[5]Buchanan and Brown, p. 3. Copyright 1967 by *Christianity Today.* Used by permission.

[6]Lanouette, p. 1

[7]Kienel

[8]Benson, pp. 83, 84

[9]James 3:1

[10]1 Thessalonians 1:5-7

[11]Burgess, p. 17. *Christian Teacher,* official publication of the Natonal Association of Christian Schools, P.O. Box 550, Wheaton, IL 60187.

[12]Miller, pp. 132, 133

CHAPTER

24

Christian Camping

As you read, think about these questions:
—What are meant by the terms, *camping, conference, centralized,* and *decentralized?*
—What are the objectives of Christian camping?
—How are objectives and program related?
—What are the elements of an effective camp program?
—What is the value of camper-counselor relationships?

Camping in twentieth-century America is big business. Mitchell and Crawford estimate that five to six million young people are involved in camping each summer. As many as 190,000 persons find vocational opportunities in camping. When various other kinds of camping (such as retreats and family camps) are added to this figure, it is conceivable that some ten to fifteen million people are involved in some form of camping.[1]

Of these millions involved in camping, a majority are involved in camp programs sponsored by religious groups. These groups have found that camping is an exciting experience through which the goals of the church can be accomplished. As a result, camping has become a vital thrust of the Christian educational program.

Definition and Purpose

Robert Rubin has defined *camping* as "communal living close to nature with a set purpose."[2] The American Camping Association's definition expands on Rubin's:

> Organized (Resident, Day) Camping is an experience in group living in a natural environment. It is a sustained experience under the supervision of trained leadership. Camping provides a creative, educational experience in cooperative group living in the outdoors. It utilizes the resources of the natural surroundings to contribute significantly to mental, physical, social, and spiritual growth of campers.[3]

Christian camping is a specific type of camping with definite Biblically-oriented goals. It is "a Christ-centered program of small-group living in a simple, controlled out-of-door environment where the camper is enabled to develop recreational, educational, and social skills and to know Christ as Savior and Friend."[4]

Christian camping is an activity the churches use to help fulfill the Great Commission Jesus gave it. In Bible-oriented churches, the camping experience stresses both initial Christian commitment and Christian growth. Its uniqueness is in the setting and the varied programming that can reach and motivate persons who otherwise would remain uninterested or uninvolved.

Objectives of Christian Camping

The objectives of Christ-centered camping grow out of this basic purpose. Four major objectives should be common to all Christ-centered camps. These objectives correspond to that statement of Jesus' balanced growth recorded in Luke's Gospel: "Jesus grew in wisdom and stature, and in favor with God and men."[5] Each camp program must have clear objectives for the *physical well-being and growth* of its campers, the *social relationships* it attempts to cultivate, the *educational growth* its Bible study programs are intended to foster, and the *spiritual commitments and qualities of life* that the total camp environment is designed to produce.

A Brief History of Christian Camping

Abraham and the other patriarchs pitched their tents and sojourned in a land into which their God had guided them.[6] Here was living out-of-doors under the guidance of the Creator-Lord of self-disclosing love. Moses directed what must have been the greatest family camp that ever existed.[7] The Law that Jehovah gave His people provided for an annual time of short-term camping when all Israel was to come to Jerusalem and dwell in tents. During this time, they would remember how God had led and provided for them after they had departed from Egypt.[8]

Although camping may have a long past, it has a relatively short history. Christian camping has its immediate background in the camp meetings of the nineteenth century. These meetings developed out of the revivalism associated with the Second Evangelical Awakening, particularly the phase that took place on the American frontier. Even after the initial wave of revivalism had passed, the camp meeting survived as a popular religious institution, especially in the South and West. Camp meetings served both religious and social purposes. As Hall notes in Texas Disciples, "Scattered settlers with little preaching available found it advantageous to gather at some camping spot, camp out for a week or two, and hear preaching day and night. Travel was slow and tedious and camping was congenial to the pioneers."[9]

These camp meetings, particularly among Methodists and Baptists, became annual affairs and were held at centrally located campsites. Evangelism was emphasized. Preaching, Bible study, and prayer were included in the religious activities of the campers. In a natural setting, religious nurture was provided for persons of all ages.

The first camping experience specifically for youth occurred in 1861. Frederick Gunn, headmaster of the Gunnery School for Boys in Washington, Connecticut, led his young cadets to nearby Milford-on-the-Sound where they camped. For two weeks, he led them in a series of activities including military training, hiking, boating, and fishing. This proved so successful that he continued this each summer until 1879. Gunn has been dubbed the father of the American camping movement.

The first church-sponsored camp was an informal program conducted in 1880 by George Hinkley. He took seven boys camping on Gardiner Island, Rhode Island. He believed that the informal living outdoors would break down barriers between these young men and himself, and enable him to win them to the Lord. The informal program he conducted included Bible teaching, sports and recreation, and an evening worship hour.

In 1885, the Young Men's Christian Association began its first summer camp. Sumner F. Dudley organized this camp on the banks of New York's Lake Champlain. This camp, now known as Camp Dudley, is the oldest boys' camp still in operation. Other parachurch and character-building agencies followed the YMCA example. After the turn of the century, the YWCA, Boy Scouts, Girl Scouts, Campfire Girls, Salvation Army, the 4-H, and other agencies began organized camping programs.

Sometime in the 1880's, Dwight L. Moody began summer conferences at his home in Northfield, Massachusetts. The Mountain Retreat Association, later known as Montreat, near Asheville, North Carolina, began a similar program in the 1890's. Other conference centers, such as the one at Winona Lake in Indiana, were also begun. These were not strictly camping, but were leisurely paced programs of Bible study set in a natural atmosphere. The founders of these programs felt that such Bible teaching was not being carried out as it should be within the local churches, so vacation time and in-depth Bible study were combined at these centers. Later several of these conferences began to sponsor boys' and girls' camps on the outskirts of their properties.

Similar in nature was the Chautauqua Conference for Sunday school teachers established in 1874 at Lake Chautauqua, New York, by Methodist bishop John Vincent and Lewis Miller school enthusiasts. This original summer program of Bible study and teacher training was expanded to include many other religious and cultural elements. It became the springboard of the Chautauqua lecture program that helped to provide adult education for many communities for several decades.

In 1912, the International Sunday School Association under the leadership of John Alexander began a leadership training conference at Lake Geneva, Wisconsin. After this, various denominations began their own camping and conference programs. Cynthia Pearl Maus inaugurated the Disciples of Christ's first conference in 1919. Other denominations began programs in the 1920's and 1930's. By the mid-thirties, many independent and evangelical groups were developing camping-conference programs. Camping is now as universal among religious groups as vacation Bible school and the Sunday school.

Forms and Varieties of Camping

Much that is done in the name of camping is not really camping, but an adaptation of the older conference idea. The Todds outline those elements that are characteristic of camps and conferences:[10]

A Church Camp	A Conference
Leisurely pace	Fast-moving
Simple, relaxed life	Designed for inspiration
Controlled environment	Less controlled environment
Small-group activity	Mass activity
Counselor centered	Platform centered
No "prima donna" as speaker	Expert speakers
Better-trained counselors	Counselors mainly disciplinarians
Simple outdoor setting	Often elaborate facilities
Nature emphasis	Nature only incidental
Emphasis on personal evangelism	Mass evangelism
Informal worship	Formal worship
Personal counseling	Group instruction
Individual worship stresses private devotions	Mass approach to worship
Development of the individual	Leadership training
Informal program	Formal program
Participation by all	Spectator status for most

Kenneth Gangel notes that a conference is meeting-centered: "The entire program—recreational, instructional, and spiritual—is superimposed upon the site so that the resulting activities are structured very carefully and centered in the meetings of the day."[11]

Most church camps are largely conference-type experiences that include some camping for variety, interest, and individual emphasis. This has come about because many evangelical churches and parachurch organizations that sponsor camping "consider the indoctrination and evangelization of their youth more important than teaching how to char a potato in coals or to sleep in a bumpy bough bed."[12]

There is probably more variation in church camping than in any other agency designed to achieve Christian educational goals. Types of camping programs range all the way from strict Bible conferences to outdoor adventure or wilderness camping; from trip camping (backpack, bicycle, horseback, canoeing) to resident camping; from camps run by an individual to extensive camp programs under strict denominational control.

Types of camping can be classified as to their sponsorship, the various age groups and other interests that they serve, and the duration and location of the camp program.

Sponsorship

Camping programs have a variety of sponsorship. Some successful Christian camps and conferences are operated by individuals who own the campground, control the program and personnel, and offer their services to churches and individuals.

Several parachurch organizations sponsor camping programs. Young Life camps and Fellowship of Christian Athlete camps are conducted with evangelistic and nurturing goals in mind, along with the specific aims of the organization (Fellowship of Christian Athlete camps are sports-oriented, yet aim for evangelism and nurture).

Probably the largest number of camping programs are church sponsored. The local camp is sponsored and controlled by a large local church, a group of cooperating churches, or a denomination.

Age Groups and Special Interests

When camp programs first began, they were mainly for adults and college youth. In more recent years camping has been expanded to serve other age levels. Day camping, which is becoming popular, has been offered for six- to eight-year-old youngsters. Family camping, encouraged by secular as well as religious interests, involves all ages in family units. The emphasis is upon helping families to grow spiritually and become a stronger Christian witness.

Research conducted jointly by Christian Camping International and Scripture Press noted that 26.3 percent of all camps researched were for junior age children (ten and eleven). High school camps made up 21.5 percent of all camps, and junior high 17.1 percent. Family camping logged in at 8.1 percent, followed by college-age at 6.7 percent, leadership training groups at 6.2 percent, and married couples at 4.5 percent.

Special interest camps range from sports activities camps to camps for the handicapped and retarded. Other special interest camps include camps and retreats for the underprivileged or the delinquent, music and/or drama camps, work camps (painting, repairing), college-credit camps, retreats for the elderly, and various kinds of youth and adult retreats (for example, engaged couples' retreats and church leadership retreats).

Duration and Location

Camping programs can also be classified as to their duration. In the research conducted by Christian Camping International and Scripture Press, it was found that almost half (47.5 percent) of all camping programs were one week in duration. Another two out of five were weekend camps and retreats. The week-long camp seems to be more popular among juniors and young teens, while the weekend camp or retreat was more popular with the high school and college ages.

More and more camp programs are conducted year-round as facilities are winterized for more extensive use. Whereas only about fifteen percent of the programs had year-round camping in 1964, in 1969 almost forty percent did, and camp directors were projecting year-round camping in seventy percent of all camps surveyed by 1974.

In times past, camping was often limited to a resident campsite. This is still the most popular. However, in recent years trip camping has grown rapidly. Campers, whether hiking, in canoes, on horseback, or in camper-trailers, do not settle in one location but keep on the move, pitching camp in different spots. Day camping and overnight camping do not need a resident camp location either, but can use a farm, a city or state park, or a friendly wooded area.

There are more church camps in the Midwest (31.6 percent) and West (29.8 percent) than in the South (18.7 percent) or East (13.5 percent). Only 6.4 percent of camps are in Canada. Almost eighty percent of all camps surveyed owned their own campsite, and seventy percent of these camps had been in existence for more than eleven years.

A wide range of camps exists, from platform to wilderness; from centralized to decentralized. Some camps are like plush country clubs with excellent modern facilities. Others are rugged, back-to-nature, rustic, and primitive. But when it comes to lasting results, what matters most is people, not facilities. When God works, He works through people sharing their commitment to God with others in the camp experience.

Administering Camp

The administration of a camp program is usually accomplished by a camp board or committee. A camp director and/or deans implement the plans made by the committee. Planning should be done in an orderly, businesslike manner, for much of the administration of the camp relates to budgets, food service and purchasing, maintenance, and securing a competent staff. The camp committee could be divided into subcommittees that would plan and carry out certain phases of camp work. Committee workbooks with guide sheets could be developed to aid in the planning process.

The camp director or manager is responsible for putting basic decisions into action and generally overseeing the camp itself. In some situations the director is the overall administrator, but each week's individual program is planned by a dean who selects his teachers and counselors and directs the actual camp program.

Better planning for camping will result when a definite planning schedule is developed. This calendar will schedule specific items that need to be done by a certain time. As the summer program is finished, for example, evaluation should be made at various levels. Reports and follow-up ideas should be forwarded to the participating churches. All bills should be paid and the books audited. As the fall months come, next year's program would be planned. The planning calendar would give direction to the camp board and director, and provide continuity and guidance for any new director or board member.

Other essential items must be administered effectively. Publicity and promotion is one of those areas. Various media must be used to share information, motivate potential campers, and secure good will and financial support among the camp's constituency. An effective public relations program will help create a favorable public image. This, in turn, helps to recruit campers and staff, and to undergird a program with prayer and financial support.

The camp administrator must be aware of governmental and legal regulations that affect camping. The camp must meet government health and safety standards. The administrator must provide Social Security and unemployment compensation for salaried employees, and collect sales tax on canteen items sold to campers. Membership in such organizations as American Camping Association[13] and Christian Camping, International[14] can provide beneficial information on many of these items. By meeting the standards set out by these organizations, member camps will generally also meet all government regulations, with the exception of local laws and codes.

Other items must also be given careful attention. They include insurance (for campers, staff, buildings, grounds, and vehicles) food services, and bookkeeping. These items must be carefully planned for, and the plans must be effectively executed.

Since there are many different phases of organizing and administering a camp program, the camp committee and director should outline those tasks that should be done before, during, and after each camp session. This outline could be coordinated with a planning calendar. Regular meetings of the camp committee should be held to assess the progress of planning and performance. Such administrative tools and tasks are designed to develop a better program and accomplish the spiritual objectives for which Christ-centered camping exists.

The Camp Program

Success is measured in the program of each camp week. The program includes everything that happens at camp, planned or unplanned, so planning can help ensure a program's success. The following are some essential guidelines for program planning:[15]

1. Provide opportunities for adventure, achievement, and social adjustment.

2. Encourage the participation of all campers, not just those who are highly skilled or athletic.

3. Allow for individual needs and unscheduled situations—be simple, balanced, and flexible.

4. Take full advantage of both the campsite and staff resources.

5. Grade activities and subject matter to the ages, interests, and abilities of the campers.

6. Provide opportunity for individual creativity, so that each camper may develop his own special interests and abilities.

7. Stay within the expectations of those churches supporting the camp, so that the camp produces compatible and contributing members for the churches.

8. Expand the program for young adults to include a wide variety of interests. Such features as music, fine arts, and exploring social problems should be provided as well as all types of outdoor activities.

9. Create and maintain favorable camp traditions.

10. Safeguard the health and well-being of the entire camp community.

Since programming is variable, an ideal program cannot be defined. What would be ideal for a more activity-centered program might not be as ideal for a small-group, counselor-centered camp week or for a week whose program centers in some theme. Camping that is conference-oriented would demand a different program than a camp that is decentralized.

However, certain general features of programming for Christ-centered camping should be included whatever the camping pattern.

The Bible should be central. Bible classes, discussion groups centering on Biblical themes, and applications of Bible truth to young people's problems are essential to Christian camping.

Evangelism must also be stressed. Whether on a one-to-one basis or a more traditional, platform-centered approach, every young person of accountable years needs to be led to a relationship with Jesus Christ as his Lord and Savior.

Music is important. A singing camp is a happy camp. All kinds of music have their place in the camp program—camp songs, silly fun songs, folk songs, choruses, gospel songs, and hymns. Camp can also be a time for training older young people in music leadership.

Camps should provide opportunities for worship. Individual, small group, and total camp worship experiences should be planned carefully.

Campfires are traditional at camp. In fact, they are so commonplace and often poorly done that their value has been eroded. It is better to plan only one or two campfires, and make them highlights of the camp week, than to have a campfire each night with little or no planning.

Recreation of various kinds is a universal feature of camping. Often it is organized around team sports and carried out in organized, competitive recreation. Other informal kinds of recreation are provided that cater to individual interests. In addition, more Christian camps include general recreational activities as swimming, crafts, and various well-planned nature programs that combine recreation with learning. A special emphasis upon world missions, development of Christian service, or leadership training should be programmed into every camp week, particularly those serving older youth.

The planners of a camp program must be aware of the camp objectives and the nature of the campers. Johnson and Kingsley stress that those formulating the program should be sensitive to overlapping, overlooking, and overloading.[16] In other words, a camp program should not overlap on what the Sunday school or regular youth program in the local church is doing. Neither should planners overlook any possible program feature that could be developed for their campsite by the wise use of resources, both personal and financial. Overloading can apply to the program and staff as well as the campers. A program should stress variety and balance, wise use of staff time and energy, and the elimination of program pressures from campers.

The key to the program is the camp staff. They help the camper to grow spiritually. They are program leaders who make the program effective. The staff includes deans, who usually are the overall leaders of a week of camping, Bible instructors, worship and activity leaders, and cabin counselors.

Camp counselors are key personnel, especially in decentralized camps. Counselors are not professionals. They are mature, spiritually committed people (at least nineteen years old, say most standards). Counselors may assist with program activities, teach assigned classes, and share in other program areas. Their main function, however, is to live with their assigned campers. As they share living quarters, they become proxy parents to them. In these informal times campers will have opportunity to share problems, insights, and feelings. In cabin devotions, rap sessions, and informal living, counselors can guide campers to develop better attitudes and can help them grow spiritually.

How can such counselors be developed? Camp personnel can be led to see that they all should be counselors. They can show their concern, share with the campers in the week's experiences, and be available whenever needed.

A counselor training program can be developed by each camp organization. Joy MacKay's excellent volume, *Creative Counseling for Christian Camp* (Scripture Press, 1966), sets forth a program that any camp could inaugurate. It features training by correspondence, with special weekend sessions and precamp sessions. Through these means, counselors are led to explore camp objectives, take part in specific camp programs, learn more about campers as persons, and discuss ways of handling specific problems. As the counselors actually work with campers, counselor meetings could be held each day for further instruction, discussion, and evaluation. Whatever training plan is followed, a rule of thumb is—a job description *before*, supervision *during*, evaluation *after*.

A camp that is conference-oriented could modify its program to allow opportunity for more small-group and one-to-one experiences. Camps that are already locked into traditional facilities can assign counselors to a certain group, housing them together in a certain area of the dormitory. The program can allow time for the counselor and his group to be together.

Every camp should have training sessions for teachers and counselors. They should be made aware of the importance of interpersonal relationships, and instructed in the principles of counseling and working with small groups.

Summary

Christian camping is growing and making a spiritual impact. Thousands of decisions leading to spiritual conversion are made each year. Through the camping experience, many young adults are led to decide that their lives should be devoted to specialized, church-related vocational service. Hence, Christian camping is a recruiter for the Christian college and for the formal ministry of the churches. Indeed, the church camp is not just a place, but an experience with God. This experience may have lifelong consequences, issuing into eternity. Christian principles, creative freedom, and sound administrative practice must be joined together to make this "experience with God" even more significant in the future.

Project

Read at least three periodicals pertaining to Christian camping. Write a brief report.

Selected Bibliography

Camping Is Education. Martinville, Indiana: American Camping Association, 1960.

Christian Education Research. *On Christian Camping Activities and Trends.* Wheaton, Illinois: Scripture Press Foundation, 1970.

Dimock, Hedley S. (ed.) *Administration of the Modern Camp* (revised edition). New York: Association Press, 1965.

Ensign, John and Ruth. *Camping Together As Christians.* Richmond, Virginia: John Knox Press, 1958.

Gangel, Kenneth. "Christian Camping," *Voice,* 43:21, June, 1969.

Goodrich, Lois. *Decentralized Camping.* New York: Association Press, 1959.

Hall, Colby. *Texas Disciples.* Texas Christian University Press, 1953.

Hammett, Catherine T. and Virginia Musselman. *The Camp Program Book.* New York: National Recreation Association, 1951.

Johnson, Ted and Lee M. Kingsley. *Blueprint for Quality: Administrative Guidelines for Camping.* Chicago: Harvest Publications, 1969.

Joy, Barbara Ellen. *Annotated Bibliography on Camping.* Minneapolis: Burgess Publishing Company, 1963.

La None, John. *A Guide To Church Camping.* Nashville: Convention Press, 1976.

Mitchell, Viola and Ida B. Crawford. *Camp Counseling.* Philadelphia: W. B. Sanders, 1961.

Peters, Raymond. *Let's Go Camping.* Elgin, Illinois: Brethren Press, 1945.

Rubin, Robert. *The Book of Camping.* New York: Association Press, 1949.

Thurston, LaRue A. *The Complete Book of Campfire Programs.* New York: Association Press, 1959.

Todd, Floyd and Pauline. *Camping for Christian Youth* (revised edition). Grand Rapids, Michigan: Baker, 1968.

---

[1]Mitchell and Crawford, p. 8
[2]Rubin, p. 1
[3]*Camping Is Education,* p. 8
[4]From CAMPING FOR CHRISTIAN YOUTH by Floyd and Pauline Todd. Copyright 1963 by Floyd and Pauline Todd. p. 34. Used by permission of Baker Book House.

⁵Luke 2:52
⁶Genesis 12ff
⁷Exodus 40:36; Numbers 9:17ff
⁸Deuteronomy 16:13-15
⁹Hall, p. 202
¹⁰Todd and Todd, p. 30 (see reference 4)
¹¹Gangel
¹²Todd and Todd, p. 31 (see reference 4)

¹³*The American Camping Association* is the professional association for organized camping in America. It grew out of a coalescence in 1935 of the Camp Directors Association (1910), the National Association of Directors of Girls' Camps (1916), and the Midwest Camp Directors Association (1921). It serves camps by providing information, instilling professional attitudes, setting up standards and accrediting camps that meet these standards.

¹⁴*Christian Camping, International* is a similar organization growing out of previous evangelical camping groups. It functions for Christian camping as the American Camping Association does for general camping. It also sponsors national and regional workshops so that help can be given at the grass roots level.

¹⁵Johnson and Kingsley, pp. 83, 84
¹⁶*Ibid.*, pp. 76, 77

25

The Campus Ministry

As you read, think about these questions:
—Why are campus ministries significant in our country?
—How did campus ministries develop?
—What are the objectives and programs for campus ministries?
—What qualifications are necessary for the campus minister?

Higher education is no longer Christian higher education. The church gave birth to higher education in medieval times and continued to nurture it for several centuries, but now the majority of higher educational institutions are secular.

More than seventy percent of all college students are enrolled in state or public institutions. Churches can no longer depend solely upon their own higher educational institutions to educate students about Jesus Christ. It became apparent that churches would have to follow students to the secular campus, to help preserve their faith in an alien surrounding and to help them witness to others in that surrounding. For this purpose, campus ministries developed.

History of Campus Ministry

At the time of the Civil War, only nineteen of America's 182 colleges were public institutions. The remaining colleges had been brought into existence by the churches and religiously-oriented private groups. They invested heavily in these private, denominational, and church-related colleges. Most young people entering college were enrolled in these institutions, and the religious flavor that dominated their atmosphere was seen as sufficient to keep these young people committed to the church.

But the Morrill Act of 1862, which granted land for the establishment of state colleges, was destined to change this picture. By the beginning of the twentieth century, the state colleges established through the impetus of the Morrill Act were taking the lead in higher education. In 1910, only two of the largest dozen schools were not state supported, and the rate of student enrollment gain in state colleges and universities was three times the rate of gain in private and church-related institutions. This flood of students into secular institutions, including more and more church youth, alerted church leaders to a new need—to follow the students to the state campus and minister to them there.

Some student work (as campus ministry was called in those years) was being done, however. The Student Volunteer Movement, grew out of the Haystack Prayer Meeting of Williams College students in 1806. By the close of the nineteenth century, it had permeated many colleges with its religious fervor, particularly its concern for foreign missions. In a quarter of a century, 4,500 missionaries sailed from the North American continent, given impetus by the Student Volunteer Movement. The Northfield, Massachusetts Conference, called by Dwight L. Moody in 1880, gave permanent form to this movement. Under the leadership of John R. Mott, a young Cornell graduate, it became the parent body to the World Student Christian Movement with twenty-two national Student Christian Movements formed throughout the world.

The bulk of religious work, even at the many private and church-related colleges, was done by the Young Men's and Young Women's Christian Associations. The first student YMCA began at the University of Virginia in 1857. Twenty years later, delegates from forty colleges gathered at Louisville to form the national student YMCA. A similar organization was formed by the YWCA in 1886. By 1900, these two organizations had 1,300 associations with a total membership of 100,000—nearly one-half of all American college students. At this time the Y's still saw themselves as "arms of the church" that served the general interests of Protestant churches. Denominations were willing to let the Y's care for their students enrolled in state institutions.

The denominational churches themselves attempted various forms of campus ministry with volunteer leadership. Most programs centered in local churches and not upon the college campus itself.

Another denominational approach was to organize student guilds or societies upon the college campus. In 1887, the Tappan Association for Presbyterians and the Hobart Guild (Episcopal) were formed at the University of Michigan. This plan was quickly adopted by the major Protestant denominations and by the Roman Catholics (Newman Clubs) at state universities in Illinois, Texas, Pennsylvania, Wisconsin, and elsewhere. These campus guilds or clubs became the basis for current patterns of campus ministries.

Another approach was the development of a Bible chair or professorship at the university. This plan was pioneered by the Disciples of Christ at the University of Michigan in 1893. Other Bible chairs were begun at the University of Virginia, University of Missouri, and the University of Kansas. These were sponsored by the Christian Women's Board of Missions. Soon this plan became generally accepted, and the Bible chairs grew prevalent. College credit offered through the chair was accepted by the university, but the chair itself was supported by an organization outside the university. The Churches of Christ throughout the south began to establish Bible chairs at every major college and university.

The most significant effect of Bible chairs was not that accredited instruction was given, but that men with ecclesiastical standing and academic preparation were sent to work full-time on major campuses. This paved the way from the student associations and denominational guilds, with their nonprofessional, voluntary leadership, to the professional leadership of university pastors and campus ministers.

The Bible chairs came at a propitious time. They began when religious education was seen largely in terms of Bible study, and were located in the geographical and cultural area known as the "Bible belt." The Bible chair was regarded as an acceptable device for teaching religion at a state institution without violating the principle of separation of church and state. Bible chairs or their equivalent arose among many of the major denominations, with Disciples, Churches of Christ, and the Mormons leading the field. At various places in the 1920's and 1930's, some of these Bible chairs banded together to form a school of religion. In a few instances these schools of religion offered accredited work through the university toward majors at baccalaureate and masters levels. In one institution, the University of Iowa, a doctorate in religion is available.

However, the Bible chair thrust has lost much of its impetus, because many state institutions have developed departments of religion. Academic study, in those areas provided earlier by the Bible chairs, is done through the university with no qualms about church-state problems.

By the close of World War II, various kinds of campus ministries existed. Most denominations had established departments of campus ministry and began campus clubs or foundations at most major university centers. Bible chairs were present in certain institutions, frequently joined to a denominational club or foundation. Local churches also ministered to the college campus, either through their own college departments or cooperatively with other local churches. In some instances, places for religious instruction, Christian fellowship, and other programs and activities were built adjacent to the campus.

On June 22, 1944, the Rankin-Barden Bill became law. This bill produced what is generally called the "GI Bill of Rights." By 1957, 2,350,000 World War II veterans had received college training, and almost six million had taken advantage of some other kind of schooling (vocational, skill-oriented, or apprentice). This impetus was to have lasting effects upon the college population.

By the end of the 1960's, fifty-five percent of all high school graduates enrolled in colleges, and most of these (seventy to eighty percent) were in public institutions. Though other forms of higher education have become increasingly popular in the 1970's and the college population has leveled off, it continues at a high level. This continuing college population has challenged the churches and concerned Christians. Church youth need help in developing Christian maturity while they attend college, and the state campus is itself a mission field.

Certain evangelical organizations such as Inter-Varsity Christian Fellowship began their ministries on American campuses in the late 30's. Bill Bright, a product of the college department of First Presbyterian Church in Hollywood, formed Campus Crusade for Christ in 1951. Young Life, the Fellowship of Christian Athletes, Navigators, and others soon entered campus work. Almost all of these operate on a club basis and are oriented toward evangelism.

American denominations have continued to promote campus ministries. Some, like the Southern Baptists in their Baptist Student Union, have done so independently with great success. Others have joined together in ecumenical partnership. In 1960, the student ministries of the Disciples of Christ, the Evangelical United Brethren Church, the United Church of Christ, and the United Presbyterian Church brought into being the United Campus Christian Fellowship. This organization and the National Student Christian Fellowship (an umbrella agency related to the National Council of Churches) began sponsoring united ministries on campuses. They tend to emphasize an ecumenical program, not in the sense of denominational cooperation, but the loss of denominational identity in a united ministry.

Because of the need for professional workers in campus ministries, Christian colleges and seminaries have developed courses and programs to prepare individuals for such ministry. Internships, workshops, and other kinds of learning experiences have also been developed to aid in this preparation.

Philosophy of Campus Ministry

The church's concern with higher education is based upon the conviction that God is the author of all truth and that He is concerned with every level of life. In the past, campus concerns of the churches were directed toward conserving the faith of church youth and providing an evangelistic witness on campus. Such concerns must be stressed continuously, but in a sense the church must also attempt to reclaim the colleges and universities for God. The church must present to the university a visible and influential example of the Christian community on campus.

In this ideal sense, a campus ministry is involved in the total academic community, not just with students. As a result, the church's ministry on campus is the same as its ministry in the local church or in the Christian college: to promote Christian education. "In the special context of higher education, a Christian is helped to see all truth and values in relationship to the Biblical truth of Jesus Christ, and is thereby freed to live as a whole person and to participate responsibly in the world of *academia.*"[1]

Any underlying philosophy and practice of campus ministry must be concerned with people. On any secular campus, the persons uncommitted to Jesus Christ must be evangelized. The Christians who teach or administer must be challenged by an effective campus ministry to take seriously their Christian responsibility. People who are hurting, confused, and caught up in problems unique to the college context must be led to see that in the Christian community on campus there is genuine love, care, and concern that can provide help for their problems. By the very nature of the current secular campus, there will be students and faculty members who operate on a faith level borrowed from family or community. An effective campus ministry will provide a robust and open exploration of Biblical and theological themes and implications.

With these basic principles in mind, the campus minister must set out specific objectives for his particular campus ministry. He must consider the type of institution (multiversity, regional college or university, community college, commuter or resident college) at which the ministry operates, and the specific needs of area churches. The following is a list of guidelines for developing a specific statement of objectives.[2] An effective campus ministry:

1. Recognizes the validity of every sincere effort to reach the academic community with the gospel, and welcomes every opportunity for cooperative effort.

2. Recognizes that the college campus must be dealt with not as a homogeneous unit but as a highly stratified, fragmented, diverse community.

3. Avoids a sectarian posture.

4. Understands the sociological aspects of the student's background, the community environment, and the climate of the individual campus.

5. Establishes a cordial working relationship with administrative officials, faculty members, and student body officers, and attempts to enlist their active support for its program.

6. Strives to make its program an integral part of campus life. Consequently, the program is tailored for high and low points in campus activity.

7. Recognizes the unsophisticated religious background of the average student and adjusts its doctrinal arguments to an appropriate level.

8. Identifies itself with the highest ideals of the university.

9. Is positive in approach and attitude.

10. Presents a faith that is life-affirming and culture-affirming.

11. Identifies itself primarily with the students.

12. Experiments, innovates, and adapts its methods.

13. Establishes itself as a ministry within the campus rather than beside the campus.

14. Rallies the effort and energy of the existing community of faith within the academic community.

15. Exercises great discretion in identifying itself with any campus issue.

Types and Programs of Campus Ministry

Each campus minister must make a thorough study of its situation and develop programming and activities accordingly. He must consider place of residence, academic relationships, extracurricular activities, and the academic environment. Although different campus ministries utilize different methods and activities, some areas of program should be universal.

Evangelism is a primary objective of the campus ministry. Evangelistic activities on the campus may range from those traditionally used in local churches to a one-to-one style in which a student or faculty member shares his faith with another. Whatever methods are used, the heart of the evangelistic task is the same—the presentation of the good news of God in Jesus Christ so that all men may accept Him as Savior and obey Him as Lord. This is the central task of the church and the campus ministry. Christian students, faculty, and university staff members must actively present Christ to other persons on campus.

Most campus ministries have developed a core group concept. Any active campus Christian group has a center or core group who are genuinely committed to Christ. These people can become the radiating influence on campus for that minstry. The campus minister himself should disciple these young people and send them forth, as Jesus did with His disciples, to minister and serve on the campus.

Much of the work of an effective campus minister will be *counseling*. In spite of the presence of professional counseling services in the university complex, many young people never consult professional counselors. Here is the campus ministry's unique opportunity. Sensitive Christian students may themselves function as counselors, or refer needy students to a campus minister who is more skilled at counseling than they are. Group discussion of common academic and moral problems may well become group therapy. Students who are helped with their problems will share with other students facing similar situations. The counseling service can become an informal, yet vital public relations tool.

Every campus ministry must stress *Biblical and theological study*. Such study can be done in programs accredited by the university or an accredited Christian college. Other ministries prefer non-credit, short-term religious study. Inter-Varsity Fellowship has done much to provide non-credit Bible and theological study, and their publishing arm, Inter-Varsity Press, provides excellent resources for study. Evangelical campus ministries can cooperate in this area by bringing in special lecturers on relevant themes or sponsoring debates on crucial religious or scientific issues. Frequently the campus ministry may share sponsorship of a special lecturer with one of the university departments.

On some campuses, a campus house where Christian students live has also become a study center. The house not only provides the place for special formal programs, but it involves residents in a deepening of their convictions through discussion and small group worship.

If a campus ministry is to be concerned with the total academic community, it must not ignore the *university faculty*. Many of these people are nominally Christian, and need a renewed and revitalized faith. Under the aegis of the National Council of Churches, the Faculty Christian Fellowship has provided an ecumenical effort toward reaching the university campus. Such publications as the *FCF Bulletin, The Christian Scholars* (a journal of the Commission on Higher Education of the National Council), and *Faculty Forum* (published by the Methodist Church to serve the whole faculty movement), are auxiliaries to this program. The Inter-Varsity Christian Fellowship, through its Faculty Fellowship, provides an ecumenical platform for those whose convictions are more Biblically con-

servative. Both of these groups stress the importance of vocation, the need to be Christian in all of one's relationships, and
the problems and opportunities of Christian witness as a faculty member.

American college and university campuses have become the
training ground for many *foreign students* in recent years. The
Smith-Mundt Act, passed in 1948, providing for a cooperative
higher educational exchange program, and the Fulbright Act of
1946 resulted in an increase in the number of foreign students.
In 1946, 15,000 foreign students were studying in United States
higher educational institutions. By 1964, this number had risen
to 75,000. The number continues to increase. These students
have come from more than 152 countries and are enrolled in
almost 2,000 different educational institutions.

Here is a golden opportunity for the church through its campus ministries. Many of these foreign students are lonely and in
need of friendship. A campus ministry could provide opportunity for acquaintance and friendship, sponsor a "host family"
program, and help foreign students adjust to the American culture. But here is also a tremendous evangelistic opportunity
with world mission implications. These foreign young people
are the higher-class, more intelligent youth of their countries. If
they are led to Christ, they may have greater influence in their
home country than dozens of American missionaries. In some
instances in which a nation is closed to traditional missionary
work, this may be the only way to send a Christian witness to
that country.

In the past it has been assumed that a ministry to college
students would necessarily be carried out by a ministry on
campus or by a church located in the university town. The
development of regional universities and community colleges
has made it possible for almost every church to minister to the
college student. It is estimated that some kind of college will
exist within twenty miles of every citizen by 1980. In such
urban areas as Los Angeles, churches will have college people
in their membership, even though these college people do not
know one another as a part of the academic community. This
has led to area-wide campus ministries, even though no attempt has been made to form structured ministries on the university campuses in the area.

These developments mean that "every church is going to be
faced with the problem of ministering to the academic commu-

nity."[3] Churches must recognize that they minister to people whatever their context or subculture. Campus ministry, then, is a ministry to persons who are involved in the academic life of the country. To be true to its Lord, the church must devise ways of reaching the people within that special context.

The Campus Minister

In most instances the key to success in a campus ministry is the campus minister. He is the motivator, the discipler, the teacher, who provides the driving force for those involved in the ministry. Because of the environment of the secular campus, the Christian commitment and leadership ability of the campus minister may need to be greater than that of other kinds of ministers.

The campus minister should be young enough to understand the students. At the same time, he needs to be emotionally and spiritually mature. He should be well-educated, with both undergraduate and graduate degrees. Work at the graduate level in counseling, apologetics, history, and theology is extremely helpful. As he ministers, he may wish to take graduate classes at the university. This gives him a feel for the academic atmosphere at the university and provides opportunities for interaction with students and faculty. He should seek other opportunities in continuing education—workshops, reading, and a perusal of the various higher education journals to keep abreast of the trends.

Above all, the campus minister must be motivated by the love of Jesus Christ. He must have a deep abiding faith and carefully thought-through convictions. He must also be intellectually honest and sympathetic toward students.

Each campus minister should be given a job description that will help define his role, his responsibilities, and his relationships to various groups. This job description must be developed in relation to the needs of the individual campus and the abilities of the campus minister. Figure 25-1 indicates the tasks in which Hammond found campus ministers involved.[4] It suggests some elements for the development of a job description:

Activity	Frequently	Occasionally	Rarely
1. Engaged in informal theological discussions with students	71%	26%	1%
2. Gave personal counseling to students or faculty	68%	29%	1%
3. Helped students to organize religious programs	60%	32%	6%
4. Led study groups on religious topics	48%	40%	10%
5. Entertained students in your home	47%	45%	6%
6. Conducted worship services for the campus	32%	24%	42%
7. Was active in our denomination's regional or national meetings on matters other than the campus ministry	20%	45%	33%
8. Had sessions for students becoming baptized, confirmed, church members, and so forth	16%	23%	59%
9. Was liaison for local church to get faculty or other adults into the life of the church	15%	37%	46%
10. Engaged in theological discussions with the faculty	14%	60%	24%
11. Helped students organize social events	13%	43%	42%
12. Helped students organize some sort of social action effort	10%	50%	38%
13. Took stands you knew your denomination would disapprove of	6%	44%	48%
14. Took stands you knew the college administration would disapprove of	5%	50%	43%
15. Guest-lectured for faculty member	1%	23%	74%
16. Had meetings for college alumni to discuss religious and social issues	1%	9%	89%

Figure 25-1. Activities of campus ministers

Summary

Campus ministries are a vital part of the church's thrust in evangelism and education. If the church is to affect the future, it must influence those centers of influence in American higher education. American churches must invest in a ministry to college and university people. We must accept and implement the challenge of reaching the university with the gospel.

Project

Write to or interview a campus minister. What does he do in his work?

Selected Bibliography

Ambrose, W. Hayden. The Church in the University. Valley Forge, Pennsylvania: Judson Press, 1968.

Beach, Waldo. Conscience on Campus. New York: Association Press, 1958.

Bolin, Gene. Christian Witness on Campus. Nashville: Broadman Press, 1968.

Cantelon, John. A Protestant Approach to the Campus Ministry. Philadelphia: Westminster Press, 1964.

Chamberlin, J. Gordon. Churches and the Campus. Philadelphia: Westminster Press, 1963.

Earnshaw, George W. (ed). Campus Ministry. Valley Forge, Pennsylvania: Judson Press, 1964.

Garrison, Charles. Forgotten Christians. Joplin, Missouri: College Press, 1967.

Guidelines for the Development of United Campus Ministries. Department of Higher Education, NCCCA, 1965.

Hammond, Phillip E. The Campus Clergyman. New York: Basic Books, 1968.

Hummel, Charles E. Campus Christian Witness. Chicago: Inter-Varsity, 1958.

Miller, Alexander. Faith and Learning. New York: Association Press, 1960.

The Study of Religion in College and University and Its Implications for Church and Seminary. New York: Department of Higher Education, National Council of Churches, 1967.

---

[1]Earnshaw, p. 20. Used by permission of Judson Press.
[2]Adapted from a paper presented by K. Don Clark for a class in Campus Ministry, Emmanuel School of Religion, 1967.
[3]Earnshaw, p. 63
[4]Hammond, pp. 65, 66

CHAPTER

26

Christian
Higher Education

As you read, think about these questions:
—What role has religion played in higher education in America?
—What has been done to prepare professional workers in Christian education?
—Define a *Bible college*. Why did these institutions come into existence?
—What is the Evangelical Teacher Training Association?

_____

Higher education was born in the church and nurtured at her bosom for centuries. It has its roots deep in medieval European society. Ancient universities developed out of medieval scholasticism and the cathedral schools of the church; these have set the pattern for modern higher education. Degrees, faculties, and courses of study still reflect the ancient pattern. In Europe, universities are still religiously oriented and often church-related. Their departments of theology are integral and vital parts of the general faculty.

The Beginning of Colleges in America

Religious Motivation
The first colleges established in America were established by the church. Harvard College was established in 1636 to train a

literate ministry. Harvard's mottoes, program of studies, and religious fervor in its early years bears witness to the religious motivation for its establishment and continuation.

Yale University, William and Mary College, Dartmouth, and many other early higher educational institutions came into being for the same reason as Harvard. Some were designed to promote a certain sect or denomination. Others were to teach Christianity in general. Not only did these early institutions provide ministers and missionaries, but they also supplied the early teachers and leaders of the colonies. The curriculum of these colleges included liberal and practical arts, but religion was the core around which the curriculum was organized.

Secularization of Colleges

The scene has changed. Today most of these privately-endowed institutions of higher learning are indifferent to Christianity. The secularization that affected state education affected these colleges as well, and religious emphasis in purpose and curricular content was soon forgotten. Religion was forced out of its central position to be handled by student organizations or second-rate theological schools.

Not only did this trend affect private institutions such as Harvard, Yale, and Columbia, but it also affected some colleges actually established and supported by church groups. In order to compete with state colleges and universities, these church-related schools developed comparable programs, sometimes at the expense of their original purpose of serving the church. In 1923, Arlo Brown depicted the state of the church-related college in this way: "It is not uncommon today to find denominational colleges requiring for graduation 20 to 30 semester hours of foreign language study and advanced mathematics while making no requirement in psychology, Bible, religious education, and similar subjects."[1]

Not all Christian colleges have surrendered to a secularistic trend. Excellent Christian liberal arts colleges, like Pepperdine, Wheaton, and Gordon, still place the Christian world view at their center, preparing Christian men and women to live the Christian lifestyle in whatever vocation they pursue.

The Teaching of Religion in American Colleges

The secularistic trend is now being reversed. Both church-related and state institutions of higher learning recognize to a greater extent the need for religious teaching.

Surveys of the Early Part of the Century

One of the endeavors of the Religious Education Association was to promote the teaching of religion in higher educational institutions. W. S. Athearn, a member of this Association, wrote in 1913:

> There is at the present time an organized effort, led by the Religious Education Association, to put courses in religion back into denominational colleges. Only a few church colleges are teaching religion. They are teaching the same subjects that state universities teach, and their students are forced to absorb religion from the atmosphere of the college chapel, the Christian associations, etc. Now that state universities are surrounding themselves with student pastors, Divinity houses, and Christian associations, the denominational colleges must either go out of business or begin to perform a task for society which the state school can not do; the task is to teach religion in every year of the college course.[2]

In 1915, Athearn conducted a survey of the teaching of religious education in 300 American colleges. Sixty-seven of them offered an average of five and one-third courses each in English Bible and literature, and thirty-eight of them offered an average of two courses each in religious education. Only seven colleges offered enough courses in Bible and religious education to constitute a major for the bachelor's degree. These seven were Carleton, Drake, Grinnell, Millikin, University of Chicago, Yale, and Eugene Bible University. Of these, only the University of Chicago, Drake, and possibly Eugene Bible University, offered enough courses to enable a student to major in religious education.[3]

In 1915 and 1916, the Council of Church Boards of Education made an independent study of 203 colleges under its jurisdiction. Of these colleges, only thirty-three were making adequate provision for permanent instruction in the Bible, and only 138 of these colleges required any Bible for graduation.

Other surveys indicated the weakness of the church colleges in regard to religious instruction. These colleges, sponsored by the churches, were supplying everything but what the churches needed—religious teachers.

Athearn led a one-man crusade against the secularization of

colleges and universities organized and supported by the churches. He took surveys and published books (such as *Religious Education and American Democracy* and *A National System of Education*) that related to this problem. He also used the convention and lecture platform to forward his crusade.

Athearn stated that the church-related college must be a school of the church, teaching young adults religion first and then other subjects. The other subjects would never be taught apart from the church's basic religious presuppositions and implications, however. Personality is the supreme emphasis of a church college: all student activities are not for the privileged few, but for all.

In the pamphlet, *Religion at the Heart of the Christian University*, Athearn (by then president of Butler University) stated four distinct tasks that must be achieved by the church college: (1) to preserve the essential disciplines and cultures of the liberal arts college; (2) to give religion and the Bible their rightful places in the college curriculum; (3) to give proper recognition in the college course to religious education and various forms of social service as vocational fields of great personal and social significance; and (4) to prepare college students for satisfactory graduate work in graduate and professional schools in the fields of religion and social science.[4]

Athearn believed that no student in the church college should be allowed to graduate without being prepared for intelligent lay service in the local church. This, he felt, could be done through students electing a "service minor in Christian service courses in addition to required biblical courses."[5]

The Christian religion and the Bible must be central to the Christian college or university. Whenever the church college is completely secularized, whenever it fails to prepare young people for effective lay service in the local church, it forfeits its right to existence.

Present Trends

Five types of programs became operative: (1) courses in religion within the curriculum of the state-supported university; (2) a department of religious education within the church-supported university; (3) a Bible college or Bible chair supported by a church or churches, the work of which is accredited by the university; (4) courses offered by independent denominational foundations accredited by the foundations; and, (5) a school of religion supported by the churches offering work accredited by the university.

Seymour Smith made a more recent study[6] of religion in higher education. The study concluded that ninety-five percent of the major state universities offer religion courses for credit. In the 1920's, tax-supported schools averaged only two and one-half courses per institution; in 1933 the average had moved to five courses; by 1958 the average had reached almost nine courses per institution.

Conservative Christians, however, should not be overly optimistic about this situation. Although state colleges and universities are teaching religion, too often it is the religion of liberal Christianity, not the religion of Biblical faith. Only about half of all college students are attending institutions where the gospel is a living force.[7] As long as this situation continues, evangelical churches must continue to foster a higher education that will give preeminence to the Bible and the Biblical faith. Such institutions as Wheaton, Trinity, Gordon, Bob Jones University, Milligan College, Westmont College, and others are still needed to give this Biblical witness to American universities and to provide leadership for evangelicalism.

Professional Training in Christian Education

Theological seminaries came into existence toward the close of the eighteenth century and developed rapidly in the nineteenth. These institutions functioned as professional training schools for the ministry. Courses in Bible, theology, and practical ministries dominated their curriculum. As Christian education became more prominent, seminaries began making some provision for professional training in this field. As early as 1906, a chair of education or Christian pedagogy was established in the College of the Bible, Lexington, Kentucky. Hartford Seminary, under the leadership of Edward Porter St. John, established a School of Religious Pedagogy at about the same time. Other institutions quickly followed the leadership of these two schools. Arlo A. Brown said of the first 15 years of the twentieth century, "There was practically no opposition to a chair of religious education in theological seminaries after the awakening at the beginning of the century. The installing of such chairs became largely a matter of when the institution could secure first the necessary funds and then the properly trained men."[8]

But what was true of the seminaries was not true in the colleges of the church. The first course in Christian education offered in a college for degree credit was offered at Drake University in 1910. By 1915, only seven colleges offered enough courses for a major in Bible and Christian education. Only the University of Chicago, Yale University, and Columbia University offered enough work for a doctorate with a major in religious education, and these institutions could do so only because of their affiliation with theological seminaries.

It was at this point that W. S. Athearn again exerted leadership. He believed that the church must develop a body of professionally trained religious educators. For a decade, he inspired and directed a creative program of professional training on the college and university level at Boston. In so doing, he became responsible for the upsurge of religious education of training in other university centers and theological seminaries.

Athearn had been called to Boston to serve as the head of a new work in religious education at Boston University in 1916. At first he served as a professor in the graduate school of the University. In the next three years, various training agencies were unified under Athearn's leadership to become the School of Religious Education and Social Service of Boston University. This school aimed at training competent leaders for the fields of religious education, social service, and general church work. By the 1928-29 school year, over 600 students were enrolled in the School of Religious Education and Social Service.

The Boston school served as a pattern for many other professional training schools. Southern Baptist seminaries, through the influence of Dr. J. M. Price of Southwestern Seminary, developed similar programs in their institutions. Today, almost all theological seminaries offer the M.R.E. degree as well as ministerial degrees. Only Hartford School of Religious Education and the Southern Baptist seminaries offer the D.R.E. Other universities and seminaries offer doctorates in religious education under the Th.D. or Ph.D. or Ed.D. program. Boston University no longer has a School of Religious Education, as all religious education courses are offered in the School of Theology or School of Education. The impact of the pioneer school at Boston under Athearn's leadership did much to popularize and standardize religious education as a profession.

The Rise of Bible Colleges and Institutes

A new form of American education has developed in the last hundred years. Since the 1880's, more than 240 Bible institutes and Bible colleges have been founded, enrolling more than 25,000 students.[9] Though given little place in the history of education, these colleges and institutes have become a decisive force in the education program of evangelicalism.

S. A. Witmer, who served as the Executive Director of the Accrediting Association of Bible Colleges for several years, has chronicled the growth and development of the Bible College movement in his book, *The Bible College Story: Education with Dimension.* He points out that two basic principles have shaped the program of Bible colleges. The first is a thorough commitment by Bible college educators to the Bible as the inspired and authoritative Word of God. The second principle is the mission of the church as expressed in our Lord's Great Commission. The practical purpose of the Bible college is to educate and prepare recruits to implement this work.

Causes of Establishment

The first Bible institutes were established to train lay people for Christian service. The movement developed out of the evangelical awakening that occurred toward the latter part of the nineteenth century. Dwight L. Moody formed the Chicago Evangelization Society in 1886. After his death, this institution was named the Moody Bible Institute. The Nyack Missionary Institute was founded in 1882 by A. B. Simpson. It had a strong missions course as well as the usual Bible and practical courses.

Most of the Bible colleges of today came into being as a reaction to the type of higher education sponsored by liberal churches. The fundamentalist-modernist controversy early in this century had drawn such sharp lines that new institutions were established to perpetuate the fundamentals of Biblical faith. Many new denominations resulted from divergences in theology, and many of these new denominations established Bible colleges for the training of ministers and Christian workers.

Though these institutions differ radically in program, course offerings, and facilities, they are alike in many respects:

1. All are wholeheartedly evangelical in theological convic-

tions. Each school is founded on the tenets of the Christian faith commonly accepted by evangelicals.

2. The direct study of the English Bible is given central place in all of these schools. Many schools require a student to have as much as thirty to fifty hours in direct Bible study in their four- or five-year degree program. Others require corresponding amounts for diploma courses (two or three year courses).

3. These colleges or institutes emphasize practical Christian service. They provide courses in Christian education, personal evangelism, and preaching. Many have Christian service programs that provide opportunities for students to engage in these activities while they are being taught.

4. These colleges emphasize missions. Some have been established for the express purpose of training missionaries, others have extensive departments of missions, and still others provide technical studies in medicine and radio to help prepare missionary volunteers. As a result of this emphasis, evangelical missionaries on the field outnumber those going out through the denominational boards by about two to one.

5. These colleges encourage additional study. In the early years, most Bible college graduates entered the ministry immediately upon graduation. Seeing a more complex world with intense demands upon ministers, many college leaders now recommend graduate study in conservative seminaries.

Accrediting Associations

In recent years these colleges have banded together to form a professional association. Under the auspices of the Bible Institute Division of the Commission on Education of the National Association of Evangelicals, a meeting was held in Minneapolis in 1946. Representatives from twenty-eight Bible colleges and institutes formed an association of Bible schools that would serve as an accrediting agency and a channel of communications.[10] The Accrediting Association of Bible Colleges is now recognized by the United States Office of Education as an association accrediting undergraduate colleges in the field of Bible education. More than sixty schools meet strict academic requirements to be fully accredited by the Association. The American Association of Bible Colleges is now a member of the Council on Post-Secondary Accreditation, the organization of accreditation for all American higher educational institutions.

The strength of Bible colleges in certain religious movements can be seen in the following example. Among the Disciples of Christ, liberalistic leadership captured most of the theological schools. Bible colleges were then organized throughout the United States to train ministers and Christian workers for a large segment of conservative Christians. The number of these colleges has increased to over forty institutions, some of them enrolling several hundred students. Fourteen of these are fully accredited, with two others holding candidate status for accreditation. The total number of students now studying in these Bible colleges far exceed the number in the older Disciple institutions who are preparing for Christian work.

The Emphasis Upon Christian Education

Bible colleges have emphasized Christian education for years. Most of these institutions have departments of Christian education in which students can prepare for a teaching ministry. Some of these colleges have degree programs or courses to prepare students for work as Christian education directors, youth workers, or leaders in other phases of education in local churches.

One important development resulting from the Bible institute movement has been the organization of the Evangelical Teacher Training Association. In May, 1931, a small group of men met in the offices of the *Sunday School Times* in Philadelphia. James M. Gray and C. H. Benson represented Moody Bible Institute, Charles G. Trumbull and Philip E. Howard, the *Sunday School Times*, Lew W. Gosnell, the Bible Institute of Pennsylvania; B. Allen Reed, the National Bible Institute; and Calvin C. Ellis, Juniata College. The group decided to inaugurate an association that would, in association with Bible colleges and institutes, put teacher training on a higher plane than any existing agency was then doing. The Association, through cooperating schools (both at college and seminary level), promotes a Standard Training Course which consists of 432 hours or units of work divided as follows: Bible, 144; Department Specialization, 48; Personal Evangelism, 36; Mission, 36; Biblical Introduction, 15; Child Study, 15; Pedagogy, 15; Sunday School Administration, 15; Bible Geography, 12; and Electives, 96. This would equal twenty-four semester hours of college work.

Since 1931, the Evangelical Teacher Training Association

has carried forth its program consistently. Through its member schools it provides a teacher-training program unequaled by any other agency.

Summary

The role of religious education in institutions of higher learning has fluctuated. Medieval universities were Christian educational institutions, but their American counterparts have largely forsaken the original pattern. As the religious education movement gained momentum, churches demanded more religious teaching in higher education. Religious education as a profession has been developed through graduate centers and theological seminaries. The Bible college or institute has arisen as a reaction to Protestant liberalism to foster an evangelical Christianity which is vitally interested in religious teaching. The Evangelical Teacher Training Association, associated with Bible colleges and institutes, has done much for teacher training. The picture is encouraging, particularly for the prospects of religious teaching in American higher education.

Project

Read the bulletins of a Bible college of your choice. How has its curriculum and program changed during its history? What courses does it offer in Christian education?

Selected Bibliography

Athearn, W. S. An Adventure in Religious Education. New York: Century Company, 1930.

_____. Religious Education and American Democracy. Senior Department of the Church School. Des Moines, Iowa: privately published, 1913.

_____. Organized Sunday School Work in America: 1914—1918. Chicago International Sunday School Association, 1918.

Benson, C. H. History of Christian Education. Chicago: Moody Press, 1943.

Brown, A. A. A History of Religious Education in Recent Times. Nashville: Abingdon Press, 1923.

Gaebelein, Frank (ed). Christian Education in A Democracy. New York: Oxford University Press, 1951.

Lotz, Philip H. (ed). Orientation in Religious Education. New York: Abingdon-Cokesbury, 1950.

Taylor, Marvin J. Religious Education: A Comprehensive Survey. New
    York: Abingdon, 1960.
_____. An Introduction to Christian Education. New York: Abingdon,
    1964.
Witmer, S. A. The Bible College Story: Education With Dimension.
New York: Channel Press, 1962.

---

¹Brown, p. 231
²Athearn, 1913, p. 10
³Athearn, 1930, p. 126
⁴Athearn, 1913, p. 3
⁵Ibid., p. 5
⁶"Religious Instruction in State Universities: a Report of Recent Trends."
Religious Education, Volume LIII, No. 3 (May-June, 1958).
7Gaebelein, p. 134
8Brown, p. 238
8Gaebelein, p. 157ff
10Ibid., p. 173

Conclusion

The teaching ministry of the church is not a new star on the religious horizon. From the very beginning of creation, God has provided ways by which a people, His people, could be taught to know and follow Him. The book of Acts, that historical record of the early expansion of the church, reveals a teaching church. All through the ages the church has stood strong, penetrating the darkness of sin, when it has taken seriously its responsibility to teach. But the church has languished in apathy and weakness during those eras when teaching was no longer deemed essential.

God's purpose and program for the church have not changed. Forms have been altered from age to age, but the task is still the same: each generation is to teach the faith to its peers and to its offspring. The task of communicating faith is never-ending. The church is always just one generation away from extinction.

Effective communication of sound doctrine results when strong foundations are built. You have explored those foundations in detail, since they are critical to the programs you will lead. The mission of the church is unique. So is the content the church teaches—the Bible. Your philosophy of Christian education is only now being formulated, but it eventually will guide your choices of programs and materials.

The communication of faith calls for understanding the audience, heeding sound teaching principles, and selecting appropriate methods and materials. You were exposed to up-to-date research findings and practical plans for communicating to particular groups of learners. You have not yet achieved skill in teaching—that will come with further study and extensive practice—but you have the basic tools to do the job.

The teaching function of the local church is made more effective with visionary planning, careful administration, and critical evaluation. Your overview acquainted you with the basic principles and, hopefully, whetted your appetite for added study.

Teaching occurs in the local church, but even so, the congregational task is aided by the wide variety of extra-church organizations that exist alongside the church. Camping, Christian schools, campus ministries, Christian colleges, publishing companies, and other extra-church concerns are cooperative efforts to serve the church or to extend the ministry of the local church. The skilled educator is aware of the available resources.

You have been given a practical overview of the educational task of the church. Most topics have received only cursory examination; all deserve a more detailed analysis. That must wait for advanced study. Meanwhile, you have the beginning tools to share in the marvelous work of God—communicating faith to others (2 Timothy 2:2).

Index

Scripture Index